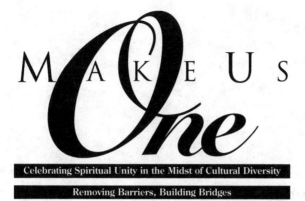

MAKE US One

Celebrating Spiritual Unity in the Midst of Cultural Diversity

Removing Barriers, Building Bridges

DELBERT W. BAKER, PH.D., EDITOR

Pacific Press Publishing Association
Boise, Idaho
Oshawa, Ontario, Canada

Edited by Jerry D. Thomas
Designed by Tim Larson
Cover photo by Sinclair/Tank
Typeset in New Century Schoolbook 11/13

Make us one : celebrating spiritual unity in the midst of
    cultural diversity : removing barriers, building bridges
    / edited by Delbert W. Baker.
        p.   cm.
    Includes bibliographical references.
    ISBN 0-8163-1267-2 (alk. paper)
    1. Seventh-day Adventists—Membership.   I. Baker,
Delbert W., 1953.
BX6154.M24 1995
286.7'32—dc20   95-18148
                                                            CIP

99 98 97 96 95 1 2 3 4 5

Dedication

To the Seventh-day Adventist Christians
in the North American Division
who are willing to make a bold commitment
to the principles of love, reconciliation, and diversity
under Christ.

Make Us One.

CONTENTS

──────*Acknowledgment*──────

*T*his project was facilitated by several wonderful people. The contributing writers were excellent to work with. They were creative, flexible, and provided helpful feedback at each stage of development. They deserve commendation for investing their thought, energy, and influence. Appreciation goes to the publishing house editors, Marvin Moore and Jerry Thomas. They believe in diversity and were willing to invest in an undertaking of this magnitude, and it was their sensitivity and patience that helped to make it all come together. Acknowledgment is given to the leadership at the General Conference of Seventh-day Adventists and across the North American Division for their exemplary efforts in studying how diversity can best impact the Church as we approach the year 2000.

Loma Linda University has provided a receptive campus climate for the ongoing diversity program, and it is here that many of the principles referred to in this book are being tested and implemented. Therefore, recognition is due to the Loma Linda University Board (LLU) for their ongoing support of diversity at LLU and to Dr. B. Lyn Behrens, president of LLU, who believes in and models diversity in her life and leadership. Appreciation is given to Isabel Leon, who provides managerial efficiency in the LLU Office of Diversity. Further, appreciation is extended to those formal and informal diversity leaders at LLU—students, faculty, and staff—who practice the principles of Christian diversity. They are proof that each of us can make a difference!

This has been a time-consuming project. Yet my wife, Susan, and three sons, David, Benjamin, and Jonathan, never wavered in their support. I am deeply indebted to them. Finally, gratitude is expressed to Christ, who has left us an eternal and perfect model of diversity.

Delbert W. Baker
Editor

Foreword

"*G*o ye therefore, and teach all nations, baptizing them in the name of the Father, and of the Son, and of the Holy Ghost: Teaching them to observe all things whatsoever I have commanded you: and, lo, I am with you alway, even unto the end of the world. Amen" (Matthew 28:19, 20, KJV).

"But in every nation he that feareth him, and worketh righteousness, is accepted with him" (Acts 10:35, KJV).

"And I saw another angel fly in the midst of heaven, having the everlasting gospel to preach unto them that dwell on the earth, and to every nation, and kindred, and tongue, and people" (Revelation 14:6, KJV).

Seventh-day Adventists are blessed with broad diversity among their worldwide constituency. SDAs now number more than eight million. They have established work in some 209 out of 236 countries. With publications and oral work, they are active with more than 700 language groups. They are going to every nation, kindred, tongue, and people. And according to Bible prophecies, there is much more diversity yet to take place before the second advent.

Not only is the SDA Church diverse, its success is tied to its becoming increasingly more diverse. In simple terms, the Church cannot be a success without being diverse. Why? Because the mission of the SDA movement is inextricably bound up with spreading the gospel and winning all people into the body of believers. Paradoxically as the Church successfully fulfills its mission and increases its diversity, it will simultaneously experience the complications and challenges that come with diversity. The task of taking the gospel to all the world will naturally expose members to people who may be very different. This is cause for celebration, but it can also result in conflict if awareness and sensitivity are lacking. One of the vexing challenges facing the Church is how to effectively respond to and manage the diversity that it now faces and will increasingly face in the future.

At a time of changing demographics and shifting paradigms, new methods and approaches based on solid biblical principles and common fairness must be reexamined and implemented. What worked in the past may not be the best approach today. A response to this challenge deserves thoughtful and prayerful consideration. The writers in this book, committed Christians who are experienced in the issues of diversity, offer practical ways for believers—members and leaders alike—to reexamine and respond to this challenge.

A Window of Opportunity

The SDA Church has a historic opportunity to be the gathering place of people of diverse backgrounds and cultures. It can model an inclusive fellowship that will be a powerful witness to the world community. There is a window of opportunity opened to demonstrate that the power of the gospel is stronger to unite than the power of culture to divide. The Church can demonstrate, in its response to the challenges of diversity, the beauty of the gospel and strength of its uniting power. Believers love Christ, and in loving Christ, they love each other. This binding love provides indisputable proof to a world desperately seeking to build bridges between different groups in society.

Relationships, based on love and fairness, become the test of the efficacy of the gospel in the life of the believer. The test with many believers may not be Church standards and doctrines. In many cases the test will be how to deal with love in spite of the differences of race, culture, and physical condition. The SDA Fundamental Belief, 13, eloquently indicates both the possibilities and challenges of diversity in the Church:

> The church is one body with many members, called from every nation, kindred, tongue, and people. In Christ we are a new creation; distinctions of race, culture, learning, and nationality, and differences between high and low, rich and poor, male and female, must not be divisive among us. We are all equal in Christ, who by one Spirit has bonded us into fellowhip with Him and with one another; we are to serve and be served without partiality or reservation. Through the revelation of Jesus Christ in the Scriptures we share the same faith and hope, and reach out in one witness to all. This unity has its source in the oneness of the triune God, who has adopted us as His children.

Diversity, then, is not just a viable option for the Church. It is not just a good idea, a new technique, or the product of the new societal paradigm; it is central to Christ's commission to His followers. It is central to our raison d'etre. It is bound with our reason and justification for existence. From the Garden of Eden to the call of Abraham to the setting aside of the people of Israel to be the bearers of God's truth on earth, diversity was integral to the divine plan and the outworking of God's providence for the saving of the human race. Fidelity to the Great Commission of Christ is realized to the extent that the Church spares no effort to see that all people have an opportunity to hear the liberating truths of the three angels' messages. Diversity is integral to the very existence of the Church.

The Dimension of Diversity

It is important that diversity is understood and appreciated for what it is. Diversity in the Christian context is all about *appreciating*, *respecting*, and *valuing* people, all people, regardless of their ethnicity, gender, culture, and physical condition in the witness and ministry of the gospel. So on one hand, it is about respecting and appreciating the talents, abilities, and perspectives that people, called by the gospel, bring to the body of Christ. It is about valuing the contributions of people regardless of their background, appearance, and physical condition. But it doesn't stop there. Diversity goes beyond attitudes of respect and appreciation and results in concrete actions concerned with *including and sharing* with diverse people. In a biblical context, diversity includes all people and then impartially utilizes the gifts and talents of the members in its ministry, governance, and administration. This is how the principles of love and fairness are demonstrated in the organizational and administrative structure of the Church.

It should be noted that there are many views and philosophies associated with diversity in various settings that may be situation specific. However, one of the significant distinctions of diversity from a Christian perspective is that all views and plans relative to diversity are screened by and submitted to the principles of the Word of God. Even if a concept is palatable from a secular perspective, before it is accepted as a part of the Christian agenda, it must square with biblical principles. The Bible tests the habits and practices of the believer, and nothing has preeminence over the Scriptures—not culture, mores, styles, or preferences. In this sense, diversity in the Church is distinctly different from other forms of diversity found in society.

A Handbook on Christian Diversity

This book, *Make Us One,* can serve as a handbook on Christian diversity and relations between different races/

ethnic groups. It is the first of its kind in the SDA Church, and it seeks to approach the subject of diversity and race relations among SDAs candidly, fairly, and in a balanced and practical manner. However, due to the enormity of the subject, this book approaches diversity in the context of the Church's North American Division. Further, it should be noted that while, in general, diversity includes issues dealing with race/ethnicity, gender, physical condition, and age, this book is specifically dealing with diversity from the aspect of race/ethnicity and culture in the Christian setting.

In these pages a deliberate attempt has been made to hear different voices speak to solutions and issues of diversity. Therefore, the authors themselves are diverse and represent a variety of viewpoints. They may differ in perspective and in opinions on some issues, but there is unanimity on the cardinal points. Each writer has a deep desire to see the gospel spread to all corners of the earth and to see a revival of practical love and unity in relationships in the body of Christ.

The content of this book is divided into a simple and reader-friendly format. First, there is an *Introduction,* which provides a context for the study of diversity and Church—*Diversity and the Divine Experiement,* by Robert S. Folkenberg, president of the General Conference of SDAs. Following are the three sections: *Understanding*, which covers subjects that enhance one's understanding, sensitivity, and appreciation for diversity and the changes that accompany it; *Growing*, which covers practical principles that identify problem areas and effective interpersonal attitudes and skills for overcoming obstacles in the areas of the family, Church, and workplace; and *Relating*, which is designed to provide biblical strategies and relationship-building approaches that focus on communication, conflict resolution, and successfully relating to SDAs from international backgrounds. The book ends with an epilogue, *Love, the Last Word*, by Calvin B. Rock, vice-president of the General Conference of SDAs.

The purpose of this book is simple. It is to help bring about unity in the Church, the body of Christ. It is to help erect bridges of understanding between diverse people in the SDA Church and to practically witness to the life-changing love of God that is to be evident in the last days, a love that will help to usher in the second advent. This theme of love and unity was eloquently set forth by Christ in John 17:21: "That they all may be one"; it was further echoed by Ellen White in *Sons and Daughters of God* (286): "Among human beings as well as among the things of the natural world, there is diversity. Unity in diversity among God's children, the manifestation of love and forbearance in spite of differences of disposition, this is the testimony that God sent His Son into the world to save sinners."

The writers of these chapters unite in saying that the answer to the challenges of diversity is a spritual one and that the path to unity in diversity is found through a selflessness and genuine love relationship with Jesus Christ.

Delbert W. Baker
Editor
1995

Introduction

DIVERSITY AND THE DIVINE EXPERIMENT

Robert S. Folkenberg

Diversity, love, and the building of relationships are a part of a divine experiment with the Seventh-day Adventist Church to prepare a people for the second coming of Jesus Christ.

*T*he Seventh-day Adventist Church is engaged in a divine experiment. What is that experiment? In a world that is becoming increasingly fragmented along racial, ethnic, age, gender, and economic lines, we are attempting to build one people, united in Jesus Christ to meet Him at His soon appearing.

The task seems impossible. Incredible from a human standpoint. But ours is not simply a human endeavor—it is a divine experiment. We believe that the Lord wants to demonstrate to a world at the end of its tether the power of the gospel to break down barriers, dissolve long-standing alienation, and sweep away prejudice and hostility.

For us, ethnic and cultural diversity isn't a problem but an opportunity, not a weakness but a strength. The more diversified we become, the more the potential for individual and corporate growth, and the greater the witness to the world of the divine experiment.

We wrote (under the impress of the Holy Spirit, I believe) diversity into the statement of faith that binds us together worldwide. The thirteenth article of our Fundamental Beliefs, "Unity in the Body of Christ," reads thus:

> The church is one body with many members, called from every nation, kindred, tongue, and people. In Christ we are a new creation; distinctions of race, culture, learning, and nationality, and differences between high and low, rich and poor, male and female, must not be divisive among us. We are all equal in Christ, who by one Spirit has bonded us into one fellowship with Him and with one another; we are to serve and be served without partiality or reservation. Through the revelation of Jesus Christ in the Scriptures we share the same faith and hope, and reach out in one witness to all. This unity has its source in the oneness of the triune God, who has adopted us as His children.

This divine experiment, this impossible dream, is preeminently a *spiritual* undertaking. Either we are building spiritually or we are building a house of cards that will collapse in ruins about us. And our spiritual building, the unity of the worldwide Seventh-day Adventist fellowship, rests on four pillars—*creation*, *cross*, *church*, and *commission*.

Creation

The biblical teaching concerning origins undergirds the Seventh-day Adventist Church. It is the first pillar supporting our incredible diversity. This teaching assures us that we all come from a royal line. We are sons and daughters of the King of the universe. We did not crawl out of a chemical soup aeons ago; we haven't lifted ourselves up by our bootstraps.

No! "God said, 'Let us make man in our image, in our likeness, and let them rule over the fish of the sea and the birds of the air, over the livestock, over all the earth, and over all the creatures that move along the ground.' God created man in his own image, in the image of God he created him; male and female he created them" (Genesis 1:26, 27).

Regardless of our color or culture, our ethnicity or socio-economic status, we all have the same Father and the same Creator. No culture is inherently superior to another, no one can rightly lord it over another. When the chips of life are down, we know that this is true. When our vital powers ebb away and we need a transfusion of life itself, we know that the blood of any other will do. The microscope can tell no difference between the blood of a White person or Black person, rich or poor, learned or unlearned. For God "hath made of one blood all nations of men for to dwell on all the face of the earth, and hath determined the times before appointed and the bounds of their habitation" (Acts 17:26, KJV).

Though marred by sin, the image of God still remains in every person. The gospel works to restore the divine image: "And we, who with unveiled faces all reflect the Lord's glory, are being transformed into his likeness with ever-increasing glory, which comes from the Lord, who is the Spirit" (2 Corinthians 3:18).

Ellen White spoke of the purpose of education as the restoration of the divine image (*Education*, 15). And referring to early church she wrote: "Every Christian saw in his brother a revelation of divine love and benevolence. One interest prevailed; one subject of emulation swallowed up all others. The ambition of the believers was to reveal the likeness of Christ's character, and to labor for the enlargement of His Kingdom" (*The Acts of the Apostles,* 48).

As Seventh-day Adventists we recognize and acknowledge that no culture or ethnic group has a corner on the divine image. The image of God is more than any individual, more than maleness or femaleness, more than this race or that. Together—in our diversity—we reflect the divine image. And together—in our diversity—that image is to be progressively restored as part of the divine experiment to demonstrate the power of the gospel.

This pillar of Creation has profound implications for the manner in which we relate to each other. It means not only that we respect each other and seek to preserve each other's dignity and build up in love, but that we realize we are incomplete without each other. Only in our totality of diversity do we find the restoration of the image of God. But we rejoice in diversity not merely because of our common origin in the Creator, but because our Creator has become our Redeemer.

Cross

Probably the greatest passage in the Scriptures that describes the work of Christ to unite human diversity in Himself is Ephesians 2:11-22. Not surprisingly, it comes from Paul, the apostle par excellence to the Gentiles. Three great ideas rule the development of his thought here—alienation, reconciliation, and the cross.

In graphic word pictures Paul describes the alienation of the Gentiles. They suffered under the designation "uncircumcised," a term of contempt the Jews used that at once labeled, pigeonholed, and excluded them as inferior. But they also were "*separate* from Christ," "excluded from citizenship in Israel," and "*foreigners* to the covenants of the promise." "Without hope" and "without God," they were "far away"— outside the pale, "foreigners and aliens." Between Jews and Gentiles lay "the barrier, the dividing wall of hostility."

Although the world has moved light-years from Paul's day, the scene he describes comes right out of our times. The alienation between Jews and Gentiles he sketched here has become cosmic, with parents alienated against children and children against parents, one ethnic group against another, one culture over the other, men against women and women against men, the "haves" against the "have nots," and the "have nots" against the "haves." Paul's account in Ephesians

2 is our world—our fractured, fragmented world.

But—and here is the miracle of the gospel—Paul moves from alienation to reconciliation. Those who were once "far away" have been "brought near." Christ has brought peace, bringing the separated parties together, making "the two one." He has destroyed the barrier, the dividing wall of hostility, and has created "in himself a new man out of the two." Thus, He has reconciled both of them to God: now "both have access to the Father through the one Spirit." No longer foreigners and aliens, the Gentiles now are "fellow citizens with God's people and members of God's household."

Here is the goal that philosophers and politicians, statesmen and social workers have sought for centuries and for which they still seek. The removal of alienation! The breaking down of barriers of hostility! No more suspicion, prejudice, tribalism, racism, and sexism! Reconciliation in the midst of diversity!

But, says Paul, reconciliation didn't simply happen. It didn't come about because of a government mandate, a Great Society program, or intensive education. God *made* reconciliation and this "through the cross, by which He put to death their hostility." In God's eternal purpose the death of Christ brought the death of alienation—not only between God and man but between man and man.

How does the cross remove the alienation? By making a new humanity, "one new man out of the two." In Jesus Christ—as we kneel at the cross and gladly accept the gift of His love—we become new men and women. "You are all sons of God through faith in Christ Jesus, for all of you who were baptized into Christ have clothed yourself with Christ. There is neither Jew nor Greek, slave nor free, male nor female, for you are all one in Christ Jesus" (Galatians 3:26-28).

In many places in his letters, Paul returned to the theme of the cross. For him it was never an add-on, a formula to be mouthed at the appropriate time and place. No! The cross gave Paul his focus for living and for mission. "May I never boast except in the cross of our Lord Jesus Christ," he said, "through which the world has been crucified to me, and I to the world" (Galatains 6:14). And to the Corinthians he wrote: "For Christ did not send me to baptize, but to preach the gospel—not with words of human wisdom, lest the cross of Christ be emptied of its power. . . . For I resolved to know nothing among you except Jesus Christ and him crucified" (1 Corinthians 1:17; 2:2).

As wonderful as Paul's account is of the reconciling power of the cross, Christian history presents a mixed record. Professing Christians enslaved others; priests, prelates, and theologians perpetuated the denigration of women and other "uncircumcised." Nor is the account of the Seventh-day Adventist Church exemplary. All too often we have chosen to go along with social and cultural norms, even when they conflicted with the specific claims of the gospel. In the United States we were slow to take up the work in the South after the Civil War; we were slow to integrate our churches. We, too, often moved only after society moved. We have not, by and large, confronted racism, casteism, tribalism, and sexism, naming them for what they are—a denial of the cross that makes us all one in Christ Jesus.

We need to get back to the cross. For it is there that we find our unity and oneness. We need to make the cross central in our living, central in our preaching. "Of all professing Christians," said Ellen White, "Seventh-day Adventists should be foremost in uplifting Christ before the world. The proclamation of the third angel's message calls for the presentation of the Sabbath truth. This truth, with others included in the message, is to be proclaimed; but the great center of attraction, Christ Jesus, must not be left out. It is at the cross of Christ that mercy and truth meet together, and righteousness and peace kiss each other" (*Gospel Workers,* 156).

For us, the cross must be more than a theme. It is the source of our power, God's weak thing by which He defeated the world and the powers of evil, His foolish thing by which He made known the wisdom of heaven. And that wisdom is very practical, impacting the way we think, the way we regard others, the way we relate to others. That wisdom issues in love, acceptance, and reconciliation. That wisdom takes diversity and makes out of the many one new person—through the cross!

Church

The third pillar on which the worldwide Seventh-day Adventist Church fellowship rests is the concept of the Church itself.

From the beginning, the new community Jesus called into being was varied in its makeup. Jesus gathered all, excluding none—those who were not part of His fellowship excluded themselves. He welcomed everyone, even tax collectors and other "sinners" (Luke 15:1, 2).

Look at the apostles whom He selected. We find fishermen, a tax collector, and a member of a radical party, the Zealots. Further, His itinerant band was accompanied by women followers as well as men. Some of these women came from the upper echelons of society; some were wealthy and helped with the financial support of Jesus' ministry. "After this, Jesus traveled about from one town and village to another, proclaiming the good news of the kingdom of God. The Twelve were with him, and also some women who had been cured of evil spirits and diseases: Mary (called Magdalene) from whom seven demons had come out; Joanna the wife of Cuza, the manager of Herod' s household; Susanna; and many others. These women were helping support them out of their own means" (Luke 8:1-3).

Jesus founded the church. It is the *ekklesia*, those "called out" from the world to follow Him and live together in bonds of fellowship. The people who make up the Church come from all sorts of backgrounds—in New Testament times from among slaves and soldiers, artisans and highborn, rich and poor, old and young, men and women. They have responded to the divine call and confessed Jesus of Nazareth as Saviour and Lord; they have been called out as His, and He is their Head.

The Bible presents several metaphors or models of the

Church, and each carries within it the idea of diversity. Thus, the Church is "God's household, built on the foundation of the apostles and prophets, with Christ Jesus himself as the chief cornerstone. In him the whole *building* is joined together and rises to become a holy temple in the Lord. And in him you too are being built together to become a dwelling in which God lives by his Spirit" (Ephesians 2:20-22).

Again, the Church is a *family*, with differences among its members but a common "blood" tie—the blood of Jesus Christ (Ephesians 3:15; Romans 8:14-16).

The Church is a *field*, or *garden,* in which various workers play a part in the growth of the plants, but God is the Gardener. "So neither he who plants nor he who waters is anything, but only God, who makes things grow. The man who plants and the man who waters have one purpose, and each will be rewarded according to his own labor. For we are God's fellow workers; you are God's field, God's building" (1 Corinthians 3:7-9).

Likewise, the Church is a *sacred temple* founded on Jesus Christ. "For no one can lay any foundation other than the one already laid, which is Jesus Christ. If any man builds on this foundation using gold, silver, costly stones, wood, hay or straw, his work will be shown for what it is, because the Day will bring it to light. It will be revealed with fire, and the fire will test the quality of each man's work. . . . Don't you know that you yourselves are God's temple and that God's Spirit lives in you? If anyone destroys God's temple, God will destroy him; for God's temple is sacred, and you are that temple" (1 Corinthians 3:11-13, 16-17).

The Church is also a *body*. Just as the body has many parts that work together in mutual support and sympathy, so the Church has many members, each one different from the other, but each with its distinctive gift and essential for the good of the whole. And Christ is the Head.

I know of no better way to express the diversity of the Church than these words of Paul as he elaborates on the body metaphor:

The body is a *unit*, though it is made up of many parts; and though all its parts are many, they form one body. So it is with Christ. For we were all baptized by one Spirit into one body—whether Jews or Greeks, slave or free—and we were all given the one Spirit to drink.

Now the body is not made up of one part but of many. If the foot should say, "Because I am not a hand, I do not belong to the body," it would not for that reason cease to be part of the body. If the whole body were an eye, where would the sense of hearing be? If the whole body were an ear, where would the sense of smell be? But in fact God has arranged the parts in the body, every one of them, just as he wanted them to be. If they were all one part, where would the body be? As it is, there are many parts, but one body.

The eye cannot say to the hand, "I don't need you!" And the head cannot say to the feet, "I don't need you!" On the contrary, those parts of the body that seem to be weaker are indispensable, and the parts that we think are less honorable we treat with special honor. And the parts that are unpresentable are treated with special modesty, while our presentable parts need no special treatment. But God has combined the members of the body and has given greater honor to the parts that lacked it, so that there should be no division in the body, but that its parts should have equal concern for each other. If one part suffers, every part suffers with it; if one part is honored, every part rejoices with it. Now you are the body of Christ, and each one of you is a part of it (1 Corinthians 12:12-27).

In all the biblical depictions of the church, we find no suggestion of homogeneity or bland conformity. Rather the opposite—we find great diversity. Diversity is the very essence of the church; without diversity, whatever type of community may exist is less than the divine plan.

Collectively, the Church reflects the image of God. That image is too rich to be limited to a single person or group. Together, in Christ who is our Head, we reflect His glory, the multiform beauty of His character and the many-hued abundance of His grace. We need each other. And in the Church, in submission to Christ, we find our true selves in relation to one another.

We come now to the final pillar in the Seventh-day Adventist Church's understanding of diversity—commission.

Commission

For Seventh-day Adventists, Jesus' marching orders to His followers, the Great Commission, isn't optional. He is our Lord, we His disciples. He commands, not invites, and we take Him seriously. "All authority in heaven and on earth has been given to me. Therefore go and make disciples of all nations, baptizing them in the name of the Father and of the Son and of the Holy Spirit, and teaching them to obey everything I have commanded you. And surely I will be with you always, to the very end of the age" (Matthew 28:18-20).

Inevitably, then, we are a people with a global vision. Only as the gospel of our dying, risen, and soon-coming Saviour goes out into the world, and as we see disciples made to Him from all the nations, can we feel that we are on the right track. We *want* diversity—the diversity that comes from a global mission—for this is the evidence that we are indeed about our Master's business.

We have heard said so often that we are a unique movement that we probably fail to grasp this fact. For we are unique—unique among Protestant churches, unique among all churches. No other Protestant church attempts to be a global fellowship. The Methodists, Presbyterians, Lutherans, and evangelical groups function as national or regional churches. If you are a Lutheran, for instance, you belong to one of the branches of Lutheranism within North America. You may not be on speaking terms with Lutherans in other synods, and you have almost no sense of closeness to Lutherans in Germany, Asia, or South America.

No Protestant church is like ours—one world communion, one gathering of the nations among the banner of Prince Emmanuel. The Roman Catholic Church is a vast world body, but it is fractured along national and regional lines, with great gaps in theology and practice among Catholics from one part of the world to another. The evangelicals, fired with missionary zeal, seek out a part of the world to receive the gospel. They do good and earnest work, but their focus is localized. Ours is global.

From our earliest days we Adventists have been inspired and impelled by a dream, a vision:

> Then I saw another angel flying in midair, and he had the eternal gospel to proclaim to those who live on the earth—to every nation, tribe, language and people. He said in a loud voice, "Fear God and give him glory, because the hour of his judgment has come. Worship him who made the heavens, the earth, the sea and the springs of water" (Revelation 14:6, 7).

We have seen ourselves in this passage. We have seen here predicted a last-day message and mission that takes up and fulfills the Great Commission. Before the Lord returns, we believe, the good news will go to every village and hamlet, will break through to every unreached people group.

What a dream! It is the impossible dream—from a human standpoint. But with God all things are possible: Jesus' victory on Calvary assures the ultimate, global triumph of His mission.

Not only does Revelation predict a global mission just before Jesus returns, it also shows the success of that mission. John saw them, a vast number of men and women and boys and girls of all races won from this planet in rebellion. "After this I looked and there before me was a great multitude that no one could count, from every nation, tribe, people and language, standing before the throne and in front of the Lamb. They were wearing white robes and were holding palm branches in their hands. And they cried out in a loud voice: 'Salvation belongs to our God, who sits on the throne, and to the Lamb' " (Revelation 7:9, 10).

Diversity—threatening? Not for us. Diversity is in our blood, diversity is in our mission.

In September 1885, Ellen White attended the third session of the European Council. Her presentations included "Love and Forbearance Among Brethren," "Unity Among Laborers," and "Unity Among Different Nationalities." The Seventh-day Adventist Church, still in its fledgling stage, was just beginning to see itself in a global context, just starting to sense something of the divine experiment to bring together the nations under the power of the gospel.

Ellen expressed her fears when she first came to Europe: "I was almost afraid to come to this country because I heard so many say that the different nationalities of Europe were peculiar, and had to be reached in a different way. But the wisdom of God is promised to those who feel their need, and who ask for it." She also said: "Though some are decidedly French, others decidedly German, and others decidedly American, they will be just as decidedly Christlike. . . . God wants the different nationalities to mingle together, to be one in judgment, one in purpose. Then the union that there is in Christ will be exemplified."

And she issued this warning: "I warn you, brethren, and sisters not to build up a wall of partition between different nationalities. On the contrary, seek to break it down whenever it exists" (see *Testimonies for the Church,* 9:179-183).

Diversity

I applaud the preparation of this book on diversity and relationship building among the races, tribes, and ethnic groups of this movement. A book of this nature can provide all of us with new understanding and tools with which we can better realize the goal of "unity in diversity." The vision of Revelation 14:6, 7 won't just happen—it takes work! Global mission won't be realized without effort, planning, boldness, and sacrifice. And the coming together of the nations under the banner of the everlasting gospel—the divine experiment—won't happen without education and planning to break down the barriers of prejudice and suspicion that society has erected everywhere and which are even deep within us, in our thinking and attitudes.

Here is our goal: "We are to demonstrate to the world that men of every nationality are one in Jesus Christ. Then let us remove every barrier, and come into unity in the service of the Master" (*Testimonies for the Church*, 9:196).

Robert S. Folkenberg, born of missionary parents in Puerto Rico, is the president of the General Conference of Seventh-day Adventists. He is an experienced pastor, evangelist, administrator, musician, and pilot. He is bilingual and has done mission service in the Inter-American Division. He and his wife, Anita, have two children.

AMERICAN DIVERSITY

The 1990 census shows that racial and ethnic groups are growing seven times as fast as the non-Hispanic White majority. During the last ten years, California, Florida, and Texas have experienced the greatest population increases in minority groups. California leads the nation with an increase of 61.1 percent. While the White population actually declined in sixteen states during the 1980s, forty-one states saw double-digit percentage increases in their minority populations. Figures show that 6 percent of the counties in the United States are now minority majority, and many more are approaching the 50-50 balance.

During the 1980s, the Black population in America grew by 13.2 percent and now comprises 12.1 percent of the population in the United States. Hispanics now account for 9.0 percent of the national census. The Hispanic population of Los Angeles County alone has increased by 1.3 million over the last decade and now totals more than three million. Asians, who account for 2.9 percent of the population, doubled in numbers from 3.4 million to 7.0 million during the 1980s, with 39 percent of them living in California. The number of Native Americans has increased 33 percent since 1980 and represents approximately .8 percent of the population. Native Americans are the fastest growing minority group. The number of foreign-born immigrants, already a large share of the nation's population growth, will continue to increase, stimulated by the legislation passed in 1990, which increases the number of immigrants allowed per year from 500,000 to 700,000.

The minority population is growing most rapidly, not in central cities, but in middle-class suburbs. More and more college-educated minorities are joining the professional ranks, qualifying for skilled jobs and living a middle-class lifestyle. As a result, neighborhoods are more likely to be segregated by income level and less likely by race.

Source: American Demographics, July 1991

SECTION ONE

UNDERSTANDING

What Is Your Diversity Tolerance?
How Tolerant Are You?

*T*olerance is something we all like to think we have. But it is not easy to define: it is not just a matter of flexibility or simply permissiveness, nor is it the bottling up of feelings that we could otherwise have vigorously expresseed. It is clearly tied up with empathy—the capacity to put ourselves into another person's shoes and see the world from his or her viewpoint. In a strange way, it is also our capacity to see how other people view us.

Tolerance is an essential quality for peaceful and harmonious living in a society that admits, within the law, many different ways of thinking and behaving. Psychologists know that intolerance is associated with authoritatrian personalities and also with narrow and limited experience of the world. But while it is easy to detect intolerance in others, it is not so easy to pin it down in ourselves. This questionnaire, however, if answered honestly and accurately, will give you some pointers.

MARK YOUR ANSWERS ON A SEPARATE SHEET

1. When a friend does something you very much disapprove of, do you

a. Break off the friendship?

b. Tell her how you feel, but keep in touch?

c. Tell yourself it is none of your business, and behave toward her as you always did?

**2. Is it hard for you to forgive someone who has
seriously hurt you?**

a. Yes.

b. No.

c. It is not hard to forgive, but you don't forget.

3. Do you think that

a. Censorship is vitally necessary to preserve moral
standards?

b. A small degree of censorship may be necessary (to
protect children, for instance)?

c. All censorship is wrong?

4. Are most of your friends people

a. Very much like you?

b. Very different from you and from each other?

c. Like you in some important respects but different
in others?

**5. You are trying to work and concentrate, but the
noise of children playing outside distracts you. Would
you**

a. Feel glad that they are having a good time?

b. Feel furious with them?

c. Feel annoyed but acknowledge to yourself that
kids do make noise?

**6. If you were traveling abroad and found that
conditions were much less hygienic than you are
used to, would you**

a. Adapt quite easily?

b. Laugh at your own discomfort?

c. Think what a filthy country it is?

7. Which virtue do you think is most important?

a. Kindness.

b. Honesty.

c. Obedience.

8. Do you discuss critically one friend with others?
   a. Often.
   b. Rarely.
   c. Sometimes.

9. If someone you dislike has a piece of good luck, would you
   a. Feel angry and envious?
   b. Wish it had been you but not really mind?
   c. Think *Good for him*?

10. When you have a strong belief, do you
   a. Try very hard to make others see things the same way as you?
   b. Put forward your point of view but stop short of argument or persuasion?
   c. Keep it to yourself unless directly asked?

11. A friend is suffering from depression. Everything in her life seems to be fine, but she complains to you that she always feels depressed. Would you
   a. Listen sympathetically?
   b. Tell her to pull herself together?
   c. Take her out to cheer her up?

12. Would you employ someone who has had a severe nervous breakdown?
   a. No.
   b. Yes, provided there was medical evidence of complete recovery.
   c. Yes, if he was suitable in other ways for the work.

13. When you meet someone who disagrees with your views, do you
   a. Argue and lose your temper?
   b. Enjoy a good argument and keep your cool?
   c. Avoid argument?

14. Do you ever read a periodical that supports political views very different from yours?
   a. Never.
   b. Sometimes, if I come across it.
   c. Yes, I make a special effort to read it.

15. Which statement do you most agree with?
   a. If crime were more severely punished, there would be less of it.
   b. A better society would reduce the need for crime.
   c. I wish I knew the answer to the problem of crime.

16. Do you think that
   a. Some rules are necessary for social living, but the fewer the better?
   b. People must have rules because they need to be controlled?
   c. Rules are tyrannical?

17. If you are a religious believer, do you think that
   a. Your religion is the only right one?
   b. All religions have something to offer their believers?
   c. Nonbelievers are wicked people?

18. If you are not a religious believer, do you think that
   a. Only stupid people are religious?
   b. Religion is a dangerous and evil force?
   c. Religion seems to do good for some people?

19. Do you react to fussy old people with
   a. Patience and good humor?
   b. Annoyance?
   c. Sometimes a, sometimes b?

20. Do you think the Women's Rights movement is
   a. Run by a bunch of aggressive and insecure people?
   b. An important social movement?
   c. A joke?

21. Would you marry someone of a different race?
   a. Yes.
   b. No.
   c. Not without thinking carefully about the various problems involved.

22. If your brother told you that he was a homosexual, would you
   a. Send him to a psychiatrist?

    b. Feel shocked and accept him?

    c. Feel shocked and reject him?

23. When young people question authority, do you

    a. Feel uneasy?

    b. Think that it is a good thing?

    c. Feel angry?

24. Which statement do you agree with?

    a. Marriage is a bad institution.

    b. Marriage is sacred and must be upheld.

    c. Marriage is often difficult but seems to meet the needs of many people.

25. Do you think you are right—in matters of belief rather than fact—

    a. Always?

    b. Often?

    c. Rarely?

26. If you stay in a household that is run differently from yours in matters of tidiness and regularity of meals, do you

    a. Fit in quite happily?

    b. Feel constantly irritated by the chaos or the rigid orderliness of the place?

    c. Find it fairly easy for a while but not for too long?

27. Do other people's personal habits annoy you?

    a. Often.

    b. Not at all.

    c. Only if they are extreme or I am edgy.

28. Which statement do you most agree with?

    a. We should not judge another person's actions, because no one can ever fully understand the motives of another.

    b. People are responsible for their actions and have to take the consequences.

    c. Even if it is tough on some people, actions have to be judged.

Now Check Your Scores
(Total your scores to find your analysis.)

1. a. 4	b. 2	c. 0	15. a. 4	b. 2	c. 0
2. a. 4	b. 0	c. 2	16. a. 0	b. 4	c. 4
3. a. 4	b. 0	c. 4	17. a. 2	b. 0	c. 4
4. a. 4	b. 0	c. 2	18. a. 4	b. 4	c. 0
5. a. 0	b. 0	c. 4	19. a. 4	b. 0	c. 4
6. a. 0	b. 0	c. 4	20. a. 4	b. 0	c. 4
7. a. 0	b. 2	c. 4	21. a. 0	b. 4	c. 2
8. a. 4	b. 0	c. 2	22. a. 2	b. 0	c. 4
9. a. 4	b. 2	c. 0	23. a. 2	b. 0	c. 4
10. a. 4	b. 2	c. 0	24. a. 4	b. 0	c. 2
11. a. 0	b. 4	c. 2	25. a. 4	b. 0	c. 2
12. a. 4	b. 0	c. 2	26. a. 0	b. 4	c. 2
13. a. 4	b. 0	c. 2	27. a. 4	b. 0	c. 2
14. a. 4	b. 2	c. 0	28. a. 0	b. 4	c. 2

Analysis

For a quick view of your level of tolerance, check the "Tolerance Thermometer."

Below 30. If your score lies in this range, you are a particularly tolerant person. You are exceedingly aware of others' problems and difficulties, and you have a natural capacity for accepting them even when they offend you. You will be a good friend and popular with others. You may find that other people abuse this sympathetic good nature because they have nothing to fear from recriminations. Even then, you do not get really cross with them.

31-60. You are a tolerant person, and people will recognize you as one. If your score is above 50, however, you are probably tolerant and broad-minded in some areas only. Actually, it is easy to be tolerant if one does not hold very firm beliefs about anything. Look through the questions again, and note where you picked up higher rather than low scores. Were these questions in which personal comfort was directly concerned or in which convictions or very strong ideological beliefs were touched upon?

61-89. You are not as tolerant as many people, and if your score is higher than 80, you are basically an intolerant type of person. This will lead to clashes and short-term friendships. It will also mean that little things trouble you far more than they should and that you may waste emotional energy on what is really rather insignificant. It is very likely that you count yourself as someone with high principles, who tends to stick to important things rather than trvia. If you can get a wider experience of life and greater genuine contact with people, however, your tolerance temperature will come down, and in the end you will feel happier for it.

Over 90. This high score indicates that you are a very intolerant person. If your score is over 100, then you are also bossy, self-opinionated, and overquick to take offense. The only kind of friends that you are likely to retain are those who are interested in your money or generosity. If you really have scored this high, ask yourself *why* you are so unable to accept the faults in others. What are the aspects of other people that offend you most? Could it be that you are really punishing yourself for faults that you see in yourself?

1

Challenges of Change and the Church Mission

Caleb Rosado

The world and Adventism are going through vast and dramatic changes. Understanding the dynamics of these changes can lead to personal and Church growth.

*T*wo battleships assigned to the training squadron had been at sea on maneuvers in heavy weather for several days.... The visibility was poor with patchy fog, so the captain remained on the bridge keeping an eye on all activities.

Shortly after dark, the lookout on the wing of the bridge reported, "Light, bearing on the starboard bow."

"Is it steady or moving astern?" the captain called out.

Lookout replied, "Steady, Captain," which meant they were on a dangerous collision course with that ship.

The captain then called to the signalman, "Signal that ship: We are on a collision course, advise you change course 20 degrees."

The captain said, "Send, I'm a captain, change course 20 degrees."

"I'm a seaman second class," came the reply. "You had better change course 20 degrees."

By that time, the captain was furious. He spat out, "Send, I'm a battleship. Change course 20 degrees."

Back came the flashing light, "I'm a lighthouse."[1]

This captain experienced a "paradigm shift"—a movement away from old explanations that no longer explain reality. When one is immediately confronted with an unbeknown dangerous coastline, a course change of twenty degrees won't do. What is needed is a complete change of direction!

As the Church rapidly advances toward the shoreline of the twenty-first century, it cannot continue to carry on business as usual. The dictum of success for the twenty-first century is this: "We cannot become what we need to be by remaining what we are."[2] We live in dynamic, changing times. Yet the old ways of doing things, even if successful, are a continual threat to the very survival of the Church. Steve Wilstein reminds us that, "It's dangerous to believe you will remain successful simply by doing the same things that once brought success. *That will be true only if the world doesn't change.* . . . To be successful over the long haul, you need to change before it stops working. It's hard because nobody wants to change something that's working."[3] Thus, most persons and organizations will not change unless forced to.

The purpose of this chapter is to show how our world is changing, and how such changes, especially in the area of diversity, offer the Seventh-day Adventist Church an unparalleled opportunity for ministry and mission. An understanding of the challenges of diversity can be helpful to the Church as it charts its course into the uncharted waters of the twenty-first century. Though the Church's journey into the twenty-first century is spiritually charted, *socially* it is not. And it is in this realm where much of the structural conflict in the Church resides, even theological conflict, which often arises out of a desire for power and control. Thus the Church needs an awareness of the social forces that impact its mission, because the Church does not function in some social vacuum. Rather, it is influenced by the society of which it is a part.

The Stages of Societal Change

To understand why issues of diversity and multiculturalism are currently challenging the foundations of our society and the mission of the Church requires the awareness that society is not a static entity but an ever-changing one. Today we live in a society different from that of generations past. A failure to understand this may result in methods of ministry that are no longer relevant to today's needs, much less tomorrow's. What are the challenges we need to be aware of in order to have a ministry that transcends the twentieth century and is relevant to the twenty-first? The following chart describes sixteen of the major sociological shifts that have impacted the Church. These shifts also illustrate the sweeping changes that have taken place in the last century.

STAGES OF SOCIETAL CHANGE

	[1850s]	[1950s]	[1990s]
1. SOCIETY:	Agrarian	Industrial	Information
2. ECONOMY:	Agricultural	Manufacturing	Service
3. WORK TIME:	Nature	Clock	Flextime
4. TRADE CENTER:	Mediterranean	Atlantic	Pacific
5. FORM:	Tribe	Town	Technopolis
6. TRAVEL:	Walking	Driving	Flying
7. WORLDVIEW:	Familial	National	Global
8. ORIENTATION:	Past	Present	Future
9. ETHNIC VIEW:	Conformity	Uniformity	Diversity
10. POWER/SOURCE:	Family/Muscle	State/Money	Individual
11. EDUCATION:	Grade School	High School	College/G.S.
12. LOYALTY:	Family	Institution	Individual
13. OPTIONS:	Minimal	Many	Multiple
14. LIFESTYLE:	Ritual	Reformation	Revolution
15. RELIGION:	Tribal	Organized	Self-Help
16. VIEW OF GOD:	Mythical	Ontological	Functional

The following sixteen areas of change are suggested as representative of the major changes which have occurred within three societal ages—agrarian, industrial, and information. The change areas have been gathered from a variety of sources and provide a helpful overview for the chapters to follow in this book.[4]

1. Society: An *agrarian* society dominated much of human history until the nineteenth century, when the economic base shifted from agriculture to industry, first in Europe in the eighteenth century, then in the United States in the nineteenth, as a result of the Industrial Revolution. The *industrial* society held sway until 1956 and 1957, when the *information society* had its beginnings. Two factors brought about the change—the rise of a professional class and the computer chip. We have now shifted from a labor-intensive economy to a knowledge-intensive one, dominated by the computer and the communications satellite. Some people think we are now entering the information society. In all actuality, we have been in it for some time and are soon to leave it.[5]

2. Economy: The economic base of the agrarian society was primarily located in *agriculture,* which involved the planting, harvesting, or extracting of raw materials. The family was both the unit of production and of consumption, as people ate what they gathered or produced. The industrial society came into being after the Civil War, when the economic base shifted to *manufacturing,* the turning of raw materials into commodities and consumer goods. Life now shifted to the cities; people no longer worked in and around their homes, and rarely did they consume what they produced, for now they were working for money.

As the economy expanded, the need for professional services grew, giving rise to a *service* economy and the processing of information. Today, less than 2 percent of the population in the U.S. is involved in farming and less than 8 percent in manufacturing.[6] The emphasis is now on consumption rather than production, and the rising standard of living encourages a materialistic or secular view of life, rather than a spiritual one.

3. Work Time: In an agrarian society, the workday was pretty much determined by *nature.* People worked from sunup to sundown. With the industrial society and the rise of factories, work went under cover, and the *clock* became the determiner of work time. Production could now take place around the clock, in shifts. Today, due to technological advances, coupled with concerns for individual needs, *flextime* is now the norm, as people adjust their work schedules around other priorities in their lives.

4. Trade Center: At the turn of the last century, John Hay, the U.S. secretary of state, declared: "The Mediterranean is the ocean of the past, the Atlantic the ocean of the present, the Pacific the ocean of the future."[7] That prophecy has now come true. Five hundred years ago, when the Taino Indians discovered Columbus, lost somewhere in the Caribbean, the world economy centered in the *Mediterranean.* With the shift to the Industrial society, the *Atlantic* became the center of commerce. It was during this period when the majority of European immigrants came to the United States. Today in the Information society, the *Pacific* has now become the new trade route of the world.

5. Form: In the agrarian society the family, the *tribe,* with its extended kinships, close-knit sense of community and homogenous communal life, dominated the structural form around which society was organized. In the shift to industrialization, the small *town,* with a strong sense of community, became the dominant form of social organization. Now in the information society, the sprawling *technopolis* with its massive network of communications and multicultural interrelations dominates society.

6. Travel: *Walking* or human/animal/wind-powered forms of transportation, dominated for the longest time in history. People did not venture too far from home, as long-distance travel was limited by the cumbersomeness and inconvenience of movement. With the Industrial Revolution, a mechanized form of travel and transportation—*driving*—superseded human powered means. With the invention of the automobile at the end of the nineteenth century, people experienced a greater freedom of movement. After World War II and the ushering in of the Information Age, *flying* became the new norm for travel and transport, with the development of computerized technology.

7. Worldview: In an agrarian society, the parameters within which people viewed reality were *familial,* not extending much beyond the tribe, the family, the small commune, due to the limitation and inconvenience of travel. The industrial society gave rise to a *national* worldview, encouraged by the mechanization of travel. With millions of immigrants coming to this country especially after the 1850s, the concern was with building a sense of unity out of all this ethnic diversity. Thus, the legend in the Great Seal of the United States found on the one dollar bill reads *E PLURIBUS UNUM* ("out of many one"). In the new information society, the worldview has shifted to *global,* with a new perspective that transcends national boundaries. In the information age, the slogan now is "think globally; act locally."

8. Orientation: In terms of time orientation, John Naisbitt declares: "In our agricultural period, the time orientation was to the *past.* Farmers learned from the past how to plant, how to harvest, and how to store. The time orientation in an industrial society is *present.* Get it out, get it done, *ad hoc,* the bottom line, and all that. In our new information society, the time orientation is to the *future.*"[8]

9. Ethnic View: An "ethnic group" is a group of people with a sense of collective identity—solidarity—who may share a common culture, history, language, religion, or national origin.

The beginnings of this country were marked by a certain intolerance toward groups that differed from the behavior and belief of the Anglo-Saxon core group. The focus of the dominant group, the English, was on *Anglo-conformity,* the most prevalent ideology of assimilation in America throughout the nation's history. Thus, in order to be an "ideal"

American, one should be White, Anglo-Saxon, and Protestant—the WASP model.

From 1850 onward, with the shift to an industrial society, the masses of White ethnics from Europe began to arrive by the millions. Their cultural and religious differences led to the development of the *melting-pot theory* of assimilation, which envisaged a biological merger of the Anglo-Saxon peoples with other immigrant groups and a blending of their respective cultures into one new indigenous American type. The essence of the melting-pot theory—uniformity— was that America was a large crucible.[9]

There were three problems with this theory. *First* of all, the crucible had already been molded between 1776 and 1789, and its shape was "Anglo-conformity." *Secondly*, not everyone was invited to the "pot party." Blacks, Hispanics, American Indians, and Asian Americans—the racial minority—were simply left out.

The *third* problem with the melting-pot theory, and the most important one, was that it gave a skewed definition of who was an American. The old and still prevailing ideology of what an American looks like was a Northern European phenotype—White, blond, and blue-eyed. Those who differed from this visual image were and still are labeled as hyphenated Americans: Native-American, African-American, Mexican-American, Asian-American, etc. The implication is that they are not quite yet Americans and have not divested themselves completely of their past to be included. Most may never be included because they cannot change their skin color.

It is this latter point that led Eduardo Seda Bonilla to conclude that there have been "two ways" of adaptation for minority groups in the United States—one for ethnic or "cultural minorities and one for racial minorities."[10] For the former, all they simply had to do to be accepted was to "discard their culture," and they would be accepted. For the latter— persons of color—the issue was more complex, it was racial, and the shedding of culture made no difference in their acceptance. They simply have not been accepted as genuine Americans.

Multiculturalism—respect for what the other brings to the communal table —is redefining *who* is an American by challenging the taken-for-granted definition of American as "White." Multiculturalism, a system of beliefs and behaviors, recognizes and respects the presence of the various racial-ethnic groups in a particular society or organization, acknowledges the validity of their different forms of cultural expression, encourages their cultural contributions and reflections.[11] It is telling the people of the United States of America that an "American" is any person that is a citizen of this country either by birth or naturalization, no matter their skin color, physical features, cultural expression, or national origin. The result is a rich cultural tapestry, a beautiful mosaic, a delicious stew, that reflects the beauty of God's family.

As we now move within the new information society, with a global worldview, the focus is on *diversity*. Diversity includes more than cultural and racial differences. By diversity is meant the biological, cultural, physical and socioeconomic differences (such as age, class, culture, education, gender, physical condition, race/ethnicity, values, etc.) that people bring to an organization, community, or society. While these differences have the potential of giving rise to conflicts, if managed well, they can result in a synergetic unity in diversity. Therefore, the effect of *all working together* will be greater than the sum total of all the parts working independently.

Managing diversity is nothing new. Today, for the Church to reach its potential, that attitude has to shift from one of exclusion, both the individual and institutional dimensions, to one of *inclusion*. If the gospel means anything, it means *inclusion!*[12] Everything done in the church, at all levels of ministry and administration, must be done with the gospel principle of inclusiveness in mind: *Because we are one with God, we are also one with each other, equal before both* (John

17:23; Acts 10; Galatians 3:28; Ephesians 2:14-22). Thus, managing diversity in the Church means that the various talents and capabilities of its diverse membership are unleashed so as to create a wholesome, inclusive environment. Such an environment is safe for differences, and it enables people to reject rejection, celebrates diversity, and maximizes the full potential of all in the unity found in Christ. In this setting Christ is honored, a powerful witness is made to the world, and everyone benefits.

Diversity, then, in its essence, is a "safeguard against idolatry."[13] It prevents one group from serving as the norm for all other groups. Only the gospel has that divine function. The Church is challenged to shift to a "futures-orientation," one that anticipates change rather than reacts to it. A new era demands new methods and new metaphors.

The *stew-pot* is a better metaphor to describe the reality of the Seventh-day Adventist Church as an ethnically diverse church. We have never been a melting-pot, which conjures up images of a homogeneous, purée-like product. Rather, we are a heterogeneous body, a rich cultural stew, where the various ingredients—while maintaining their distinctiveness—have contributed their unique ethnic flavors, all richly blended by the heat of group tension. This is what makes a stew a stew, not just the ingredients tossed in together as in a cold salad, but the application of heat to the pot. Managed carefully, the heat of group tension will bring out the creative juices of the various ethnic groups, resulting in a special cultural blend that gives the Seventh-day Adventist Church its unique spiritual character in the world today.

10. Power/Source: Here lies much of the problem in interhuman relations. "Throughout history, power has been associated with institutions," declares Naisbitt,[14] first with *families,* then with the *state,* and today with the *individual.* In each period, one type of power tended to dominate. In the past, the amount of power people had was largely determined by virtue of their position in the family. During the agricultural revolution, violence or *muscle,* was the main source of power. This was the primary method by which people of old gained their wealth.

In the development of nation-states, the state was the repository of power, and *money* was the main source. Today the source is knowledge, the *mind*. Authority now rests with those who have the knowledge and the information. We are moving from a "capital-intensive" society to a "brain-intensive" one.[15] This shift in power has been made possible in part by the increase of education.

11. Education: For the greater part of our history as a nation, a *grade-school* education was all that was needed, as the economy did not require much education beyond the ability to read and write. With industrialization, *high schools* emerged to bring the immigrant experience in line with the dominant culture. Today, the needs are such that a *college* education, even graduate school, is becoming the new requirement for social and occupational advancement. We have become a "credential society,"[16] where people need the necessary credentials—a diploma— to get a decent job, even though the education received may not necessarily have prepared them for that job.

12. Loyalty: In an agrarian society, loyalty was to the *family,* as this was the locus of activity and the place where work centered. When the economy shifted to the factory, loyalty shifted to the company, the corporation, the *institution.* The result was the rise of The Organizational Man[17]— the person who would always be loyal to the company, the organization, the institution. The focus is now on the *individual,* the new locus of loyalty.[18] Name brands in products or churches are not even safe anymore, as people will go to where their needs are better met.

The impact on religion is that people are no longer denominationally loyal.[19] There was a time when if one left the Seventh-day Adventist Church, there was nowhere to go. Today, growing up Adventist is no guarantee that a person will continue to be an Adventist. People tend to gravitate toward those religious groups that will meet their spiritual needs irrespective of the church's message. The rapid increase of independent/nondenominational, community churches is an example of a rise in generic, non-brand loyal churches. The point: The spirit of individualism of our time is moving people toward those religious expressions that enable them to develop spiritually, even if it means leaving the church of one's childhood.

13. Options: The matter of choices and available options is often determined by the type of society we live in. Options increase as we move from an agrarian/rural society to an urban/technological one, from *minimal* to *many* to *multiple.* Urbanization contributes to the freedom of choice, which also requires the need for discipline, because one cannot exercise all the available options. Religion, the Church, is challenged to help people cope with this reality.

14. Lifestyle: The age of *ritual,* where things were done by rote, following traditions handed down from one generation to the next without much thought involved, is over. But so is *reformation,* concerned with improving things, without necessarily transforming them. Today we are living by *revolution,* a transformation of the present in view of the needs of the future. This does not mean, however, that everything must be overthrown. The idea is to save from the past that which is functional to the needs of the present and has a usable future, while at the same time constructing that which did not exist but is now needed. This change has an immense impact on the Church.

15. Religion: There was a time when entire communities reflected the same religious tradition, went to the same or similar church, and were of the same faith. *Tribal,* rural societies tended to be this way. Religion was a guiding force in the life of the community.

With industrialization, *organized* religion became more prominent and the mode of religious expression. Religion and ethnicity often went hand in hand. The English were Episcopalians and Baptists, Scots were Presbyterians, the Germans and Swedes were Lutherans, the Irish, Italians, Poles and Mexicans were Catholics, etc. Denominational loyalty was high, as each church claimed to have the "truth." But as brought out under Loyalty, the focus was more on the institution than on the individual; institutions were more concerned with their own survival and institutional needs than those of the individual members. Institutions failed to grasp the Sabbath principle, a most important principle given 2,000 years ago by Jesus in Mark 2:27, when He declared: "The Sabbath was made for humankind, and not humankind for the Sabbath." Simply stated, the Sabbath principle declares that: *The institution exists for the purpose of meeting the needs of individuals and not individuals the needs of the institution.*

People today in the information society are moving away from organized religion to *self-help* forms of religion, the religion of a fast-food society. Much like a competitive market economy as a result of deregulation, the religious scene in America today resembles more of a "spiritual supermarket," with the various groups competing with each other for customers.[20]

The change helps to explain why New Age religion is so attractive to many people today—according to some estimates, 15 percent of the population. It is an example of a self-help, do-it-yourself, self-service type of religion, consistent with the fast food, information society we live in.

In my many years of teaching sociology of religion at secular state universities in the midwestern, eastern, and now western sectors of the United States, I have discovered that students are not interested in organized religion as much as in self-help spirituality. The result is a tendency to develop or gravitate toward those forms of religious expression that are compatible with their cultural lifestyle and social behavior and/or which give meaning to their existence.

16. View of God: The reduction of our world to a global village by an international communications network and the interdependence of nations has raised new questions about God. Now the exploited nations and the deprived peoples of the world are able to see how the rest of the world lives and how the few benefit at the hands of the many. These people, primarily from agrarian societies in less developed countries, who for centuries have had a *mythical* understanding of God (God and nature inextricably linked), are now waking up, bypassing the *ontological* phase (God as separate being). In other words, they are leaping from an agrarian society to the information society, bypassing the industrial society (not necessarily in terms of economics, but in terms of information), and are raising *functional* questions about God in relation to their experience. On whose side is God? Is this all we have, or is there more? Is not God the One who hears the cry of the oppressed and stands up against Pharaoh and demands justice? And so the voices of liberation, feminist, ecological theology, raising functional questions of God, are heard from all corners of the world—Latin America, Africa, Asia, Black and Hispanic America, the female world, and indigenous peoples.

There are a couple of factors that are bringing about an increase and interest in religion—demand and supply.[21] The first is the result of rapid social change and the gravitational pull of the year 2000, the *millennium.*[22] Social earthquakes—societal change—like their geological counterparts, create insecurity in people, sending them in all directions in search of social anchors. Religion is one of those anchors. During periods of great social upheaval, political change, and economic uncertainty, people turn to religion as a spiritual anchor to provide a sense of social stability in their lives. This reflects the demand side of religion.

On the other hand, a shift in societies gives rise to new religious markets, opportunities, and movements. This is the supply side of religion. The shift from an agrarian to an industrial society, for example, brought about the development of several new religious groups in American society such as the Mormons, the Seventh-day Adventists, Christian Scientists, and Jehovah's Witnesses, as well as transcendentalism and spiritualism. The same happened in the 1960s in the shift to the information society. The lowering of immigration restrictions resulted in an increased immigration from India and a wave of gurus bringing Eastern religions and the emergence of New Age movements.[23]

As we move toward the twenty-first century, both factors—demand and supply—will give rise to numerous new religious groups. "In turbulent times, in times of great change [and of social and economic uncertainty], people head for the two extremes: fundamentalism and personal, spiritual experience."[24] The closer we get to the year 2000, the more we will see apocalyptic cults emerge in society, such as the two ill-fated groups, the Branch Davidians in Waco, Texas,[25] and the Solar Temple in Switzerland, both claiming to be spiritual anchors in the midst of social storms.

These are the stages of societal change, which give the Church an understanding into the nature of society and challenge its mission. These stages of change demonstrate why diversity is now a social reality and therefore a necessity to be taken seriously and not merely an option. The problem we are facing in the Church, however, is that while we are living in the information age, we are still thinking with an agrarian mindset and value system, all the while utilizing methodologies from the industrial age. The paradigm of uniformity of past ages cannot serve the needs of a diverse church and society. To be relevant, the Church must be current in both *mindset* and *methodology*. How well the Church is able to communicate with this ever-changing society is determined by how willing the Church is to not only respond to these changes, but to anticipate them.

What Will the Future Look Like?

The above is merely a mirror of the past and the present. What will the future look like? Let me give you a brief glimpse. Again, it just reflects a sociological perspective, but one which we need to take seriously if the Church is to survive into the twenty-first century.

STAGES OF SOCIETAL CHANGE

Late 1990s into the twenty-first century

1. SOCIETY: Global
2. ECONOMY: High-Tech
3. WORK TIME: Relative

4.	TRADE CENTER:	Trilateral
5.	FORM:	Neo-Village
6.	TRAVEL:	Teleporting
7.	WORLDVIEW:	Planetary
8.	ORIENTATION:	Future/Past
9.	ETHNIC VIEW:	Mutuality
10.	POWER/SOURCE:	Team Synergy/Empowerment
11.	EDUCATION:	Grad./Tech.
12.	LOYALTY:	Group
13.	OPTIONS:	Myriad
14.	LIFESTYLE:	Reliance
15.	RELIGION:	Spirituality
16.	VIEW OF GOD:	Inclusive

---

1. Society will shift to *global*.[26] In fact, to a large extent, we are already there, due to a global economy.

2. The Economy itself will eventually become *high-tech* once the super information highway becomes fully operational. Yet in a highly alienated society, people are increasingly finding themselves alone. Thus in an age of *high-tech,* people need *high-touch*—strong attachments and social bonds that give people security, dignity, and self-worth. People thus will turn to that person, group, or object they believe will give them the greatest stability, connection, and meaning to life.

3. Work Time will shift to *relative* time in that with computerized technology, work can now be fitted around personal needs.

4. Trade Center is becoming *trilateral*—NAFTA, the European Community, and the Pacific Rim. The remainder of the world, the have-nots, will have to be included, or else they will become the centers of disruption and the displaced.

5. Organizational Form of urban living will be, and is even now, shifting to a *neo-village*. This is a new form of urban planning which seeks to recover the sense of community lost with the rise of industrialization.

6. Travel will shift to *teleporting,* meaning that as a result of computerized technology, interactive multimedia, and virtual reality, an illusory, artificial, computer-generated parallel world will be created, giving people a sense of being in remote locations in the physical world. People will be able to go anywhere and do anything they want to do, without leaving their homes. It will be an exciting but frightening world, with tremendous implications and opportunities for the mission of the Church.

7. Our **Worldview,** because of environmental concerns, will shift to *planetary.*

8. Time **Orientation** will be both *future and past,* meaning that with the help of technology, humans will realize that they cannot plunge headlong into the future without consideration for lessons from the past.

George Santayana reminds us that: *"Those who cannot remember the past are condemned to repeat it ."*[27] Can we not learn from the past, so as to have an unfogged future? Ellen G. White said we can, using words similar to Santayana's. "We have nothing to fear for the future, except as we shall forget the way the Lord has led us, and His teaching in our past history."[28]

9. Such learning will impact our **Ethnic View** in relation to diversity. A whole generation of children and youth are now being educated within a diverse and multicultural curriculum. The result will be an attitude and sense of *mutuality—* oneness resulting from giving and taking and learning from each other. This will not necessarily eliminate racism. For racism is the deliberate structuring of privilege by means of an objective, differential, and unequal treatment of people, for the purpose of social advantage.

Racism involves competition over scarce resources that results in an ideology of supremacy which justifies power of position by placing a negative meaning on perceived or actual biological/ cultural differences. Thus, if the essence of racism is the refusal to accept the "other" as an equal, then to eliminate racism one would have to give up the societal rewards of *pride of position,* social *power,* and structural *privilege.* This is not possible without the basic institutional alteration of society, because it is a culturally and structurally sanctioned reality.

If racism has nothing to do with biology but has everything to do with socially structured beliefs and behavior, then it can also be socially *unlearned* and *unstructured*. The key factor for success in this process, however, is to work through the primary social institutions that perpetuate such learning and behavior: the family, the school, the church, the workplace, and government. These institutions must undergo a dramatic transformation for racism to be eliminated.

Long ago, Karl Mannheim reminded us that: "To live consistently, in the light of Christian brotherly love, in a society which is not organized on the same principle is impossible. The individual in his personal conduct is always compelled—in so far as he does not resort to breaking up the existing social structure—to fall short of his own nobler motives."[29] This is why the Church, the primary moral institution in society, has to lead the way. Adventism, as the most ethnically diverse religious organization in the world, is in a position to lead the way, if it will only be true to its mission in view of this vision.

10. This brings us to **Power** and its **Source**. As we approach the twenty-first century, power will shift from the individual to *team synergy,* for individuals can no longer go it alone. Yet team synergy is on the way in, while the "lone ranger" is on the way out, for as Thomas Kayser suggests, "None of us is as smart as all of us."[30] Team synergy is a product of valuing and effectively managing diversity, where, as mentioned earlier, the effect of *all working together* is greater than the sum total of all the parts working independently.

The new paradigm shift of the twenty-first century is one of *inclusiveness* and *interconnectedness*. This is a cultural, spiritual bond—our common frailty—that connects us to each other and to our physical, ecological environment, for we are all in this together, "united we stand, divided we fall." The source of this new power of team synergy is *empowerment:* the process of enabling people to be self-critical of their own biases so as to strengthen themselves and others to achieve and deploy their maximum potential.

11. The demands of society will alter **Education.** Not only will *graduate* education become normative, but also *technological* education, especially at the high-school and community-college levels. One function of education will be to develop in students a sense and practice in how to be a "world citizen." A world citizen is a person who is able to transcend his/her own racial/ethnic, gender, cultural, and sociopolitical reality and identify with humankind throughout the world, at all levels of human need. S/he is a *transcending* person who knows no boundaries and whose operating life principle is compassion.

12. Loyalty will shift away from the individual to *group*. The super information highway, with sources such as Internet, will create a new cadre of "global groups" throughout world society.

13. This, of course, will have a tremendous impact on **Options** as these now become *myriad*.

14. Lifestyle will be greatly impacted as well, moving nations and peoples away from revolutions to *reliance,* meaning that no nation or people can go it alone anymore, a factor which brought about the end of Russian communism and apartheid.

15. All of this will give rise to a new paradigm of **Religion**—a concern with *spirituality*.

16. An *inclusive* **View of God**, the result of the interconnectedness of humankind, is the support for the concern with spirituality. The late 1980s and early 1990s have seen the return of spirituality, in a global concern for connectedness and communalism. A new paradigm or way of perceiving our world, has emerged as a "global spirituality" focused on the interconnectedness of all of life, both human and environmental. This holistic view of life—which is very biblical (Genesis 1, 2; Romans 8) and is at the core of three biblical doctrines, the Doctrine of Humankind, the Sabbath, and Creation—has a profound spiritual undergirding.

In an unstable age of rapid sociopolitical change, people are desperately searching for an anchor to the soul. Many are now seeking for it in spirituality. *Spirituality is that intangible reality and animating force that connects us to God, however defined, and to each other, resulting in a state of security and in a sense of worthful purpose.* But this area can be just as bankrupt as science, if people, Adventists included, place at the center of their life that which is not eternal and divine. Thus, true spirituality needs to be centered in God, who does not change but is the same yesterday, today, and forever. This *spirituality* is none other than the Holy *Spirit,* who creates a longing and yearning for God in the human heart and who centers our life in the person of Jesus Christ.

Conclusion

We live in dynamic, changing times, as illustrated by the Stages of Societal Change. This presents a challenge to the Church as to the way it must carry out its mission. While the Church must be sensitive to the various forces influencing change, it must not allow these forces to be the *main* criteria for change. Thus the need for restructuring the Church must not be driven by economic or political forces but by the egalitarian factors of the gospel. The central dynamic which must guide the Church through the uncharted waters of change is the inclusive principle of the gospel—"unity in diversity in Christ" (Galatians 3:28).

Michael Fullan, at the University of Toronto, reminds us that "change is mandatory, growth is optional." Such changes are placing new demands and constraints on the Church as a spiritual/social institution to be relevant to the times in which it exists. Diversity is no longer an option for the Church but a necessity because of the paradigm shifts society has undergone. Because of the paradigm shifts just discussed, twenty degrees of change will not do. These are merely cosmetic. The Church itself needs to undergo a major paradigm shift consistent with the gospel and relevant to the needs of society.

The gospel demands an "incarnational" model of ministry, one that is able to take on flesh in its diverse hues. God's challenge to the Church then is: "Worship me in *any* cloth, for I am not tailor-made. Who told you that I was?"[31]

It is the mission of the Church, therefore, to prepare today's generation of members to not only understand these social changes, but more importantly to anticipate them so as to respond proactively rather than reactively. Such action will enable our churches, our schools, our institutions to become catalysts for change. The ultimate change, however, will be a translation from this earth to the heavenly one soon to come. In view of this ultimate change, the words of Gandhi are most fitting: "We must live the change we desire to see in the world."

Caleb Rosado, Ph.D., is professor of sociology at Humboldt State University, Arcata, California. He is the author of three books and has pastored for more than twenty years and established the multicultural congregation, the All Nations Church, in Berrien Springs, Michigan. He is an international consultant and speaker on issues of diversity and multiculturalism. He and his wife, Ronnie, have three children.

Endnotes

1. Cited by Stephen R. Covey, *The 7 Habits of Highly Effective People* (New York: Fireside, 1990), 33.

2. Max DePree, *Leadership Is an Art* (New York: Doubleday, 1989).

3. Steve Wilstein, "Getting What It Takes to Win," *Hemispheres*, June 1994.

4. Among the many sources from which this material was drawn are the works of Harvey Cox, *The Secular City* (New York: The MacMillan Company, 1965); John Naisbitt, *Megatrends: Ten New Directions Transforming Our Lives* (New York: Warner Books, 1982); John Naisbitt and Patricia Aburdene, *Re-inventing the Corporation* (New York: Warner Books, 1985); John Naisbitt and Patricia Aburdene, *Megatrends 2000: Ten New Directions for the 1990s.* (New York: William Morrow and Company, Inc., 1990); Alvin Toffler, *Powershift* (New York: Bantam Books, 1990); Cornelis A. van Peursen, "Man and Reality—the History of Human Thought," *Student World,* No. 1, 1963, 13-21; and by the same author, "The Concept of Truth in the Modern University," *Student World,* No. 1, 1963, 344-353; and Hedley Beare and Richard Slaughter, *Education for the Twenty-first Century* (London: Routledge, 1993).

5. An outstanding article that covers the same ground as this article but with a different slant is the one by Peter F. Drucker, "The Age of Social Transformation," *The Atlantic Monthly,* November 1994.

6. Alvin Toffler, *Powershift* (New York: Bantam Books, 1990), 70.

7. Ibid., 179.

8. *Megatrends,* 18.

9. Milton M. Gordon, *Assimilation in American Life* (New York: Oxford University Press, 1964), 120.

10. Eduardo Seda Bonilla, Ethnic Studies and Cultural Pluralism, in *The Rican,* Fall 1971, 56-65.

11. For a fuller explanation of the concept of multiculturalism, see Caleb Rosado, "Multicultural Ministry," *Spectrum: The Journal of the Association of Adventist Forums,* April 1994, 23:5, 27-34.

12. See Caleb Rosado, *Broken Walls* (Boise, Idaho: Pacific Press Publishing Association, 1993).
13. Brian Wren, "What Language Shall I Borrow? Worship: Language & Gender." The Second International Conference on Adventist Worship, April 7-10, 1993, La Sierra University.
14. *Megatrends,* 309.
15. Toffler, 129.
16. See Randall Collins, *The Credential Society* (Orlando, Fla.: Academic Press, Inc., 1979).
17. William H. Whyte, Jr., *The Organization of Man* (New York: Simon & Schuster, 1956).
18. Paul Leinberger and Bruce Tucker, *The New Individualists* (San Francisco: Harper Collins, 1991).
19. Wade Clark Roof, *A Generation of Seekers: The Spiritual Journeys of the Baby Boom Generation* (San Francisco: Harper Collins, 1993).
20. For a discussion of this religious economy paradigm to explain the religious character of the United States, see: Roger Finke and Rodney Stark, *The Churching of America, 1772-1990* (New Brunswick, N.J.: Rutgers University Press, 1992); R. Stephen Warner, "Work in Progress Towards a New Paradigm for the Sociological Study of Religion in the United States," *American Journal of Sociology,* 98:5, March 1993, 1044-93.
21. Roger Finke and Laurence R. Iannaccone, Supply-Side Explanations for Religion," *The Annuals of the American Academy of Political and Social Science,* 527, May 1993, 22. See Chapter 9 of *Megatrends 2000.*
22. Finke and Iannaccone, 36.
24. Ibid., 277.
25. See Caleb Rosado, "Lessons From Waco," *Ministry,* July and August 1993; also published in the *Adventist Review,* 29 August 1993.
26. Peter F. Drucker, in an important article on the same theme this article touches on, "The Age of Social Transformation," *The Atlantic Monthly*, November 1994, combines both the Information Society and the Global Society into one, which he calls the "Knowledge Society." While this is useful, I still felt that it makes more sense to separate the late twentieth century from the beginning of the twenty-first, since the distinctions will be transformational.
27. George Santayana, *The Life of Reason* (New York: Dover Publications, Inc., 1980 [first published in 1905]), 1:284.
28. Ellen G. White, *Life Sketches of Ellen G. White* (Boise, Idaho: Pacific Press Publishing Association, 1915), 196.
29. Karl Mannheim, *Ideology and Utopia* (New York: Harvest Books, 1936), 195.
30. Thomas Kayser, *Building Team Power* (New York: Irwin Professional Publishing, 1994).
31. Words from a poem that Wintley Phipps shared with me.

2

Adventism's Rainbow Coalition

Roy Branson

An understanding of the roots of the diverse groups in Adventism, particularly its largest ethnic community—Black Adventists—will help us to better appreciate each other's struggles and concerns.

*P*robably no church in the world embraces more ethnic communities than Seventh-day Adventists. One hundred and fifty years after the Great Disappointment, almost 90 percent of Seventh-day Adventists now live outside the United States. Adventists worship in more countries than any other church but Roman Catholicism. Even among the 10 percent of the Adventist denomination living in the United States, the majority will be non-Whites as early as 1998.

Embracing fellow believers who look, talk, and act differently from ourselves has been one of Adventism's more dramatic pilgrimages. The road to ethnic diversity has sometimes been a rough one—and it may get rougher. We can learn from how our founders wrestled in the United States to combine appreciation of cultural differences with a sense of unity and common purpose.

Adventism was begun, and initially led in the nineteenth century, by WASPS—White Anglo-Saxon Protestants—living in New England and upper New York State. For a few years after the Great Disappointment, they believed that God would take to heaven only those who had accepted Him before 1844. In effect, their Shut-Door teaching permitted primarily WASPS into heaven. Even when they changed their minds and opened the Shut Door, Adventists took several years to actively welcome Whites other than Anglo-Saxons.

White Ethnics

In 1856, twelve years after the Great Disappointment, James White, J. H. Waggoner, and Uriah Smith took Adventism's first step toward ethnic diversity. They prepared a tract for German immigrants in their own language. Among the waves of European immigrants landing on the Eastern shore of the United States, those who joined Adventism came primarily from those Protestants who had dissented from established European state churches. The first Norwegian and Swedish immigrants, baptized in 1858, included a Baptist preacher and forty members of his congregation. John Mattson soon also converted a Danish Baptist preacher to Adventism.

In the 1870s, Adventists expanded their work among German and Scandinavian immigrants. In 1871, the first Adventist periodical in a foreign language appeared—the Danish *Advent Tidende*. Danish converts convinced fellow emigrants from Germany to the Dakotas to become Adventists. In 1872, a lay leader in a Nebraska Church of the Brethren brought several other German immigrant families into Adventism. That same year, a former Baptist preacher organized the first Swedish American church in the United States. Concurrently, the *Svensk Advent Harold* (Swedish Adventist Herald) began publishing.

During the next decade, Bible schools were started for

Scandinavians in Chicago (1885) and for Germans in Milwaukee (1886). Scandinavian and German departments were also instituted at Battle Creek College and then at Union College (1891). At the turn of the century, the Anglos continued to regard immigrants as foreigners. When denominational leaders came to organize departments at the 1901 General Conference, they created what they called the North American Foreign Department, specifically "for the work among the German and Scandinavian nationalities in North America, and for others as necessity may demand."[1]

In 1910, no less than three foreign-language seminaries opened for classes: Danes and Norwegians in Hutcheson, Minnesota; Swedes on a farm in Broadview, Illinois; Germans on 112 acres near Clinton, Missouri. These seminaries grew through World War I and after. By 1922, the Danish-Norwegian Seminary had grown from a beginning of 82 students to 188, and the Swedish Seminary from 22 to 200 students. The German Seminary achieved the largest enrollment—225 students. During these years, when the United States had the highest percentage of foreign-born and second-generation citizens in its history, the Anglo Adventists reported that those they designated as "foreign" members comprised over 16 percent of the SDAs in the United States.

Scandinavians came to dominate the leadership of the Foreign Department. By 1918, S. Mortenson, a Danish American, noted that immigration patterns had changed—in his view, for the worse. In the 1870s, he said, people from northwestern Europe formed 99 percent of the immigrants to the United States, but "we find that in 1914 the figures had so changed that the people from northwestern Europe made up only 25 percent, while those from southeastern Europe constitute 75 percent of the immigration."

Mortenson regarded the latest immigrants with at least as much suspicion as Anglo-Saxon Adventists had earlier regarded the German and Scandinavians, like Mortenson. "On an average, 37 percent of them are illiterate. They are practically all Roman or Greek Catholics, and in their ideals, customs and habits they differ widely from their northern neighbors and from us." Mortenson looked on the newcomers from southern Europe as culturally unequal. "It is true many of them are outwardly unlovely, uncultured and unpolished, but the raw material for sparkling jewels is there. The privilege is ours to grind and polish the rough surface and bring out the inner beauty."[2]

Deteriorating economic conditions in the United States forced first the German Seminary in Clinton, Missouri (1925), and then the Danish-Norwegian Seminary in Hutcheson, Minnesota (1928), to move to the Swedish Seminary at Broadview, Illinois. As late as 1932, the secretary of the General Conference Foreign Department felt it necessary to assure the Scandinavian Adventist membership that this did not mean a breakdown of ethnic distinctions. "One question that was raised was the objection to having Danish-Norwegian young people mixed up with representatives of the Latin races. . . . Marriages between Nordics and Latins at Broadview are very rare (only 7 Italians and 4 Poles are in attendance at Broadview)."[3]

During the Depression and World War II, immigration declined. By 1933, the percentage of Adventists in the United States designated as ethnics slipped below 10 percent. Also, the second generation of immigrants from across Europe was assimilated rather easily into the American Adventist Church. Descendants of Scandinavian and Germans immigrants came to serve in many leadership positions, including vice-presidents and president of the world Church. By 1951, the Foreign Department was disbanded.

Native Americans

Anglo Adventists lumped the original Americans with foreigners. C. W. Parker reported in an 1893 *Review and Herald* that in Pine City, Minnesota, "last Sabbath we had in our meetings Scandinavians, Americans, and Indians, which shows that the message is going to the people, tongues and languages." He also reported the first Native American converts to the

Seventh-day Adventist denomination, an unnamed Chippewa couple.[4] By 1897, the first congregation of Seventh-day Adventist Native Americans had been organized.

Adventists have directed most of their money and attention involving Native Americans toward Navajos. To this day, it is regarded as a mission effort. The North American Division supports a twelve-grade school in Holbrook, Arizona, that teaches farming, gardening, plumbing, carpentry, electronics, and auto welding. The division has provided scholarships for Indians in other parts of the country to attend the academy in Arizona.

After World War II, at about the same time the denomination started the school in Arizona, it also began a dispensary in Monument Valley, Utah. It was not until 1969 that the denomination ordained an Indian, Tom Holliday, who became pastor of the Adventist church in Monument Valley. Interestingly, in spite of these efforts in Arizona and Utah, as of 1992, the vast majority of Native American Adventists lived in the North Pacific Union—992 of the 1,791 Native Americans in the North American Division.

Jewish Americans

It is assumed that even fewer Jews than Native Americans comprise North American Adventism. One person was responsible for Seventh-day Adventists first paying special attention to Jews: F. C. Gilbert, a London-born Jew, who in 1889 converted in Boston to Seventh-day Adventism. For half a century, Gilbert, as secretary of the Jewish Department and then field secretary of the General Conference, pleaded for more work to be done for the Jews. Gilbert wrote articles in the *Review and Herald* and many tracts for fellow Jews. From Gilbert's time to the present, the denomination has published a special magazine for Jews, now called *Shabat Shalom*. Still, so few Jews were ever converted, the Foreign Department never even kept figures of how many North American Adventists were Jews.

It was not until 1949, three years after Gilbert's death, that the first Jewish Adventist congregation was organized in New York City. J. M. Hoffman, a Jewish convert who first became active in evangelism in the South, moved to the Bronx, where he organized 25 members into a congregation. He wore the Jewish prayer shawl and yarmulke, replaced all Sabbath offerings and Ingathering campaigns with a congregation-wide double-tithe, and built up the membership to over 130. In 1959, Hoffman moved the congregation from the Bronx to mid-Manhattan, into a multipurpose building that included a 400-seat auditorium. Hoffman called the new facility the Times Square Center.

Eventually, because of objections from New York rabbis, Hoffman had to relinquish his Jewish vestments. After Hoffman retired, the membership of the congregation dwindled to 25 Jewish members. While F. C. Gilbert, and now Clifford Goldstein, the editor of *Liberty* magazine, have gained prominence within Adventism, and Jewish Adventists report that they constantly meet denominational leaders and members who are wholly or partly Jewish, no ethnic community within American Adventism remains less visible than Jews—and less threatening to other ethnic groups.

Asian Americans

During the 1992 riots in south central Los Angeles, Korean American Adventists were among those whose stores were demolished. That is not surprising, since Korean Americans now comprise the largest group within American Adventists of Asian origin. Over half of Asian American Adventists live in California (12,000 of the division's 20,000).

California is where the first Asian Americans became Adventists and organized their first congregations. In 1892, T. H. Okahira was baptized in an evangelistic campaign in Paso Robles, California. He attended Healdsburg College (now Pacific Union College), and four years later the first Japanese American convert became the first Seventh-day Adventist missionary to Japan. His son was responsible for starting the initial Japanese American church in Los Angeles. In 1922, the first Japanese American churches were organized in northern California—a congregation of fifteen members in Mountain View and one of twenty in San Francisco.

External forces were responsible for significant increases in Asian American Adventists. The first was the imprisoning of Japanese Americans in California concentration camps during World War II. The Foreign Department sent three full-time workers and 120,000 pieces of Japanese language literature into the concentration camps. Two hundred Adventists went into the camps, 350 walked out—a 75 percent increase.

More liberal immigration laws in the mid-1960s led to an even greater number of Asian American Adventists. This increase paralleled a climbing percentage of Asians among all immigrants to the United States. From 1,000 members in 1965, Adventists of Asian origin increased within a decade by over 150 percent. Then, from 1980 to 1990, Asian American Adventists increased by another 252 percent. By 1992, although Asian Americans constituted only 2.6 percent of the division membership, they had expanded to over 20,000 members in the North American Division.

The concentration of Asian American Adventists in California is reflected in the fact that Asian American Adventists send a much higher percentage of their children to Adventist colleges in California than do other ethnic groups. (Although Adventist schools of higher education in California also admit a significant number of foreign students from the Pacific Rim countries and enroll some non-Adventist Asian Americans, most of their ethnic Asian students are from American Adventist families.) In the 1992–1993 school year, Asians and Asian-Americans made up 14 percent of the enrollment at Pacific Union College, 20 percent of the students at Loma Linda University, and 36 percent of the student body at La Sierra University. Asians constituted a larger percentage at all three schools than any other ethnic group but Anglos.

Hispanic Americans

As with so many of the ethnic groups, Hispanics started becoming Adventists in the late nineteenth century. As might be expected, it was in the Southwest, near Mexico, that Hispanics first found Adventism. In 1898, a Methodist pastor in Tucson, Arizona, brought his church of Spanish-speaking members into the Adventist denomination. Shortly after 1900, Hispanic churches sprang up along the Rio Grande—El Paso, San Antonio, Laredo, Corpus Christi, and Mission, Texas. In the 1920s, more Hispanic congregations appeared in such picturesque-sounding towns as Las Cruces, San Marcial, Socoro, and Raton. Hispanics in California organized their first congregation in 1906 and in Colorado two years later. Up to World War II, Mexican Americans in the Southwest, California, and Colorado remained the core of Hispanic American Adventists.

The church had Mexican Americans in these areas primarily in mind when it twice established schools for Spanish-speaking Adventists in the Southwest. First, in 1920 the Spanish-speaking Training School opened near Scottsdale, Arizona, in conjunction with what later became Thunderbird Academy. The school closed thirteen years later during the Depression. The second attempt by the General Conference—Seminario Hispano-Americano, near Albuquerque, New Mexico—lasted only ten years. It was sold to the Texico Conference and became the Sandia View Academy.

After World War II, the world of Hispanic Adventists became much more diverse. Puerto Rican Adventists immigrated to New York City. In the 1960s, Cuban Adventists moved into Miami. In the mid-1960s the same immigration laws that admitted vastly more Asians did the same for Latin Americans. Hispanics of different nationalities, particularly Central Americans, found their way to North America.

Hispanics have not attempted to organize their own ethnically defined conferences. Instead, a pattern emerged of directors or vice-presidents for Hispanic members within the existing conferences and unions. Since the 1960s, Hispanics have grown rapidly. By the early 1970s, Hispanics consti-tuted one-third of the Texico Conference and 40 percent of the Greater New York Conference. From 1980 to 1990, Hispanic members in North America increased 127 percent. By 1992, Hispanics had become 17 percent of the Pacific Union mem-bership, 15 percent of the Southwestern Union, and 12.5 percent of the Atlantic Union. Among North American Adventists as a whole, Hispanics were a more modest 8.5 percent of the membership. But if growth patterns hold steady, by the year 2000, there will be 150,000 Hispanic Adventists in the North American Division, comprising 14.5 percent of the division membership.

African Americans

As in the United States as a whole, the most complicated ethnic relationship among Seventh-day Adventists has been between Whites and Blacks. At least in America, the relation-ship has formed a recurring pattern: The general society is changing the relationship of Blacks and Whites, some event creates a crisis in Black-White relations within Adventism; Black members make certain demands; the White majority refuses; instead, the Whites institute the changes Blacks had demanded during the previous crisis in racial and ethnic relations. The dynamics of the race relations and encounters between Whites and Blacks in the Adventist Church have had far-reaching effects and considerable historic impact on the entire denomination. Therefore, considerable discussion is here given to the development of the Black work as it reveals the prevalent attitudes on the subject.

Millerites and Abolitionism

Black Adventists trace their roots back to the Millerites. William Foy, a Black man, received visions (1842–1844), that were similar to Ellen White's early visions in 1844. Ellen White said that Foy had four visions and that she talked to him after she had spoken at a meeting. She said Foy told her he had seen some of the same scenes she saw. She recalled hearing him speak in Portland when she was a girl and said he bore "remarkable testimonies." For years it was believed Foy refused to share his visions, gave up Christianity, and died in 1845 after the Great Disappointment. Foy lived until 1893. These and other misconceptions are cleared up in the book *The Unknown Prophet* by Delbert Baker.

The Founders' Theology on Race

Only six years after the Great Disappointment, Ellen White urged civil disobedience in the cause of anti-slavery. When the U.S. Congress passed the Fugitive Slave Act in 1850, Ellen White told Sabbath-keeping Adventists in no uncertain terms that "the law of our land requiring us to deliver a slave to his master, we are not to obey."[5] When she learned that an Adventist defended slavery, she bluntly admonished him: "You must yield your views or the truth.... We must let it be known that we have no such ones in our fellowship, that we will not walk with them in church capacity."[6] At a time when many, even in the North, considered slavery a commercial or political issue, Ellen White regarded slavery as a moral outrage.

Ellen White could have believed in the abolition of slavery and still not regarded the Black persons as equal to whites, but she was unequivocal: "Christ came to this earth with a message of mercy and forgiveness. He laid the foundation for a religion by which Jew and Gentile, Black and White, free and bond, are linked together in one common brotherhood, recognized as equal in the sight of God."[7] Not only were redeemed Christians equal in Christ, but Blacks and Whites were equal brothers because of a common creation. God wants us, she said, to remember "their common relationship to us by creation and by redemption, and their right to the blessings of freedom."[8]

James White, the organizational leader of Sabbath-keeping Adventists, declared that oppression of slaves in America was significant evidence that the beast in the book of Revelation, chapter 13, was the United States, a beast that looks like a lamb but speaks like a dragon.

When the Civil War began, President Lincoln had not yet announced his Emancipation Proclamation and said that he was fighting the rebellion only to save the Union, not to free the slaves. Uriah Smith, who succeeded James White as editor of the *Review and Herald,* used the pages of Adventism's official church paper to pronounce an anathema on the sitting President of the United States for not acting immediately to free the slaves.

The first Black Seventh-day Adventists were scattered through northern churches. The first congregation of Black members was organized in the South. Harry Lowe, a former Baptist preacher, joined a biracial church in Edgefield junction, Tennessee, near Nashville. Then in 1886, because of racial tensions, he led in the formation of a Black congregation of ten members. The first Black Seventh-day Adventist to become an ordained minister, C. M. Kinney, was born a slave in Richmond, Virginia; converted to Adventism in Reno, Nevada, and then attended Healdsburg College for two years. Kinney preached in Kansas before moving on to a successful ministry in Kentucky and Tennessee. By 1890, a second predominately Black church was organized in Louisville, Kentucky.

In the early 1890s, Ellen White spelled out for the General Conference officers what equality between whites and blacks, based on her theology of both redemption and creation, meant in the practical life of the church.

> It will always be difficult matter to deal with the prejudices of the White people in the South and do missionary work for the colored race. But the way this matter has been treated by some is an offense to God. . . . You have no license from God to exclude the colored people from your places of worship. Treat them as Christ's property, which they are, just as much as yourselves. They should hold membership in the church with the White brethren.[9]

James and Ellen White's older son took his parents' theology of ethnic and race relations seriously. The result was crucial for relations between Whites and Blacks in the American Adventist Church. In 1895, Edson White built a boat, called it the *Morning Star*, and with some White colleagues, sailed it down the Mississippi River. He and his friends conducted for Black Southerners along the river towns of Mississippi, not only religious meetings, but health clinics and classes in reading, writing, and farming.

However, in 1895, opposition to Edson's *Morning Star* mission came not only from White plantation owners. Black preachers, fearful of losing members, also incited Whites against the Adventists. The result were violent attacks, burnings, and attempted lynching. Edson White had sailed into what some historians of the South have called the "Crisis of the Nineties." It was a time, says Yale's C. Vann Woodward, when "a great restiveness seized upon the populace, a more profound upheaval of economic discontent than had ever moved the Southern people before, more profound in its political manifestation than that which shook them in the Great Depression of the 1930s."[10] Economic, political, and social frustrations pyramided social tensions, which broke out into aggression against Blacks—and sometimes against their White friends.

Finally, in 1899, Ellen White reluctantly began counseling caution. "As far as possible, everything that will stir up the race prejudice of the white people should be avoided. There is a danger of closing the door so that our white laborers will not be able to work in some places in the South." She did add the famous promise to Black Adventists: "Let them understand that this plan is to be followed until the Lord shows us a better way." Ellen White remained committed to equality between Blacks and Whites based on both God's work of salvation and creation, but after the experience of her son in the midnineties, she became more pragmatic in how to apply racial equality to specific circumstances.[11]

The Creation of the Negro Department

By the time of the 1909 General Conference session, there were about a thousand Black Adventists, and the first crisis in relations between Whites and Blacks had hit the denomination. L. C. Shaefe, formerly a Baptist preacher, and probably the most prominent Black preacher in Adventism, had been invited to pastor the integrated, though predominately Black, First Seventh-day Adventist Church of Washington, D.C. One of its members was the daughter of Frederick Douglass, the most famous Black person of his time, and a witness, he said, to the falling stars of 1833.

Prominent members of the Church felt that the newly elected General Conference president, A. G. Daniells, wanted Black and White Adventists to worship in separate congregations. As the newly reorganized General Conference was moved from Battle Creek to Washington, D.C., the officers left First Church to organize other, White congregations. The General Conference committee refused to assign a White pastor to assist Shaefe in an evangelistic campaign. Dr. J. H. Howard, a Black physician in First Church, expressing views shared by Shaefe, wrote to Daniells that "it is difficult to see why it is necessary to make a race line in the Adventist denomination in face of the fact that the truth involves a positive protest against any such thing in the church."

By the time of the 1909 General Conference session, the demands of the Black leaders had become specific. J. K. Humphrey, pastor of the Harlem First Church, made his case on the floor of the session by appealing to the denomination's earlier efforts on behalf of White ethnics. "As I studied the situation, I found that the other nationalities were getting along first-rate. . . . It encourages you to listen to these reports of how the work is going among the Germans, Danes, Scandinavians and others; but when it comes to the Negroes, do you hear anything?"[12]

A. G. Daniells strongly supported the creation of the Negro Department. Like Humphrey, he cited the precedent of the Foreign Department. The first signer of the "Appeal," Sydney Scott, made the fieriest speech of the discussion, concluding that "there ought to be a just and fair representation in that department from the local mission clear to the head" and that the name of the department should be "Afro-American."

Scott, and the other Black leaders, got their department, but not the suggested name. Nor did they get representation. The first secretary leading the Negro Department was a White man, as were many of his successors. It would be nine years before the first Black leader, W. H. Green, would head the department.

After World War I (1914–18), crowds in America's cities cheered returning Black regiments. But when the Black veterans began claiming the rights and privileges of American citizens, Whites fiercely resisted. Between 1916 to 1918, one-half to a million southern Blacks migrated to northern jobs. In just two years (1919–1920), 100,000 Whites joined Klu Klux Klan chapters in twenty-three states. In the summer of 1919, no less than twenty-five major riots broke out in American cities. One in Chicago lasted for thirteen days, wounding hundreds and killing thirty-eight people.

Crisis in Harlem

At the same time that Adventists, and Americans generally, were regressing in race relations, Blacks in northern cities were becoming more militant. This was the time of social and literary activity in New York City. The post–World War I period was also the beginning of the Harlem Renaissance, a flowering of artistic and literary talent that included a number of Caribbean immigrants and later, an author from an Adventist minister's family, Arna Bontemps. He served as principal of Adventist Harlem Academy and taught briefly at Oakwood College before becoming writer in residence at Fisk University and visiting professor for six years at the University of Chicago and Yale. In 1928, during this period of increasing ferment, W. H. Green, the first Black secretary of the Negro Department, died. He had led the department for a decade. Black Adventist pastors were disappointed in how little had been accomplished by the department since 1909. They proposed that the General Conference abolish the Negro Department and replace it with Black conferences; one

Black General Conference leader would be succeeded by several Black conference presidents.

The most obvious candidate for president of a Black conference was J. K. Humphrey. Nineteen years before, in the aftermath of Schaefe's departure from the denomination, Humphrey had stood with A. G. Daniells, the General Conference president, and helped him create the Negro Department. Humphrey, originally an ordained Baptist pastor in the Island of Jamaica, pastored the Adventist First Church of Harlem. The church was made up primarily of West Indian immigrants, in a Harlem being ignited by West Indian ideas of self-determination. Under Humphrey's leadership, the congregation became the largest in the Greater New York Conference. He had also started three other congregations.

A spring 1929 meeting of General Conference leaders in Washington, D.C., failed to approve the creation of Black conferences and instead created a commission of sixteen to study the matter (eleven Whites and five Blacks), to bring a report to the 1929 Fall Council. Humphrey quickly concluded that although he was on the commission, Black conferences were dead. He proceeded to pour his energies into promoting and soliciting funds for Utopia Park, located forty-five miles south of New York City, in New Jersey. It would include three lakes and facilities for an orphanage, a home for the aged, a training school, an industrial area, and private residences. It was time, Humphrey was convinced, for Black Adventists to create their own institutions. When the conference president inquired into Utopia Park, Humphrey wrote back that "I thank you very much for your expressions of kindly interest and your desire to cooperate in this good work, but it is absolutely a problem for the colored work."[13]

During the year, the commissioner of Public Welfare for New York City had asked the Greater New York Conference what the Utopia Park promotion was all about, and the city made permission for soliciting the Ingathering more difficult. In the fall of 1929, after consulting with the Atlantic Union, the Greater New York Conference requested that Humphrey give up plans for what the conference president had called a "colored colony." When Humphrey refused, the conference committee fired the pastor of its largest congregation.

The dismissal took place on a Friday. The following Saturday evening, the First Church of Harlem gathered to hear the news. Not only did the Greater New York Conference president attend, but the president of Atlantic Union, the secretary of the General Conference, and the revered president of the General Conference himself, W. A. Spicer. The meeting lasted five hours. According to an internal report of the General Conference leadership, the entire congregation supported the pastor. The *New York News* reported to the public that "the meeting soon became uncontrollable and bid fair to develop into a riot, which was prevented by the quick action of the pastor himself."[14]

After the 1929 Autumn Council, in the midst of confrontations with Humphrey, J. L. McElhenny, vice-president of the General Conference for North America, wrote a twenty-eight-page printed "Statement Regarding the Present Status of Elder J. K. Humphrey." He defended not only the denomination's actions concerning Humphrey, but its refusal to approve separate Negro conferences. In less than twenty years, McElhenny would again face a crisis in race relations within the church and would propose Humphrey's solution of Black conferences.

However, on January 24, 1930, the Harlem First Church its pastor were expelled from the denomination. Most of the members stayed with Humphrey, calling their congregation the United Sabbath Day Adventist Church. The district attorney's office cleared the Utopia Park project, but it was never developed.

Creation of Black Conferences

The election of Franklin Roosevelt and the beginning of World War II had a dramatic effect on American Blacks, and indirectly on race relations within the Adventist Church. From 1933 to 1946, the number of Black employees on the federal payroll increased from 50,000 to 200,000. Some Black leaders called Roosevelt's presidential order of June 25, 1941, the most important document affecting them since the Emancipation Proclamation: "There shall be no discrimination in the employment of workers in defense industries or Government because of race, creed, color, or national origin." For the first time, during World War II, Blacks were integrated into units of the army, navy, and marines.

By contrast, at the end of World War II, at General Conference headquarters in the Washington, D.C., metropolitan area, the only Black among General Conference leaders was the leader of the Negro Department. He and other visiting Black leaders of the church were still not permitted inside the Review and Herald Publishing House cafeteria, the place General Conference leaders routinely ate lunch. Both the nearby Adventist institutions, Columbia Union College and Washington Sanitarium and Hospital, did not admit Blacks.

In this environment, the almost predictable incident catalyzing a change in relations between Black and White Adventists occurred. A Black Adventist woman visiting relatives in Washington, D.C., suddenly fell ill. Her sister drove her to the closest Adventist hospital, the Washington Sanitarium and Hospital. The emergency room staff refused to care for a Black patient. The sister, now desperate, drove her to the Freedman's Hospital in another part of the city. Before they arrived, her visiting sister had died.

The Black press reported the incident to the country. Outraged Black Adventists organized a Committee for the Advancement of World-wide Work Among Colored Seventh-day Adventists. Among the prominent Black laity signing an eight-page set of demands from the committee to the General Conference was Eva B. Dykes, the first Black woman to complete a doctorate in the United States—from Radcliffe College at Harvard University.

The statement contrasted the integration of colleges and hospitals outside the church to denominational institutions to which Black members contributed tithes and offerings. Three principal demands were made: integration of Adventist institutions, greater Black representation at all levels of denominational administration, and greater accountability from denominational leadership of Black members' financial contributions to the Adventist Church.

With the press following developments, and prominent Black laity across the United States demanding action, the General Conference president met with representatives of the committee. He then convened a meeting to consider the future of the Black work in America. Just before the 1944 Spring Council of the Church's top leadership, prominent Black pastors, leaders of union Negro Departments (appointed after the Church's previous racial crisis), prominent Black laity, some White union presidents, and General Conference leaders gathered in April at the Hilton Hotel in Chicago. Presiding was J. L. McElhenny, president of the world Adventist Church. Fourteen years before, as vice-president for North America, he had been involved in dealing with the demands of J. K. Humphrey for Black conferences and his subsequent expulsion.

The General Conference leaders informed the assembled group that integration of the Adventist Church on the scale outlined by the committee of Black laity was impossible to achieve. Instead, McElhenny proposed implementing the 1929 demand of J. K. Humphrey and others to create Black conferences. Each Black conference would have jurisdiction over Black members then within several White conferences. In many cases, Black conferences would coincide with the territory of entire unions. Integration was unattainable, but there could be increased self-determination of Black clergy and conference committees. What was being proposed fell between two alternatives found in Protestant American churches: the commitment to integration at all levels, found among what remain predominantly White Episcopalian and Presbyterian denominations, and the completely separate Black and White denominations, found among Baptists and Methodists.

The head of the General Conference Colored Department, G. E. Peters, supported the creation of Black conferences. By the time a vote was taken, so did a strong majority of the entire committee. The 1944 Spring Council, meeting immedi-

ately afterward, approved Black conferences, voted to elevate
Oakwood to senior college status, and appointed Louis B.
Reynolds to be the first Black editor of *Message,* the Black
missionary magazine.

Before the end of 1944, the Lake Region Conference was
already established within the Lake Union. By the end of 1946,
five Black conferences had been created. Within a year of the
organization of these Black conferences, the percentage of the
U.S. Black population that was Adventist exceeded, for the first
time, the percentage of U.S. Whites who were Adventists.

Through the late 1940s and early 1950s, integration advanced gradually in the United States, and even more slowly
within the church. In 1950, McElhenny's successor as president
of the world church, W. H. Branson, tried to speed things up. He
released an unprecedented letter—reminiscent of a U.S.
President's executive order—addressed to all union and local
conference presidents and managers of Seventh-day Adventist
institutions in North America. In this letter he appealed to
Church leaders to redouble effort in the area of human relations.

> Perhaps no religious group in the United States or
> the world, claims so loudly that it is international in
> its attitudes and services as do the Seventh-day
> Adventists and yet, in this matter of Negro segregation, we are trailing behind the procession. We seem
> afraid to venture any changes in the relationships
> which we maintained a half century ago, notwithstanding the fact that the whole world about us had
> made and is still making drastic changes.
>
> Shall we be the last of the Christian bodies to break
> away from our historic attitudes and chart a new
> course in our human relationships?
>
> ... We wish to appeal to the managing boards of our
> publishing houses, sanitariums and schools in the East,
> North and West, to give immediate study to this matter.
> We believe that in most places in these sections of the
> country there can be complete integration of the races in

our institutions without serious difficulty.

We understand that in the deep South a few of our institutional boards have voted to discontinue segregation. . . . In some places it will require some courage to launch into such a program but the entire country is headed in that direction. The government, the churches, and the business world are leading the way, and why should we hesitate to follow?[15]

A month later, the Supreme Court of the United States unanimously declared in Brown v. Board of Education that segregation in public schools was unconstitutional. Through the remainder of the 1950s, administrators responded to Branson's letter and trends in the society by gradually integrating more and more Adventist institutions. It was later in the 1960s that Adventist schools were integrated, and the General Conference session (1962) in San Francisco elected the first Blacks to the positions of associate secretary and general vice-president of the General Conference.

Or course, Martin Luther King, Jr., stepped up the pace of integration, with the 1956 Montgomery, Alabama, bus boycott, followed by other direct actions. In Tampa, Florida, a young pastor of the Black Adventist church, Warren Banfield, accepted the presidency of the local chapter of the National Association for the Advancement of Colored People (NAACP). He organized the Black citizens of Tampa so well that his threat to lead a bus boycott was sufficient to integrate the public transportation of the city. He persuaded the city to build public housing for the poor Black people of Tampa.[16]

Not surprisingly, a specific incident soon recrystallized race relations within North American Adventism. Almost twenty years after an Adventist Black woman was turned away from the emergency room of the Washington Sanitarium and Hospital, Frank Hale, chairman of the Department of English at Central State College at Wilbeforce, Ohio, and Burrell Scott, a successful Ohio contractor, tried, at the beginning of the 1961–1962 school year, to enroll their Black daughters at Mount

Vernon Academy in Ohio. They were refused, and no denominational officials rectified the situation.

As in 1944, the Black Adventist laity organized, this time as the Laymen's Leadership Conference. In 1961, the General Conference president refused to even meet with the Black laity. It was a mistake. Mylus Martin, a Black member and reporter with the *Cleveland Press,* helped to facilitate news coverage. The first Saturday of the 1962 General Conference session, both San Francisco daily newspapers ran front-page stories, printing the demands of the Laymen's Leadership Conference: rethinking Adventist appropriations for Black churches in the United States; abolition of unofficial but real racial quotas proscribing Blacks in Adventist schools; and the complete and immediate desegregation of all Adventist organizations and institutions. More stories appeared in the local newspapers and in the national press on Friday, Saturday, and Sunday. On Wednesday, the General Conference president held a press conference affirming that the SDA Church would desegregate.

The Church had taken a major step toward responding affirmatively to demands it had said, sixteen years earlier, in 1944, were impossible to achieve—election of Blacks to all levels of denominational administration.

During this decade, Black Adventist leaders were being influenced by more than what they saw in the media. Black Adventist pastors in the South helped organize boycotts of merchants who segregated their facilities. They participated in the famous 1965 Selma to Montgomery march that led to the passage of federal legislation guaranteeing voting rights to Blacks. The South Central Conference, the Black Adventist conference in the deep South, made sure that its mobile medical unit from Mississippi was a part of Martin Luther King's March on Washington and that it was parked in the shadow of the Lincoln Memorial to provide emergency medical care.

The Black Union Issue

At the 1968 annual meeting of North American Black Adventist leaders, the Regional Advisory Council, several younger leaders proposed that the General Conference give greater financial support to Black conferences and also create two Black unions in North America. They ran into the determined opposition of the General Conference president, Robert Pierson, who for years had worked with Black leaders to expand the racial integration of the church. In 1969, a special interracial commission to study the issue rejected Black unions in North America but accepted the "Sixteen Points" that listed a series of measures that would strengthen the Black work. The next year, Charles C. Bradford became the first Black secretary of the North American Division. Black leaders were elected secretaries, or the second highest administrators, of unions across North America. In 1979, Charles Bradford succeeded Neal Wilson as the first Black President of the North American Division. The next year, the Lake Union elected Robert Carter the first Black president of a North American Union. In the 1990s Black leaders have been elected presidents of predominately White conferences.

Growth patterns of Black Adventists in North America reveal that membership took off after 1944, when Black leaders took over the running of Black conferences. There was another upturn in the mid-1960s, a period when Black laity and clergy were increasingly asserting themselves inside and outside the denomination. Even as Black Adventists have become increasingly upwardly mobile—educationally, economically, and professionally—they have continued to grow in numbers. By 1992, Black members constituted more than twice the percentage of U.S. Adventists (25 percent) as the percentage of Black citizens in the nation.

Brown and Yellow, Black and White

A glance at the roots of ethnic diversity in North American Adventism suggests that currents in society and culture can lead us to rediscover important parts of our Adventist heritage. Responding to shifts in our cultural environment helps us recover and appreciate important aspects of our community that we had forgotten were powerful and revitalizing.

Also, growth and vitality more often flow from cultivating diversity than from seeking unity. The more self-determination Adventist ethnic leaders in North America have achieved, the more they have cultivated their communities, the more the Church as a whole has grown.

Finally, we can only embrace the strangeness of others when we respect the surprising as an expression of God's irresistible creativity; when we participate in God's unquenchable delight in shapes, colors, and points of view; when we capture God's joy in the diversity of creation.

Roy Branson, Ph.D., a senior research fellow at the Kennedy Institute of Ethics, Georgetown University, is director of the Washington Institute, editor of *Spectrum,* and an adjunct professor at the Center for Christian Bioethics, Loma Linda University. He has edited several books, and his articles appear in such publications as the *Dictionary of Christian Ethics*, the *Encyclopedia of Bioethics*, the *Journal of the History of Ideas*.

Endnotes

1. *Review and Herald*, 8 June 1905, 6.
2. "Report of the North American Foreign Department," *Review and Herald,* 30 May 1918, 17.
3. Campbell, North American Foreign Department, 1932.
4. J. 0. Corliss, "What the Indians Need," *Review and Herald,* 6 June 1891, 6.
5. *Testimonies for the Church*, 1:202.
6. Ibid., 359, 360.
7. *Testimonies for the Church*, 7:225.
8. Ibid., 223.
9. *The Southern Work,* reprinted by Review and Herald Publishing Association, Washington, D.C., 1966, 15.
10. *The Strange Case of Jim Crow* (New York: Oxford University Press, 1966), 77.
11. *Testimonies for the Church*, 9:214, 207.
12. *Review and Herald,* 17 June 1909, 7.
13. J. K. Humphrey to Louis K. Dickson, 20 August 1929, quoted in Joe Mesar and Tom Dybdahl, "The Utopia Park Affair and the Rise of Northern Black Adventists," *Adventist Heritage* (1974), 1:1, 37.
14. Ibid., 39.
15. W. H. Branson to all union and local conference presidents, managers of SDA institutions in North America, 13 April 1954.
16. Conversations with Warren Banfield.

3

Ellen White, a Pioneer in SDA Race Relations

Delbert W. Baker

One person can make a difference even in the challenging area of diversity and race relations. With love and commitment, one can model the character of Christ. Ellen White modeled Christ's example in diversity and race relations and provided an example to every member in the body of Christ.

What advice would Ellen White have given on how to build relationships between the diverse groups in the Adventist Church? How would she have recommended we approach some of the sensitive challenges facing the Church in the area of diversity and race relations? Had she lived during the 1990s, what counsel would she have provided to achieve organizational equity among the diverse groups in the Seventh-day Adventist (SDA) Church? Most important, are the race-relation principles she advocated still relevant in the multicultural society in which we live?

During Ellen White's adult life, several historic events in the area of civil rights and race relations occurred in the U.S. and in the SDA Church. In the U.S.—slavery, the Civil War, the Emancipation Proclamation, and the Reconstruction and post-Reconstruction periods are a few key events. In the Church members struggled with the slavery issue, combat in the Civil War, responsibility to the Black race, and the issues of discrimination and segregation, evangelistic and humanitarian responsibility in the South, and to Black people in particular. During this period, race relations in the Church were among the more prominent issues.

During this time, the work among Black people in the South started in earnest under the leadership of James Edson White, Ellen White's son. Simultaneously, during the post-Reconstruction period, segregation as a system became institutionalized in America. During this time, Ellen White spoke and wrote extensively on the race subject and left thousands of pages of counsel. Thus we have the opportunity to examine Ellen White's role as a pioneer of race relations in the SDA Church and to examine her views on issues relevant to cultural diversity and multiculturalism.

This chapter will explore the questions stated earlier. First, diversity will be examined in light of the Bible and the SDA mission. Then we will view selected vignettes that provide a window into Ellen White's attitude toward people of different ethnic backgrounds from her own. Then Ellen White's role in the controversy over slavery and relations in the Church between Whites and Blacks will be explored. Next will be an overview of some defining components that may have impacted Ellen White's worldview on race and ethnicity. Finally, we will deduce a strategy on how to achieve unity in diversity from the Bible and the writings of Ellen White.

Diversity and the SDA Mission

In diversity literature there is deliberate emphasis on the need for people to develop broad and inclusive attitudes toward diversity. Equally emphasized is the need to cultivate actions consistent with one's attitude. Diversity is all about attitudes and actions in society and organizations that have *respect* for all people regardless of their race/ethnicity or culture; it emphasizes *appreciation* of the differences in people rather than seeking to make them conform to a particular culture. Diversity, then, building on the above two emphases, highlights the need to be *inclusive* of different people, and this involves sharing of responsibilities, resources, and opportunities. Many people, inside and outside the SDA Church, find this emphasis threatening. Others feel this emphasis is long overdue.

Regardless of one's position, diversity is vital to the mission and interest of the Church. Diversity has everything to do with its raison d'etre, the reason for our existence. The invitation of the three angels' messages in Revelation 14:6-7 clarifies God's diversity plans for His Church. "Then I saw another angel flying in midair, and he had the eternal gospel to proclaim to those who live on the earth—to every *nation, tribe, language and people.* He said in a loud voice, fear God and give him glory, because the hour of his judgment has come. Worship him who made the heavens, the earth, the sea and the springs of water" (NIV). One of the identifying signs of God's true Church is its diversity.

It follows, then, that the SDA Church is successful when it is actively involved in creating a diverse body of believers. When the Church is spreading the gospel to all the world, winning and nurturing believers to Christ, then it is involved in the work of creating and managing diversity. Spiritual diversity is the work of the Church. In this sense, diversity is not new. It is as old as the command to spread the good news of salvation, starting with Adam in the Old Testament, extending to the apostles in New Testament, and finally, to Christians in our day.

Attitudes on Race and Ethnicity

How did Ellen White respond to the biblical command to facilitate diversity in the Church? Did she understand the big picture of diversity? Were her actions consistent with her words? Did her life bear the fruit of genuine love for all people, regardless of their ethnicity? The answer is an emphatic "yes!"

Her words and works indicate that she did respond to the command to bring about diversity. She did see the big picture. Her actions were consistent with her words. She did show genuine love to all people. Though the term *diversity* had a different meaning in her day, she conceptually understood what diversity was all about. Ellen White was far ahead of her times in the area of what we now call diversity and multiculturalism.

The following vignettes highlight different aspects of Ellen White's sensitivity to principles of equity and diversity and illustrate her role as a pioneer in SDA race relations.

Committed: During the late 1700s and the early 1800s, laws were enacted designed to maintain the system of slavery. One such law, the Fugitive Slave Act of 1850, required "all good citizens" to return runaway slaves to their masters. To fail to do so would result in heavy penalty. Though this law was somewhat circumvented by the Underground Railroad, resistance was dangerous and fraught with misunderstanding, especially in the South but also in the North.

During this critical period, Ellen White took a firm position on the controversial law in favor of the ostracized Black race. She said that the "law of the land requiring us to deliver a slave to his master, we are not to obey; and we must abide by the consequences of violating this law." Her rationale was straightforward: "The slave is not the property of any man. God is his rightful master, and man has no right to take God's workmanship into his hands, and claim it as his own" (*Testimonies for the Church,* 1:201, 202). Referring to the slaves who sought to escape, she said, "They would never venture to leave their master and expose themselves to the difficulties and horrors attending their recapture if they had not as strong a love for liberty as any of us" (*Testimonies for the Church,* 1:257).

Ellen White based her stand on the biblical position of

moral disobedience. She reasoned that when the laws of humans conflict with the Word and law of God, we are to obey God, whatever the consequences may be. This type of reasoning was not new to Adventists, who routinely applied the principle of prioritizing the Word of God above the laws of humans (see Acts 5:29).

At the risk of persecution and ridicule, Ellen White believed that dignity and freedom for the Black race was an issue to be addressed. With forthrightness she spoke on behalf of the escaped slave in spite of the law that required otherwise. To Ellen White, diversity was not pedantic; it involved humanitarian principles that demanded a response.

Inclusive: In the pre–Civil War days, virtually all White citizens—whether for or against slavery—were sensitive to the dangers of promoting equality and interaction between the races. Subsequently, as a practice, Whites and Blacks didn't associate on a social basis. This was definitely true with Southerners, but it was also true with Northerners. Even many abolitionists felt the same way.

In January 1859 Ellen White, along with Elder and Mrs. J. N. Loughborough and their daughter, were visiting the western Michigan churches. It was snowing, which made travel difficult. As they journeyed southward, they took advantage of the hospitality of the Hardy family. Not an unusual occurrence, except that the Hardys were Black.

The travelers were kindly received by the Hardy family, and Ellen White's reflection on the visit reveals her sensitivity and openness. She penned these words in her diary: "We were heartily welcomed by the family. A good dinner was soon in readiness for us of which we thankfully partook. This is a colored family, but although the house is poor and old, everything is arranged with neatness and exact order. The children are well behaved, intelligent, and interesting." She then added, "May I yet have a better acquaintance with this dear family" (*Diary*, 25 January 1859).

In another example of multiracial interaction, Ellen White is credited as having been instrumental in winning Charles

Kinney, a convert who is considered to be the father of the Black work in the SDA Church. Kinney (1855–1951), the first Black person to be ordained as an SDA minister, was baptized as a result of attending evangelistic meetings conducted by Ellen White and J. N. Loughborough in Reno, Nevada. He remained supportive of Ellen White's ministry and was grateful for his connection with her. Long before the Church had established a work among the Black race in the South, Ellen White had been instrumental in winning Blacks to the three angels' messages.

Ellen White was active in many other ways. Discrimination and bigotry were practices that she opposed. She spoke on behalf of the rights and dignity of the Black race; she challenged the Church leadership to become active in working for Blacks; she gave from her personal funds to support the Black work; she consistently supported her son and daughter-in-law, James Edson and Emma White, who worked in the South; and she was instrumental in the founding of the *Gospel Herald* (forerunner to *Message Magazine*), Oakwood College, and other activities for establishing the work with Blacks.

Bold: In 1859 the slavery question was increasingly volatile. Race relations were reaching explosive levels. During the same year, John Brown was hung for conspiring with former slaves to create an insurrection at Harper's Ferry. Highlighting the tension of the time, Brown, on the way to the gallows, handed his jailer a note that predicted more bloodshed. It said: "I, John Brown, am now quite certain that the crimes of this guilty land will never be purged away but with blood. I had, as I now think, vainly flattered myself that without very much bloodshed it might be done."

Two years earlier, the Supreme Court (with the majority of justices from the South) decided that the Dred Scott case and the Missouri Compromise were unconstitutional. The Court declared that Congress had no power to limit slavery in the territories. Three justices held that a Negro descended from slaves had no rights as an American citizen and therefore no standing in court. This far-reaching decision outraged the North and excited the South. The decision further inflamed the sectional controversy over the slavery issue. The country was rapidly moving toward the Civil War.

Ellen White's statements on race relations ranged from human rights to theological concerns. They often had an air of prophetic and social significance. In her testimonies to the Church, she confronted SDAs who supported the institution of slavery. She stated that some SDAs held the same views of White superiority that were in vogue at that time. "They rank these slaves as cattle and say that it is wronging the owner just as much to deprive him of his slaves as to take away his cattle." She went on to express that "God gave him [the slave master] no title to human souls, and he has no right to hold them as his property. Christ died for the whole human family, whether White or Black." In reference to the Civil War (1861–65), she said, "God was not with the South" in the war, and "He would punish them dreadfully in the end [of the Civil War]," and the North would be punished for allowing slavery to last so long (*Testimonies for the Church*, 1:356-359).

She clearly articulated her views on those SDAs who were sympathetic to the institution of slavery. "There are a few in the ranks of Sabbathkeepers who sympathize with the slaveholder. When they embraced the truth, they did not leave behind them all the errors they should have left. They need a more thorough draft from the cleansing fountain of truth. Some have brought along with them their old political prejudices, which are not in harmony with the principles of the truth." She went on to say, "Some have been so indiscreet as to talk out their proslavery principles—principles which are not heaven-born, but proceed from the dominion of Satan. These restless spirits talk and act in a manner to bring a reproach upon the cause of God."

Committed to the Bible support of her position and convinced of the necessity of the Church taking a firm stand on the issue, she said, "Unless you undo what you have done, it will be the duty of God's people to publicly withdraw their sympathy and fellowship from you, in order to save the impression which must go out in regard to us as a people. We must let it be known that we have no such ones in our fellowship, that we will not walk with them in church capacity" (*Testimonies for the Church*, 1:358-360).

As far as Ellen White was concerned, the responsibility for the system of slavery and its concomitant negative results rested squarely on the slave master and those who countenanced the system. "The slave master has dared assume the responsibility of God over his slave, and accordingly he will be accountable for the sins, ignorance and vice of the slave. He will be called to account for the power which he exercises over the slave." Reiterating, she said, "The Colored [people] are God's property. Their Maker alone is their master, and those who have dared chain down the body and the soul of the slave, to keep him in degradation . . . will have their retribution."

Ellen White's views were clear and concise. She advocated that (1) all races are equal and deserve equal treatment; (2) slavery was a sin; (3) SDAs should not support any form of slavery—subtle or blatant; (4) SDAs and all Christians should assist slaves and former slaves "to improve their condition." One cannot understand Ellen White's views on issues relative to diversity and multiculturalism without understanding her position on the race issues of her day. Whether one looks at Ellen White from the perspective of the SDA Church or from society in general, one can see she believed in the principles of diversity. She saw these principles as having theological and moral overtones.

Throughout her ministry, Ellen White consistently interacted with people from every nationality and ethnic group. She freely mingled with all people, understanding that the gospel was not to be confined to one group or area. The SDA Church absolutely could not be monocultural and fulfill its mission. If it was to be biblical, it had to be multicultural in its mission. Ellen White was of the conviction that the SDA Church was to be a Church for all people. She supported this position even though it was unpopular in the country and Church.

In the final analysis, Ellen White is an exemplary diversity role model for Church leaders. She had a broad and inclusive worldview that was Christocentric (centered on Christ) rather than ethnocentric (centered on one's own ethnic group). She was able to speak to both sides of racial issues. She challenged White as well as Black members.

Further, Ellen White had a cosmopolitan ministry, having traveled widely overseas to England, Germany, France, Italy, Denmark, Norway, Sweden, and Australia. All together, Ellen White spent more than a decade in mission work in other countries. So the Black work was by no means the only ethnic cause she championed. Undoubtedly, it was one of the most difficult. And it was in this context that she articulated some of her most descriptive and revealing insights about what we refer to as diversity issues today.

"There is no person, no nation, that is perfect in every habit and thought. One must learn of another. Therefore, God wants the different nationalities to mingle together, to be one in judgement, one in purpose. Then the union that there is in Christ will be exemplified" *(Ellen White,* **Historical Sketches,** *136, 137).*

A Pioneer in Race Relations

SDA history shows Ellen White was an advocate for work among diverse groups and played a pioneering role in SDA race relations. She stood up for the disadvantaged and had a deep commitment to helping those who had little or no access to the gospel. History bears out that Ellen White was outstanding in her support of the issues of diversity in her day. One might question, Why did Ellen stand so firmly in behalf of the disadvantaged? Discovering the answer may help to inspire and instruct modern SDAs, as the need for cultural sensitivity increases.

Taking a Stand

Few Adventists thought of the disadvantaged Black race as a priority for the Church until Ellen White gave her ground-breaking presentation in 1891. Entitled "Our Duty to the Colored People," the message was given to the thirty leaders at the twenty-ninth session of the General Conference in Battle Creek, Michigan. The presentation was bold, courageous, and far-reaching. After describing how the Lord had repeatedly shown her things about the Church and its responsibility to Black people, Ellen White observed: "I know that which I now speak will bring me into conflict. This I do not covet, for the conflict has seemed too continuous of late years; but I do not mean to live a coward or die a coward, leaving my work undone. I must follow in my Master's footsteps."

She went on to share a theology and strategy for work among Black people in particular, and all disadvantaged in general. Unflinchingly, she reasoned, "It has become fashionable to look down upon the poor, and upon the colored race in particular. But Jesus, the Master, was poor, and He sympathizes with the poor, the discarded, the oppressed, and declared that every insult shown to them is as if shown to Himself." Not to have her comments generalized away, she went on to exclaim, "I am more and more surprised as I see those who claim to be children of God possessing so little of sympathy, tenderness, and love which actuated Christ." Then Ellen White set forth a challenge that, if believers understood and followed, would answer the diversity challenge. "Would that every church, North and South, were imbued with the spirit of our Lord's teaching" (*The Southern Work*, 10, 11).

Church historians generally refer to this document as among the most influential in eliciting a response from the leadership of the Church. It contained the major principles for developing work among Black people.

Copies of this message were distributed to key leaders, ministers in the South, and laypersons. This document was circulated in manuscript form and later printed in a leaflet. As a result of reading this message, James Edson White, Ellen White's son, was impressed to begin working for the neglected Black people in the South.

Ellen White continued to appeal for the building of the Black work even after she left for Australia after the 1891 General Conference session. She wrote a series of ten articles for publication in the *Review and Herald* (published in 1895 and 1896) that supplemented the basic appeal of 1891. As work in the South continued, Ellen White continued to write counsel. The appeal of 1891 along with other counsel on the Black work was complied together in what is called *The Southern Work*.

What motivated Ellen White to speak as she did? It wasn't politically correct. It didn't make her work easier. Possibly one could begin to explain it by pointing to her conversion experience, divine communication, or the obvious need of the Black race. Surely these factors are all part of the answer. But there was more.

Ellen White's background, experience, and molding events all contributed to her worldview—one that superseded racial and cultural concerns. Under the influence of the Holy Spirit, God providentially used her life experiences to develop within her a compassionate empathy for others. God used her to show to the Church what could happen when a person lets go of prejudice and narrow views to live out Christ's teaching of practical benevolence. While one cannot define a person by events and circumstances, those circumstances may offer insight as to what might have helped shape their values and worldview.

Building Blocks of a Diverse Worldview

The following are significant facets in Ellen White's life that may help to explain her sensitivity. According to race relations and sociological studies, a person's past experience can positively or negatively contribute to a broad and inclusive view of the world. Again, a Christian's worldview is composed of a conglomerate of experiences, fashioned by God's providence. So while these factors can help to explain Ellen White's role as an advocate, they fall short of explaining the total person. As Ellen White observed: "Again and again I have been shown that the past experiences of God's people are not to be counted as dead facts. We are not to treat the record of these experiences as we would treat last year's almanac. The record is to be kept in mind; for history will repeat itself. The darkness of the mysteries of the night is to be illuminated with the light of heaven" (*Publishing Ministry*, 175).

Early environment: Ellen White's birthplace, Portland, Maine, was certainly an influencing factor. Maine was a free state and never had the blight of slavery. It was known for its progressive and humanitarian views and was a hotbed of reform movements and free thinkers.

Home influences: Robert Harmon and Eunice Gould Harmon were of New England background. Residing in Gorham, Maine, located outside of Portland, they, too, were doubtlessly influenced by the independent and free-thinking atmosphere of the area. Ellen's parents were spiritual people of conviction. They gave up their membership in the local Methodist Church because of their acceptance of the advent teachings of William Miller. The Harmon family taught that one should stand up for their convictions and be willing to pay the price.

Religious experiences: Ellen White had a transforming spiritual experience during her early teen years. She, like many advent believers, was ostracized from the churches of her day when she embraced the teaching of the soon advent of Christ. She, too, experienced the Great Disappointment of 1844 and learned firsthand what it meant to be a part of a misunderstood group. SDAs, like the Millerites, had opportunity to develop deep sensitivities for those who were mistreated and misunderstood.

Molding associations: Ellen White indicated acquaintance with Black people from an early age. Portland had a significant Black population, so she would have known about Black people in her early years. Ellen White reminisced that when she was around fifteen her father took her several times to hear William Foy, a Black Millerite preacher, speak about the soon advent of Jesus Christ and share what he had seen in vision. She recounted that he gave "remarkable testimonies." She said that "father always took me with him when we went to hear Mr. Foy lecture, and he would be going in a sleigh." Foy received four visions (between 1842–44) prior to the beginning of Ellen White's ministry. As a child, Ellen remembered sitting by Foy's wife in one of the meetings while he was preaching (Ms 131, 1906). One might gather from this experience and other childhood vignettes that the Harmon family associated with and taught respect for all people.

Childhood experience: A traumatic experience occurred when Ellen White was a young child that surely contributed to her capacity for understanding the disadvantaged. Once a cheerful, buoyant, active child, at the age of nine she was injured by a stone thrown by a classmate. She suffered a broken nose (and probably a concussion) and was unconscious for three weeks. The experience left her disfigured, ill, and debilitated. Nervous, unable to write and attend school, her formal education ended at the age of twelve.

Humanitarian outlook: Ellen White was a compassionate person who believed in helping people. She often assisted the poor and the disadvantaged. Her diary is interspersed with incidents of how she helped those in need. Clearly she loved people, all people, and sought to help where the need was the greatest.

Biblical commission: Ellen White was converted and therefore chose to follow Christ's command to love. And one of her motives in assisting the disadvantaged was her conviction to follow Christ's charge to take the gospel to all the world. She believed that overlooking Blacks was a direct violation of the charge that Christ had given to SDAs and Christendom in general. Based on the messages given her,

Ellen White repeatedly said God had impressed her with the necessity of working on behalf of the oppressed. She saw her role and the role of the SDA Church as like that of Christ's, described in Luke 4:18-19 (NIV): "The Spirit of the Lord is on me, because he has anointed me to preach good news to the poor. He has sent me to proclaim freedom for the prisoners and recovery of sight for the blind, to release the oppressed, to proclaim the year of the Lord's favor." She saw no way that the SDA Church could receive God's approbation if they neglected this vital part of their mission.

Ellen White's challenge in the area was exemplary. Why? Because she said and modeled what needed to be done. She practiced what she preached. People knew that the medium was consistent with the message. She was effective, and as a result positive change happened in the Church. That is not to say that others didn't help to influence the Church. They did. However, when the Church neglected to do its duty, it was Ellen White who came to the forefront and made a difference.

The message is clear. We can make a difference. Different circumstances, time, place, but the fact remains. The same God who helped Ellen White make a difference will help anyone who wants to make a difference!

"There are no two leaves of a tree precisely alike; neither do all minds run in the same direction. But while this is so, there may be unity in diversity.... Look at the flowers in a carpet, and notice the different colored threads. All are not pink, all are not green, all are not blue. A variety of colors are woven together to perfect the pattern. So it is in the design of God. He has a purpose in placing us where we must learn to live as individuals" **(Ellen White, Review and Herald, *July 4, 1899*).**

Building Relationship Principles

The SDA Church is blessed to have more than eight million members worldwide. This is a signal blessing. It is also an awesome challenge. The blessing is the attracting power of the gospel; the challenge is how to manage the tremendous diversity.

A principle-centered approach to reading Ellen White's writings will lead the reader to search for universal truths. This approach is especially helpful when perusing her writings on the subject of race relations (i.e., cultural diversity issues). Most of Ellen White's comments refer to White-Black relations, since that was the diversity issue of her day. However, when one uses the principle-centered approach, they discover that the principles apply to the plethora of diversity issues facing the Church today.

The following list of eight diversity principles—spirituality, strategy, expectations, communication, commitment, relationship, evaluation, and trust (**SECRET**)—have been deduced from Ellen White's writings and the Bible. The purpose of this list is to apply spiritual counsel on the subject of diversity and relationship building. This list can provide the reader with the opportunity to compare their own behavior with diversity principles. By so doing, aspects of mutual respect and relationship building can be enhanced.

Spirituality (1)

The solution to the challenges of diversity is a spiritual one. Popular diversity training and materials may be helpful as far as they go. But in the context of the Church, diversity should be viewed differently than in a secular organization. In a spiritual context, the Holy Spirit is the One who will bring about genuine and lasting change. A believer, utilizing a spiritual approach to diversity, will accept the reality of differences in the body of Christ. These differences are not discouraged in the Word of God and should be accepted for what they are—differences. Differences are not necessarily good or bad, superior or inferior. It is therefore wise to examine the reasons why differences exist and to be sensitive to them.

In the midst of differences, it can be helpful if the believer remembers the value of the person and the importance of his or her being called by Christ. Diversity assessments, evaluations, and literature are important. However, it must be remembered that these means will not be able to accomplish the task alone. "Not by might, nor by power, but by my spirit, saith the LORD of hosts" (Zechariah 4:6, KJV).

As the Holy Spirit is poured out in the last days, we are assured that the diversity challenges will grow less and the unity of a diverse membership will increase. "Through the Spirit the believer becomes a partaker of the divine nature. Christ has given His Spirit as a divine power to overcome all hereditary and cultivated tendencies to evil, and to impress His own character upon His church" (*The Desire of Ages,* 671). The real strength of diversity is found in Christ-centered spirituality. The Church that goes through the time of trouble will not be a church divided by factional loyalties.

Strategy (2)

Fear, force, leverage, power, and intimidation are not strategies for Christian diversity. Love is! Pure, simple love. Love, the unselfish, benevolent concern for the well-being of another is what Paul described in 1 Corinthians 13 as a "more excellent way." This love is supported by the principles of the Word of God. It is the strategy that Christ has outlined. That doesn't mean that a Christian is to be taken advantage of. A love balanced by principles will be tough, firm, and resolute. It will deal with a problem with conviction. It will stand up and be counted. It is not cowardly and beholding, but it will not resort to the manipulations of secular society to get its way. Love will motivate the Christian to valiantly strive to find the best for all parties concerned.

This love is rooted in a principle that says that regardless of how I feel or what I've been taught, I will love even as Christ has loved me. Love reveals itself in an attitude of cooperation and collaboration. It models an example of Christ, who lived

His life in selfless service for others (see John 17).

In interpersonal relations the believer will share his or her love and nurture a spirit of vulnerability. In the organizational setting, love will share resources, responsibility, and decision making. Love will find a way to dismantle the hate and animosity found in situations where Christ is a stranger. It is a love that finds its happiness in the happiness of others and in doing the will of Christ. God's remnant is in love with Jesus. That love reveals itself in love for each other.

Expectations (3)

You can expect certain realities when building relationships or developing a spirit of diversity. First, know that you must be "effortful"—establishing the bridge will take time, and you will need patience. Expect the eventuality that you may need to learn and relearn about the differences found in the persons with whom you are interacting. Diversity attitudes are often viewed with suspicion because they are new and different. Some people will have a tendency to resist and misunderstand your best efforts. Anger may develop over practices considered to be wrong. Therefore, be prepared to control your anger and "righteous indignation" so that emotions will not escalate. Expect to listen and learn, though there is the tendency to talk and share what you believe to be the situation.

"With all thy getting, get understanding" (Proverbs 4:7, KJV). Understanding will help you to be sensitive to the dynamics of relationship building. Understanding will help you to be able to submit yourself one to the other and to be accountable. It will help you to keep foremost that the diversity process is similar to sanctification. It is a daily experience of ever learning, ever growing. "But the path of the just is as the shining light, that shineth more and more unto the perfect day" (Proverbs 4:18, KJV). "When the character of Christ shall be perfectly reproduced in His people, then He will come to claim them as His own" (*Christ's Object Lessons*, 69).

Commitment (4)

Obligating oneself to follow the principles of the Word in dealing with others is an act of commitment. Diversity and relationship building work when one is committed to the twin goals of *humility* and *service*.

When the atmosphere is tense and understanding breaks down, the spirit of commitment causes the believer to refuse to give up on finding a resolution. When tempers are hot and words are reckless, commitment gives a soft answer because it values the person over the problem. "The cultivation of a uniform courtesy, a willingness to do to others as we wish them to do to us, would annihilate half of the ills of life" (*Patriarchs and Prophets*, 133). Commitment is the glue that causes relationships to grow and mature. Commitment supports the effort to diversify the Church by spreading the gospel to every nation, tribe, language, and people (see Revelation 14:6).

Communication (5)

Communication is an inescapable aspect of relationship building in a multicultural setting. Love prompted by the Holy Spirit causes a follower of Christ to be open to listen as well as to share concerns and burdens. Believers who make communication a priority will *speak* (with patience and candor), will speak the *truth* (from the heart with honesty and conviction), will speak the truth with *love* (with an attitude of sensitivity and flexibility) (see Ephesians 4:15).

Communication is the bridge that unites the body of Christ into a dynamic unity. But the goal is to rid the mind of self so that communication will be authentic and effective. "If pride and selfishness were set aside, five minutes would remove most difficulties" (*Early Writings*, 119).

Relationship (6)

Relationship in the context of Christian fellowship implies a deep and meaningful connection between spiritual family members. This connection is discovered in the commonality in Christ and the mutual hope of eternal life. Relationship does not mean that there will be no conflict or stress. There will be. However, the believer who has made relation building a priority will set aside pride and selfishness and focus on preserving the relationship and resolving whatever the problem may be.

The motivating power to keep things in perspective is the fact that oneness is found in Christ and anything but a spirit of love will destroy that oneness. Negative feelings, suspicion, and dark emotions will be controlled with the help of the Holy Spirit. The believer will make apologies, amends, and restitution when necessary. Forgiveness will be applied liberally. The model for relationship preservation found in Matthew 18 will be used when expedient. "If we would humble ourselves before God, and be kind and courteous and tenderhearted and pitiful, there would be one hundred conversions to the truth where now there is only one" (*Testimonies for the Church*, 9:189).

Evaluation (7)

The Bible encourages the believer to constantly examine himself to know (see 1 Corinthians 11:28; 2 Corinthians 13:5). A Christian is sensitive that she or he does not act out of selfishness, malice, or retaliation when interacting with a fellow believer.

In the area of diversity, the individual and the organization evaluate internally and externally to ensure that they are being fair and sensitive to the diverse needs of their brothers and sisters in Christ. Is sharing taking place? Are the various groups adequately represented to give voice to the various sectors of the Church? Does leadership reflect the diversity of the body? Evaluation asks the hard questions. Is money, politics, or position the motive over love and selfless service? Evaluation constantly checks to see that love is the basis for action and that spirituality is the goal. "There is no limit to the usefulness of one who, by putting self aside, makes room for the working of the Holy Spirit upon his heart, and lives a life wholly consecrated to God" (*The Desire of Ages*, 250, 251).

Trust (8)

When you have done your best trying to develop this kind of relationship with others, trust God. Believe that all things will work out for the best. Problems will occur and certain situations will never be resolved to your satisfaction. Still, you trust God with the results. Dealing with minds can be the most difficult work. In faith you can confidently thank God for the outcome.

The person most successful in relationship building is the one who does his or her best and then trusts in Christ to do what he or she cannot do. In the family of God, you have the unique opportunity to develop character as you work through people problems. The Church provides the opportunity and obligation to relate to diverse people and situations as a means of developing character. It provides the believer with the occasion to overcome prejudice, discrimination, and narrow thinking. It is the training ground to prepare us to spend an eternity together.

> Keep your wants, your joys, your sorrows, your cares, and your fears, before God. You cannot burden Him; you cannot weary Him. He who numbers the hairs of your head is not indifferent to the wants of His children. "The Lord is very pitiful, and of tender mercy." James 5:11. His heart of love is touched by our sorrows, and even by our utterances of them. Take to Him everything that perplexes the mind. Nothing is too small for Him to notice. There is no chapter in our experience too dark for Him to read; there is no perplexity too difficult for Him to unravel. . . . No sincere prayer . . . [can] escape the lips, of which our heavenly Father is unobservant, or in which He takes no immediate interest (*Steps to Christ*, 100).

Love, the Divine Prescription

God is good. The Bible is replete with principles and strategies and methods on how to manage the tremendous diversity found in the Church. But this should be no surprise. It should be absolutely clear why such provisions were made. God commands His followers to make disciples of the diverse peoples of the world. We know that He doesn't give any command for which He has not made provision. Therefore, it is divinely appropriate that He gives the necessary guidance in the Bible (and the writings of Ellen White) to show us the best way to facilitate the love and unity that we so badly need and that He so badly wants us to have. Let us accept Christ's challenge to "love one another as I have loved you" (John 15:12). It would do us well to begin the process here that we want to continue there . . . for eternity.

Delbert W. Baker, Ph.D., is special assistant to the president and director of diversity at Loma Linda University in Loma Linda, California. He is a professor on the faculty of religion and also teaches in the Schools of Public Health and of Medicine. He has been a pastor, teacher, editor, and administrator. He is the author of four books. He regularly does organizational and human relations training internationally. He and his wife, Susan, have three sons.

4

Diversity, Relationships, and Eschatology

James W. Zackrison

The challenge of diversity in these last days calls Christians to new levels of loving, relating, and resolving problems. The Bible offers models of ministry and reconciliation to help us achieve oneness in Christ.

*A*dventists believe that the Lord's return is imminent and that all human problems will be resolved when that event occurs. In our estimation, we are pilgrims and strangers on planet Earth (Hebrews 11:13). It is the New Earth that really counts. As our pioneer Adventist hymn says, "I'm but a Stranger Here, Heaven Is My Home."[1]

In the meantime, however, we find ourselves earthbound. We fight the same traffic on the freeways as the non-heaven bound, and we sometimes lose our cool and let our opinions be known in no uncertain terms. We come down with the same illnesses as everyone else. We have to qualify for mortgages and stand in the line with other earthbound humans at the supermarket checkout. We look forward to angel's wings, but for now we are attached to the earth by the same automobile tires as the next person. There is a tension between the expectation of a better world to come and the realities of surviving the present.

Diversity and Eschatology

In a church I once pastored, I was suddenly surrounded by a unique controversy. A church member had recently visited New York City and become enamored with a group called the United Sabbath Day Adventist Church. Though raised an Adventist, I had never heard of that organization. Only later did I learn the story of J. K. Humphrey and the Utopia Park incident.[2]

While still working our way through the repercussions of Humphrey's influence on our church, a young-adult former member whom I had befriended engaged in a three-hour debate on the steps of the church with a visiting Church executive over his unfortunate experiences of racial bias at a well-know Adventist college. The Church executive maintained that no prejudice existed in the Church, while the former student's argument was, "Hey, I was there! I know what I went through." I frankly didn't know what the debate was all about. There I was, a missionary, the white pastor of an all-Black church, listening to a debate about prejudice and ethnic diversity. I couldn't remember even a passing mention of the development of ethnic churches in any denominational history class I took in academy or college.

I did know about another ethnic debate, however, because I grew up hearing about it. Around the turn of the century, the Scandinavian and German-speaking Adventist churches in North America launched a strong movement to establish separate conferences. Failing in that effort, they established a school (now Union College) with separate classes in each language and separate dining rooms for each ethnic group, a total of four. This arrangement fed fuel to an already smoldering fire and led to untenable overcrowded conditions. It soon became apparent that four language groups, plus English, was an unworkable combination.[3] Caleb Rosado points out that these long-standing ethnic animosities may well have engendered some of the demeanor at the 1888 General Conference.[4] Growing up as part of the Scandinavian community in the 1940s, I well remember how deep some animosities ran.

Early Adventist Anti-Slavery Activists

In contrast to some of the stories I heard from my church members and my family, I learned that Joshua Himes, Congregational minister and William Miller's second-in-command, had a close connection with the abolitionist movement, and his Chardon Street Chapel in Boston was used as a meeting place for an abolitionist convention.[5]

Henry Jones, another Millerite preacher, was an active advocate of temperance, dress and dietary reforms, and abolition. He lumped all these issues together under the title "Public Moral Reform" and felt that they would certainly wake up "a tremendous opposition of Satan's kingdom." Joseph Bates, a key Millerite preacher and one of the principal founders of the Seventh-day Adventist Church, was an active abolitionist as early as 1832. John Byington, the first president of the General Conference of Seventh-day Adventists, was an abolitionist and maintained a station on the underground railroad on his farm in upstate New York.[6] Edson White and his mother, Ellen G. White, pioneered the Adventist message to the Black population in the South through the work of the *Morning Star* boat plying the Mississippi River.

Key Questions

How does our belief in a "new heavens and a new earth" relate to our relationships in the here and now? How is it that early Adventists were proactive on multiethnic and multicultural issues, while later Adventists often held separatist views? How is it that even White ethnic groups, who can hardly be told apart by appearance, could engender such deep feelings of animosity while at the same time preaching the gospel?

Today, we North Americans live in the world's first truly multiethnic and multicultural society, created in part by a massive wave of immigration that since 1965 has changed the face of North America.[7] By the year 2000 the Anglo component of the church, up until now the majority group, will become a minority; it is projected to be approximately 47 percent of the total membership of the North American Division.[8] The church will be a majority-less composite of Asian, Black, Hispanic, and Anglo members. Many congregations, especially in urban areas, already reflect that diversity. How does this diversity affect the church? What models of ministry should we develop to meet the realities of population diversity?

The Search for a Biblical Model

This chapter will attempt to develop a biblical model for churches in a multiethnic and multicultural society. Our goal is to find a way to integrate belief in the imminence of the second coming of Jesus with the here-and-now realities of everyday life as members of a diversified, pluralistic society.

It is noteworthy that the three angels' messages, our Adventist theological framework, have a sociological dimension built into them. Consider the following diagram of the elements included in Revelation 14:6-12 (NIV).

**DIMENSIONS OF THE
THREE ANGELS' MESSAGES**

The everlasting
gospel to preach:
|
The sociological   Nation
dimension   ―――――――   Tribe
| Language
| People

The prophetic dimension	————	Babylon is fallen
|		
The theological dimension	——	The faith of Jesus The commandments of God

---

The point is that the three angels' messages contain a sociological dimension involving people groups. A nation is not the same as a tribe or a "people." Each is a different kind of social group. Each needs its own variety of needs met, its own kind of methodological approach. This is done most effectively in its own language. At the same time, it is the everlasting gospel that binds human diversity together within the framework of the faith of Jesus and the commandments of God.

An Evangelistic Imperative

Acceptance of the everlasting gospel makes possible the management of diversity because it has the power to produce a changed mind-set and a Christian personality. Only the gospel has the power to change a person's thinking patterns to the point that they can truly understand the brotherhood and sisterhood of humanity as God originally designed it. The gospel, "the power of God for the salvation of everyone who believes" (Romans 1:16), is the core of Christianity.

According to the Bible, there is no salvation apart from a personal acceptance of Jesus as Saviour. The great commission, the command to pass on the everlasting gospel, constitutes the marching orders of the Church. The command to preach the everlasting gospel gives priority to evangelistic outreach as the first step in managing diversity. Communicating this truth was the focus of Jesus' ministry and the continual emphasis in the early church. No amount of ethical improvement or social change, in and of itself, as valuable as it may be, can replace the imperative of individual salvation.

There is, however, yet another way to look at a linkage between the eschatological hope and the realities of everyday life. The Creation story indicates that humanity was actually given two mandates. One was to serve God and give glory to Him, the other to care for the earth and its population as a steward of God's ownership. Cain, for instance, knew he was supposed to be "his brother's keeper," or he would not have asked the question (Genesis 1:15, 28). So humanity has a built-in responsibility to humanity itself. Ellen White's affirmation of the outreach system that works best is based on this perspective. It first befriends people and then asks for a commitment: "Christ's method alone will give true success in reaching people. The Savior mingled with men as one who desired their good. He showed His sympathy for them, ministered to their needs, and won their confidence. Then He bade them 'Follow me.' "[9]

The Biblical View of Diversity

How, then, should we relate to a multiethnic/multicultural population within and outside the Church? What are the biblical perspectives?

Old Testament Perspectives on Diversity

In the Old Testament, the Lord always placed His followers in situations that allowed them to preach the everlasting gospel, no matter how diverse the population or difficult the circumstances. This is what Paul meant when he said: "From one man he [God] made every nation of men, that they should inhabit the whole earth; and he determined the times set for them and the exact places where they should live. God did this so that men would seek him and perhaps reach out for him and find him, though he is not far from each one of us" (Acts 17:26, 27).

Ellen White comments that the assignment of boundaries is for purposes of worship rather than national sovereignty or ethnic distinction. Thus the purpose for determining time and place is neither ethnic nor political, but rather to give maximum opportunity for close acquaintance with God.[10]

Managing Diversity

Abraham was called to be "a blessing to all peoples" (Genesis 12:3). God led him to a region inhabited by an entire spectrum of tribes, each of which, in turn, encompassed numerous clans and families (Genesis 15:19 mentions ten by name). Besides these, some thirty other peoples, spread from Egypt to Chaldea, are mentioned by name in the first thirty-six chapters of Genesis. More ethnic subdivisions of human-kind are given specific recognition in these thirty-six chapters than in any other section of comparable length anywhere else in the Bible!

Abraham was personally very conscious of his eschatological status as an alien (Hebrews 11:13). Nevertheless, God continued to promise that through him all peoples on earth would be blessed (Genesis 12:3). In this sense, Abraham, the alien, becomes a unifier of aliens. He takes away the status of strangerhood and unites all aliens under the banner of the King of heaven.

From a sociological perspective, in the law of Moses, the Lord went out of His way to make sure that diversity would be respected. The Mosaic legislation mandated that Israel have the same laws for aliens and native-born (Leviticus 24:22). *Aliens* in Israelite culture was an overarching term for all non-Israelites, much as we use the term *ethnic* today. Aliens were not to be mistreated (Exodus 22:21) or oppressed (Exodus 23:12) because the Lord defends their cause (Deuteronomy 10:18). The person who withholds justice from aliens is cursed (Deuteronomy 27:18). Numbers 15:15 clearly states, "The community is to have the same rules for you and for the alien living among you; this is a lasting ordinance for the generations to come. You and the aliens shall be the same before the Lord." This was true of the sabbatical year (Leviticus 25:6), the sacrificial system (Numbers 15:15, 16), Sabbath rest and/or work (Exodus 20:10), the application of justice (Deuteronomy 1:16; 27:19), and the benefits of the Cities of Refuge (Joshua 20:9). In his prayer of dedication at the inauguration of the temple, Solomon specifically prayed that the Lord would hear and answer the prayer of foreigners who wished to honor His name (1 Kings 8:41-43).

Inclusiveness

The psalmist affirms that the Lord watches over strangers (Psalm 146:9), and Isaiah tells aliens who have joined themselves to the Lord that they need not feel that "the Lord will surely exclude me from his people" (Isaiah 56:3). To the contrary: "The foreigners who bind themselves to the Lord to serve him, to love the name of the Lord, and to worship him, all who keep the Sabbath without desecrating it and who hold fast to my covenant—these will I bring to my holy mountain and give them joy in my house of prayer. Their burnt offerings and sacrifices will be accepted on my altar; for my house shall be called a house of prayer for all nations" (Isaiah 56:6, 7).

Jeremiah's appeals for repentance included a call to "do no wrong or violence to the alien" (Jeremiah 22:3). Ezekiel says that one of the sins that led to the Babylonian captivity was that the people "mistreated the alien, denying them justice" (Ezekiel 22:29). In his idealized picture of the restored Israel, Ezekiel says that aliens with children would be considered as native-born, and "in whatever tribe the alien settles, there you are to give him his inheritance" as if he were an Israelite (Ezekiel 47:23). The Old Testament, then, is clear in its teachings that all peoples are to be treated with respect and vested with equality.

In spite of the Lord's teaching, actual practice is often a different thing. For instance, the Bible says that when it came to building the temple and his own palace, Solomon, in spite of his eloquent prayer (1 Kings 8:41-43), conscripted Canaanites under his control as slave labor while he used Israelites as soldiers and government officials (1 Kings 9:20-23). He would not allow his Egyptian wife to live in the palace because the ark of the Lord had once been there (2 Chronicles 8:11). Solomon is an unfortunate example of dedication to the letter of the law, but not to the spirit of the law in practice.

New Testament Perspectives on Diversity

It is significant that Jesus' first recorded sermon (Luke 4), taken from Isaiah 61, focused on the sociological perspectives of the everlasting gospel, recognizing diversity, preaching to the poor, proclaiming freedom to prisoners, recovery of sight to the blind, and release for the oppressed. Some commentators have remarked that these categories are metaphors for spiritual release, spiritual blindness, etc. Be that as it may, healing the blind and preaching to the common people are exactly what Jesus did during His ministry. Jesus successfully combined this kind of ministry with an eschatological hope for the future.

Paul's Teaching on Diversity

Paul's statement in Galatians 3:28, "There is neither Jew nor Greek, slave nor free, male nor female, for you are all one in Christ Jesus," is a summary statement of biblical teaching, not an innovative concept.[11] Paul records six basic statements that summarize his theology of multiethnic ministry to Gentiles. In the New Testament, *Gentiles* refers to non-Jews. Paul's basic argument is that before God all people are equal. This is true because (1) from one man God made every nation of men (Acts 17:26) and because (2) all are under sin (Romans 3:9) and (3) in the person of Jesus, God revealed a "righteousness" never known before (Romans 3:21) that applies to Jew and Gentile alike (Romans 3:29) and "made the two one and has destroyed the barrier, the dividing wall of hostility" (Ephesians 2:14).

Paul shows that the proofs of this equality for Gentiles come from the Old Testament itself. The promise to Abraham, he says, was for "all who believe" (Galatians 3:8). In his discourse on Jews and Gentiles in Romans 15, he affirms the salvation of Gentiles because the Old Testament says, "The name of the Lord will be praised among the nations" (Psalm 18:49); "all nations" will rejoice with the Lord (Deuteronomy 32:43); "all you nations" are admonished to praise the Lord (Psalm 117:1).

The perception of diversity as synonymous with separation

is deeply ingrained in the human personality. It is amazing that the pull of ethnicity and tradition was so strong, even in Paul, that toward the end of his life, he would still see both the Messiahship of Jesus and the gospel to the Gentiles as "mysteries" (Romans 16:25; Ephesians 3:4-6). In 1 Timothy 3:16, he joins the two mysteries together and calls them the "great" mystery of the ages:

> Beyond all question, the mystery of godliness is great: He appeared in a body, was vindicated by the Spirit, was seen by angels, was preached among the nations *[ethnos]*, was believed on in the world, was taken up in glory.

Paul's Statements of His Theology Regarding Gentiles

Gal. 3:28	There is neither Jew nor Greek, slave nor free, male nor female, for you are all one in Christ Jesus.
Col. 3:11	Here there is no Greek or Jew, circumcised or uncircumcised, barbarian, Scythian, slave or free, but Christ is all, and is in all.
1 Cor. 1:24	But to those whom God has called, both Jews and Greeks, Christ [is] the power of God and the wisdom of God.
Rom. 1:16	I am not ashamed of the gospel, because it is the power of God for the salvation of everyone who believes: first for the Jew, then for the Gentile.
Rom. 10:12	For there is no difference between Jew and Gentile— the same Lord is Lord of all and richly blesses all who call on him.
Eph. 2:14	For he himself is our peace, who has made the two one and has destroyed the barrier, the dividing wall of hostility.

This should be enough evidence to show that the Bible teaches only solidarity and unity. There are no inferiority/superiority paradigms anywhere in the teaching of Scripture.

Human beings unfortunately invent and practice inferiority/ superiority paradigms, but they are a result of the sin problem, not the teachings of the Bible.

How Will the New Earth Be Organized?

An additional point needs to be considered. We Seventh-day Adventists tend to envision the new earth as a garden inhabited by people dressed in white robes who spend eternity doing . . . something? It is an idealized picture built partly on artists' perceptions of the Garden of Eden and partly on the nineteenth-century idealization of rural country life as the plan of God for humanity.

It is significant, however, that Revelation 21:24 talks about the nations appearing regularly at the New Jerusalem, a city, to replenish their spiritual energies at the feet of Jesus and their physical existence at the Tree of Life (Revelation 22:2).[12] Stephen Haskell, an early Adventist pioneer, was of the opinion that "all nationalities, all tribes, and all peoples will, for the first time, gather together and with one common language worship our God. The fruit and the leaves of the tree of life will bring all together."[13] There is a danger in this view, however. If the leaves of the tree of life are for the healing of the nations (Revelation 22:2), does Haskell imply that nationhood, i.e., ethnic or national identity, is something that needs to be "healed"?

There are some Seventh-day Adventist historians who lend credence to the above view. One, for instance, believes God assigned specific places where specific races should live (based on Acts 17:26,17). According to this historian, all history subsequent to the Tower of Babel incident has been a struggle to rectify these bounds of habitation. "Any plan to unite people of different racial lineage," he writes, "is always attended with severe conflict," since in his estimation any such plan is a violation of divinely set bounds of habitation.[14]

Nationhood, however, implies ethnic diversity, so the restored earth will in all likelihood be multiethnic and diversified into nations. Fortunately, the effects of sin will be eliminated, and all people will live together in peace and harmony, with no vestiges of prejudice or inferiority/superiority paradigms left.

Diversity in These Last Days

Having looked at the biblical picture of diversity as a normal part of the history of humanity, and knowing that in North America we live in the world's first truly multiethnic and multicultural society, how do we handle the natural tension that exists between the eschatological hope and the real present?[15]

Diversity in North America

Diversity has always played a major role in U.S. history. Since 1901, for example, 30 percent of the U.S. Nobel Prize winners have been first-generation immigrants. The same is true for the religious panorama. African immigrants worship the fire god in South Carolina while Hindus build elaborate temples in Malibu, the very heart of the mostly anti-religion film industry. Islamic schools flourish in the Illinois heartland, and an incredibly beautiful mosque rises from the farmlands outside Perrysburg, Ohio, inspiring a *Time* article entitled "One Nation Under Gods."[16]

Intermarriage between people groups is no longer a phenomenon. For instance, Japanese Americans marry non–Japanese Americans about 65 percent of the time. Since 1981, the number of babies born in the U.S. with one Anglo and one Japanese parent outnumbers the babies born to two parents of Japanese ancestry.

The teen culture in the U.S. reflects the same diversity. This cultural and religious diversity means that we need styles of ministry that will meet all these needs. This calls for creativity, innovation, and determination to find, and allow, new ways of doing things.

Inclusive Style of Ministry: A Goal

Inclusive style of ministry means working together toward common purposes. It means organizing churches, especially in urban areas, that reflect the diversity of the community the church wishes to serve. In this structure, diverse people groups worship under one roof as members of one church while designing ministries to meet various target audiences, based on their uniqueness and receptivity to the gospel.

In this model, diverse "congregations" work out the best methodologies for winning receptive people with common social ties, whether language, national origin, or whatever. The church may provide a variety of worship services in different languages or styles, depending on the target audiences and the space available.

The internal management of the church is shared. For instance, the membership committee has members representing all segments of the church. The pastoral staff is multiethnic and/or multicultural, as are all church offices. Even if there are a variety of language ministries in the church, periodically, the entire body comes together for joint worship. These periodic festivals focus on what is happening in each congregation and music, fellowship, and testimony. They unite the eschatological hope with the realities of this world, becoming "Sounds of Heaven" in the here and now.

Eschatology and diversity are not mutually exclusive. Before we get "angel's wings," we have the challenge and opportunity to relate and serve together here, in preparation for the eternity we will spend together there in the new heaven and new earth. God designed diversity into the human race. Heaven will reflect that same diversity. He gave Adventists a message delivered by angels that reflects that original plan. Our job, as born-again Christians, is to teach as many people as will listen what the new earth will be like and to model in our churches what we preach.

James W. Zackrison, D.Min., is associate director of church ministries and co-director of personal ministries and Sabbath School for the General Conference. He is an author and has been a pastor, teacher, and administrator in a number of multicultural settings. He has more than twenty years of mission work experience in the Inter-American Division. He and his wife, Sonia, have one son.

Endnotes

1. *Seventh-day Adventist Hymnal*, 445.

2. For the story, see Joe Mesar and Tom Dybdahl, "The Utopia Park Affair and the Rise of Northern Black Adventists," *Adventist Heritage*, 1:1, Jan. 1974. J. K. Humphrey, pastor of a large Black church in Harlem, tried to organize "Utopia Park" as a benevolent association offering a medical facility, a retirement home, and other services.

3. Lewis Harrison Christian, *Sons of the North* (Boise, Idaho: Pacific Press Publishing Association, 1942), 176.

4. Caleb Rosado, *Broken Walls* (Boise, Idaho: Pacific Press Publishing Association, 1990), 89, 90.

5. Francis D. Nichol, *The Midnight Cry* (Hagerstown, Md.: Review and Herald Publishing Association, 1944), 188-191.

6. Arthur W. Spaulding, *Origin and History of Seventh-day Adventists* (Hagerstown, Md.: Review and Herald Publishing Association, 1961), 1:314.

7. A new immigration law was enacted in 1965 that opened up the U.S. borders as never before in history.

8. Roy Branson, "Brown and Yellow, Black and White," *Spectrum*, 23:5, April 1994, 2.

9. *Ministry of Healing*, 143. For an extended discussion of Jesus' method, see Philip G. Samaan, *Christ's Way of Reaching People* (Hagerstown, Md.: Review and Herald Publishing Association), 1990.

10. *The Acts of the Apostles*, 238.

11. The "oneness" in Galatians 3:28 is sometimes seen as only a "spiritual" oneness. This is not exegetically sound, nor does it follow from Paul's teachings. The point of the book of Galatians is that no one has to practice "Jewishness" in order to be Christian. That is sociological as well as spiritual.

12. Early Adventist writers saw nations as literal groupings made up of saved people. See Uriah Smith, *Daniel and Revelation* (Hagerstown, Md.: Review and Herald Publishing Association, 1944), 768, and Stephen N. Haskell, *The Story of the Seer of Patmos* (Nashville, Tenn.: Southern Publishing Association, 1905), 353. George Eldon Ladd understands it to be a reference to the great multitude in Revelation 7:9, who, however, "will not lose their national identity," *A Commentary on the Revelation of John* (Grand Rapids, Mich.: William B. Eerdmans Publishing Company, 1972), 284. Siess categorizes them as literal nations, albeit sanctified and saved—J. A. Seiss, *The Apocalypse* (Grand Rapids, Mich.: Zondervan Publishing House, 1900), 501.

13. Stephen N. Haskell, *The Story of the Seer of Patmos* (Nashville, Tenn.: Southern Publishing Association, 1905), 353. It is possible, of course, to argue that the word *nations* is a metaphor or a symbol for saved people in general. Even taking that view, however, the scene does not change. It is still a multiethnic population that inhabits the new earth.

14. George Edgar Shankel, *God and Man in History* (Nashville, Tenn.: Southern Publishing Assocation, 1967), 136.

15. See *Time*, Special Issue, Fall 1993, for an exposé on the new configuration of U.S. society.

16. Ibid.

GROWING

Profile of a Christian Diversity Leader

A Diversity Leader is someone who is committed to (working toward) the follow characteristics:

1. Is committed to building meaningful relationships with all members in the body of Christ.
2. Understands that the call for diversity in the name of the gospel has been a part of the plan of God since the very beginning.
3. Accepts the responsibility to share the gospel with all nations, Revelation 14, anytime and in all possible ways.
4. Is willing to be instructed by 1 Corinthians 13 and the three books of John.
5. Is committed to the equality and rights of all believers.
6. Is open to learn from the input and feedback from diverse people and groups.
7. Is committed to creating "pockets of understanding and cooperation" throughout the Church.
8. Is committed to the spiritual principles of love, a Christlike respect, and inclusion for all people.
9. Has a basic understanding and awareness of diversity issues and is willing to learn more.
10. Is committed to treating people fairly, opposing prejudice, and eliminating discrimination.
11. Is willing to articulate and act toward a diversity vision in their home, church, or community.
12. Is willing to talk positively about diversity principles as often as possible.
13. Creates positive change by being a role model and builds trust by "walking the talk."
14. Is willing to take criticism and misunderstanding for their convictions in support of diversity.
15. Is committed to being a problem solver and solution-oriented.
16. Is willing to challenge organizational assumptions and institutional biases wherever and whenever they may appear.
17. Inspires and motivates people to keep moving in the desired direction and participating in the change process.
18. Supports the changing of policies, procedures, and practices for the purpose of eliminating barriers to diversity attitudes and actions.
19. Understands the power of acting, doing something, making a difference in their sphere of influence.
20. Is willing to update old attitudes, myths, and stereotypes about people and their abilities.
21. Understands that heaven will ultimately personify the very best there can be about diversity.

5

Effective Steps
to Lasting Transformation

Ramona Perez Greek

We don't ever have to be prisoners— individually or institutionally—to racism and prejudice. We can experience freedom to do and be our best for Christ by thinking and acting in purposeful ways.

*H*ow is this change of hue in America from White to Brown, Black, and Yellow going to impact the church? According to researcher and church-growth expert, George Barna (1990), the church has found itself at a crucial time in history. For decades the Church in America has set forth Christianity as a White man's faith. If it is to survive the rapid changes of today and stem its current decline in numbers and influence, the Church must embrace minorities not only as equals but as a vital key to future impact in ministry and Church growth.

Will the Church rise to the occasion and assume a proactive stance in seeing glimpses of tomorrow? Will it discern future trends so that it can provide meaningful ministries and Christian service to others? By taking intentional steps to learn and understand future trends and demographic shifts, the Church can prepare to move into the twenty-first century with contemporary ministries that fit the diversities of our time.

The demographics on diversity are considerable. Here are a few examples. The native-born Caucasian (White) population (Pope and Associates, 1994) is expected to continue to experience a declining fertility rate, reaching zero population growth rate by 2000. Trends indicate both the Asian and Hispanic populations are likely to increase by 35 to 40 percent this decade. The Black population is expected to increase by 15 percent. As a whole, the proportion of minorities will increase from 23 percent of the population in 1990 to 26 percent in 2000. By the year 2050, people of color will comprise 50 percent of the U.S. population (U.S. Census Bureau, 1992).

It has been said that the church is a microcosm of society. Recent statistics bear this out in the SDA Church as well. Statistics from the NAD Office of Human Relations (1993) indicate that while White Adventists comprise approximately 58 percent of the SDA Church in the NAD, they comprise only a little more than 11 percent of the world membership. These trends are projected to continue into the year 2000. Thus the non-White population in the SDA Church will reach a majority status faster than the larger society. This does not take into account that already 90 percent of the SDA membership lies outside of North America. The majority of that percentage is people of color.

So then, how should the Church respond to the rapid changes and incorporate minorities as equals in ministry, leadership, and church growth? How can the Church be more inclusive? How should it set aside racism and prejudices in interpersonal and organizational settings? How can it have increasingly positive interaction between cultures and ethnic groups?

In order to create change and get to the root of the problem of racism and prejudice, one must be willing to begin with the self (the individual and the institutional self), to be vulnerable, and to search one's soul. This process can be experienced through the following four steps:

1. Self-Examination

The Church cannot begin to change unless it first examines itself. There must be an examination of "old" ways of thinking and shared assumptions that have worked in the past but no longer work today (the old paradigm). These ways of thinking must be compared to where we want to be as a Church and as individuals in Christ (the new paradigm).

The Bible invites the process of self-discovery when it says, "Know thyself." This task, then, is to prayerfully start at the foundation of our souls. We have to seriously ponder our mission, question assumptions, and discuss the unspoken. Questions that aid in this process might be: Who are we? What do we value? What do we believe in? Why are we here? What do we practice?

The task is one of redefining our basic values and assumptions. It is about asking the hard questions and seeking the authentic answers to those questions. In the context of racism, prejudice, and discrimination, the following thought questions have the potential for stirring us into change in the personal, organizational, and relational areas:

Personal
• As a Christian, how can I help shape my future and the future of my Church?
• How does change take place with individual mind-sets, intergroup relationships, and organizational policies and structures?
• What are some sources of limitations to growth within me/my Church?

Organizational
• What is the mission of the Church?
• What does the gospel commission really mean when it says, "Go ye into all nations"?
• What shapes how we think, act, and interact in the Church?

• Can the Church organization reward inquiry (encourage the asking of tough questions that may challenge but need to be asked)?

• Can the Church build a "shared" vision without systems thinking?

• "Systems thinking" has to do with understanding how our actions shape our current reality. In this light, can we create a different reality in the future for the Church?

• Who benefits best from our present system?

• Who decides the rules in a system?

• For whom is this system functional? Who stands on the sidelines uninvolved?

• Does the church honor the unique abilities, capabilities, perspectives, and contributions of every individual? Do I?

• What values determine our policies and our actions?

Relational

• What are the benefits of creating the fair and voluntary exchange of human resources to motivate behavior and outcomes at all levels of the Church (people want to help but don't)?

• Do I/we believe that one person, one culture, one nationality, one leader can solve all the problems, or that all are needed to be allowed to come up with new ideas and ways of doing business that fit the challenges of today?

• What do I hope will change in me and in the Church? What do I hope for as a result of this change?

• What is difficult for me when it comes to "change"?

• What is rewarding in a "change" experience?

• What makes me think the way I do?

• Am I aware that the most powerful source of change may be people having the *opportunity* to give of themselves?

• Are "relationships" and "integration" key to a healthy functioning of the Church? What are some creative ways this can be done?

• Do any prejudices exist in the Church? In me?

• Is racism alive within the Church arena?

No denials in answering the questions. The closer we come to truth, the freer we will be to be what we were meant to be in God's divine plan. Besides, our values and expectations impact every decision of our lives every day. Understanding them is understanding what drives us.

Working Definitions

Important to the understanding of the dynamics of racism, prejudice, and discrimination when developing a transformation strategy is beginning on a common ground of definitions. The following are five key definitions.

Prejudice is an inflexible, rational attitude that often in a disguised manner defends privilege, even after evidence to the contrary. It positions itself in a socially advantageous posture and feels privileged over others who are perceived as different, and thus nondeserving (Rosado, 1994). The operating dynamics of prejudice occur at three levels: (1) cognitive level—what people believe about others, (2) emotional level—the feelings that the "other" arouses in an individual, (3) behavioral level—the tendency to engage in discriminatory behavior (Kraemer, 1949).

Discrimination is the unequal treatment of individuals or groups on the basis of some attribute such as race, ethnicity, gender, religion, age, or social class membership. When the prejudicial attitude results in an action, it becomes discrimination. Together, prejudice and discrimination are fundamental to racism

Racism is the deliberate structuring of privilege by means of an objective differential and unequal treatment of people, for the purpose of social advantage over scarce resources, resulting in an ideology of supremacy that justifies power of position by placing a negative meaning on perceived or actual biological/cultural differences. It is cultural, structurally sanctioned strategies that defend the advantage of power, prestige, and privilege (Rosado, 1994). (It should be noted that sexism has the same meaning as racism. However, when relating to the female gender, it has to do with the differential and unequal treatment of women. The reasons for discrimination becomes one of gender versus "skin color.")

Racism and sexism justify their existence by giving "differences" in physical appearances, for example, a negative meaning of inferiority. The difference that has now become negative justifies the treatment of others as inferior. A clear illustration of this is seen in the TV documentary entitled "A Class Divided," in which a schoolteacher chooses to teach her students the value of diversity by placing negative value on "blue eyes" for a day, then reversing the negative value on "brown eyes" for the following day. Students respond by improved performance when "blue eyes" versus "brown eyes" are given positive value. The same students' performance decreases when given negative value for "blue eyes." The same pattern emerges with the "brown eyes" students: with negative value given to "brown eyes," performance decreases; with positive value given to "brown eyes," performance increases. "Performance" here means the students improved academically as well as socially in their relationships with others.

The experiment and the results have far-reaching implications for an understanding of race relations. Collins (1988) states "power comes from the ability to control the definition of situations." For example, if Hispanics are perceived as incompetent and culturally deficient, the behavior that follows may become a self-fulfilling prophecy. The meaning assigned to a reality, whether it is true or not, encourages people to behave in the same manner as perceived. The "meaning," then, is in the culture's values and beliefs that are passed on from one generation to another. These values and beliefs with their attached meanings form the basis for attitudes of prejudice and the actions of discrimination that follow and that result in racism both in the society and in the Church.

Racism and power: At the core of racism is the concept of group competition: the quest for power. The word *power*, in the context of racism and prejudice, can have two meanings:

(1) capacity to act, or (2) the capacity to act in a way that influences the behavior of others even against their wishes. When these two elements are present, racism is occurring. Judith Katz (1978) declares racism and power as intertwined. Thus, powerless individuals are merely prejudiced or discriminating but are not racist, since they have no power to act.

Institutional racism is injurious and strongly influential because it permeates the entire system. In this context, racism is structured into the social system of an institution through such things as training, income, and differential education. The elimination of racism will be difficult at best if planned change is not aimed at core institutions. These institutions include the family, the school, the church, the health system, and the workplace. Reinvention is not enough; complete transformation at the root level must occur if change is to take place. This calls for the pouring of new wines into new wineskins, as opposed to pouring new wine into old wineskins (Luke 5:37, 38).

2. Vision/Mission/Goals

From self-examination and as part of the process of transformation, a sense of direction evolves, called "vision." Vision is powerful and compelling. A Holy Spirit–guided vision for the Church gives us a whole new sense of where the Church is going and how to get there. The vision becomes the catalytic force, an organizing principle for everything that the people in the Church organization do. Vision and mission work closely together. *Vision* tells us where we are going. *Mission* clarifies our purpose for existence. *Goals* tell us how to get to where we want to go.

Being in Sync
People's hearts can be inspired to work toward realizing a vision only if there is a real mission or sense of purpose. When people feel *included,* they are more likely to feel in sync (harmony) with others in the larger organization. Thus, they

work to their full capacity. Being able to identify with the Church organization's purpose, you experience *ownership* through the building of a *shared* vision. Experiencing ownership helps people find themselves in doing their life's work instead of just "doing time" in living life. It clears our direction.

The shared vision brings to life the old ways of thinking and the need for a new paradigm shift. For example, the model of *exclusion* of yesteryear no longer works for the contemporary needs of today. The old paradigm places emphasis on keeping ourselves apart. It focuses on our differences and emphasizes exclusiveness. This old paradigm bases worth of self and others on accomplishments and the use of only some gifts/ talents. This approach utilizes outdated modes of ministry that are not reflective of diversity and are not current with the time and circumstances. The time has come to respond to and promote change as part of the new way of doing things in the Church if we are to stay alive, relevant, meaningful, and growing. Our members must see change efforts as an integral ongoing part of our responsibility and accountability as Christians with a mission.

The new way of doing things can be found in the new paradigm of *inclusion* where all are valued, utilized, and recognized in appreciation for their contributions. The new paradigm places emphasis on working cooperatively with all and focusing on values we share. Inclusion emphasizes the importance of people (human value priorities) and bases worth of self and others on Christ and His sacrifice for us. In this new paradigm, people believe the energies and talents of everyone are needed to meet the challenges of our changing world. Therefore, people take responsibility because they are personally empowered. Finally, this approach uses contemporary ways of ministering to people in today's time. It is relevant, and it celebrates diversity.

In 1963, John F. Kennedy supported diversity when he said in his report to Congress outlining a Civil Rights bill, "It must be supplemented as well by enlightened private citi-

zens, private businesses and private labor and civic organizations, by responsible educators and editors, and certainly by
religious leaders who recognize the conflict between racial
bigotry and the Holy Word" (Friedman, 1967).

This new paradigm of synergy is an effective way to
eliminate racism and prejudiced attitudes as one experiences
a paradigm shift away from the old to the new ways of doing
things. The new paradigm or way of thinking can be found in
the Christ-Centered Model of Diversity recently developed by
the North American Division Multicultural Commission of
the Office of Human Relations. The model is being field-
tested currently, but when implemented, should be a great
aid in helping the division move more rapidly toward unity in
diversity in Christ.

A Christ-Centered Model of Diversity

This model is best expressed in the following way: the
model centers on the *cross* of Jesus Christ as that which not
only draws all people (John 12:32) but is the foundation on
which all find a oneness in Christ (Galatians 3:28).

The inner graphic is an ellipse. An ellipse has two *foci*. The
two foci of our bifocal vision symbolically represent God and
humankind. In Matthew 22:34, 40, Jesus makes clear the two
foci of our lives. " 'You shall love the Lord your God with all
your heart, and with all your soul, and with all your mind' "
(NRSV). This is the greatest and first commandment, and a
second is like it: " 'You shall love your neighbor as yourself.' " Our vision is to be bifocal: love to God and love to
humankind.

This perspective will give rise to the fellowship (*koinonia*)
and Christian oneness found in the early church. It is here
where our differences (racial, ethnic, cultural, biological,
physical, and social) that normally divide us in society find
the level ground of the cross in a spirit and behavior of
equality. The arrows that reach out from the center and back
again are symbolic of our mission to the world in bringing
people into the fold of fellowship: the Church.

The solution becomes clear: Christ is the center, to which all should be attracted; for the nearer we approach the center, the closer we shall come together in feeling, sympathy, and love, growing into the character and image of Jesus. With God, there is no respecter of persons (see *Selected Messages*, 1:259). The strength of the Church lies in diversity in Christ. This means working for unity while diversity is valued and respected. God's plan in Creation is based on diversity.

Diversity is the biological, cultural, physical, and sociological differences such as race/ethnicity, age, gender, disabilities, class, education, values, religion, etc., that people bring to an organization, community, or society, which have the potential of giving rise to conflicts, but if managed well can result in synergetic unity in diversity.

To clarify this point, *diversity* does not mean "separation," but "distinct" and "unique." It does not mean that one person or group is better than the other, simply, that they are different yet of equal worth and value. If we perceive *unity* to be uniformity and sameness, we omit God's creation of human uniqueness and distinctiveness.

On the other hand, if we understand *diversity* to mean magnifying differences and separation, then we exclude the common shared humanity that God created by design. Because we are one in Christ (John 17:23; Galatians 3:28), one in doctrine, fellowship, love, equality, standing before God, purpose, and mission, we therefore value diversity in character, racial/ethnic differences, gender, age, different abilities, experience, worship styles, social status, and educational accomplishments. Only "in Christ" can the two dynamic dimensions of "unity in diversity" be maintained in balanced tension, without erring on either side.

The end result of this model is a reflection of the gospel in a membership that exemplifies the unity Jesus prayed for in the garden, which would reveal to the world a correct picture of God as a loving, caring friend; a God of all nations (John 17). Ellen G. White (1939) states, "No nation or person is perfect in every habit and thought, therefore, we need to learn from each other." This presents a challenge and opportunity for the Church to proclaim the gospel in ways that are relevant to the diversity of people's culture-specific needs. This means the Church must either change the ways we do God's business or not grow. Not growing means not accomplishing our reason for being here, not accomplishing our mission.

3. Total Involvement

Building on self-examination and vision/mission/goals, the key to success in motivating others to implement the model is Total Involvement of all. This means the entire church, all members in the organization, are involved in the transformation process. Thus, a *process* must be created whereby others are actively involved in building a vision as they each envision the future they want and can achieve for the Church. This encourages people to adopt the vision as their own. This is called the "systemic" approach to change. Rather than dealing with issues such as racism and prejudice on a piece-meal approach, research indicates that the systemic approach is more effective on a broader scale.

Science has discovered that there is a direct correlation between "level of buy-in" (commitment and ownership) to "level of involvement" (participation). Being involved in a personal way to bring meaningful change increases personal interest, which results in commitment and high motivation. Widespread involvement from all parts of the organization increases the chances of acceptance and *action* toward new initiatives.

In the systemic approach (Hamel and Prahalad, 1994), people are given the opportunity to have significant involvement in planning and implementing change. A sense of ownership is experienced in the entire organization when people see how they individually or as a team can envision a future for themselves and their organization. This participation helps them understand the need for change and how to be a part of the process. This makes them committed to *action*.

Our country and Church have become multicultural. This helps to explain why the systems method has proven to be effective in supporting change efforts within cultures as well as between cultures. This is because an important dynamic results when people of diverse backgrounds from all parts of the organization come together to integrate their thinking. Valuable insights happen. This collective flow of creativity develops into new ways of doing things, new mind-sets, and new ideas on how work gets done in the Church organization for effectiveness.

The Reward of Ownership

A sense of ownership happens when people have been consulted and involved in the process of deciding which changes need to be made from their unique cultural perspectives. Top-down strategies, visions, and plans often fail, regardless of their polish. Why? Because people were expected to listen to someone else's ideas, dreams, and plans. Collaboration and commitment happen when people feel personal ownership.

When each individual's perspective is valued, a closer view of the reality of the organization is developed. In this increasingly complex world, each person's perspective, talents, and gifts are needed. The most complete picture of reality includes the most perspectives. Remarkable support will occur, assisting leaders who alone cannot shift the future course of an entire organization.

Involving everyone unleashes extraordinary energy and optimism. This results in productivity. When people are highly energized for action, everyone wins. Guided by the Holy Spirit, people's imaginations, thoughts, ideas, and feelings are set free to create a vision for the future. Creativity and synergy are unleashed. The whole Church organization moves together into its future, truly reflecting a "shared" vision.

The comment "None of us is as smart as all of us" (Kayser, 1994) reflects the team approach to organization of today as the most effective way in turbulent, changing times. When the potential power of a team is harnessed, the results are greater success in achieving mission and objectives. There is power in collaboration.

This is team synergy at its best. A diverse group of people utilizing their own creativity, innovation, judgment, intuition, and brain power can do a better job than a lone star. Team synergy is in; the lone ranger is out. Nature teaches us this. For example, geese heading south for the winter months fly in V formation. Scientists (Kayser, 1994) tell us that as each bird flaps its wings, it creates an uplift for the bird immediately following. When the birds fly together in V formation, the whole flock adds at least 71 percent greater flying range than if each bird flew on its own. One goose may fall out of formation. When it does, it suddenly feels the drag and resistance of trying to go it alone and quickly gets back into formation. When it is ill or hurt, two geese fall out of formation and follow it down for protection. All work together creating synergy!

However, when groups of people (departments, etc.) focus on their own turf and needs, this creates different teams headed in different directions. What is needed is everyone working together, accessing each other's expertise, and all moving in the same direction with the same vision, mission, and goals. Attempting to see the world through each other's eyes and listening to each other can lead to greater understanding of ethnic differences, alignment, commitment, ownership, and openness—characteristics that produce healthy teams working in harmony toward that common goal. When the people have the vision, they are motivated to make it a reality.

Everyone is valued and needed. Trends in demographic shifts present opportunities for groups of people who have not had the opportunity to achieve their full potential in the traditional mode, such as different ethnic groups, women, older people, and the poor. When people are supporting each other's change efforts through harmonious thought and action, change is more palatable. It no longer becomes threatening. Now changes can be substantial across the entire Church organization.

4. Policies-Practices

The final step in the transformation process deals with policies-practices. Effective and sensitive organizational leaders will model the value of diversity. This will be demonstrated in the operational policies and practices of the Church. The efforts to reflect heterogeneity and empowerment of all the groups within the Church membership will be decisive and by clear design, thus reducing the potential societal influences of unconscious prejudices and discrimination to take hold. The practice of multicultural ministry begins with the practice of a new paradigm in Christ at the decision-making level.

Any Christ-centered model of diversity calls for servanthood leadership, which has its focus on service to others. As we noted earlier in the chapter, racism has at its base a desire for control, for power. This human element has been with us since the beginning of time. During Christ's day, E. G. White, says, "In the kingdoms of the world, position meant self-aggrandizement. The people were supposed to exist for the benefit of the ruling classes. Influence, wealth, education, were so many means of gaining control of the masses for the use of the leaders. *The higher classes were to think, decide, enjoy, and rule; the lower were to obey and serve.* Religion, like all things else, was a matter of authority. *The people were expected to believe and practice as their superiors directed. The right of [people as humans], to think and act for [themselves],* was *wholly unrecognized*" (*The Desire of Ages*, 550, emphasis added).

This brings to mind a comment a university professor once said, "When 'no' is not an option, 'yes' has no meaning." Under these circumstances, people have no options from which to choose. Thus, their responses are meaningless. The beauty of Christ's model is that He always allows us the freedom of choice; the power of the will; individuality; the power to think and do. He is not about force or arbitrary rule. "*In Christ's kingdom there is no lordly oppression, no compulsion of manner.* The angels of heaven do not come to the earth to rule, and to exact homage, but as messengers of mercy, to cooperate with [human beings] in uplifting humanity" (*The Desire of Ages*, 550, emphasis added).

As we can see, "Christ was establishing a kingdom on different principles. *He called [people], not to authority, but to service,* the strong to bear the infirmities of the weak. Power, position, talent, education, placed their possessor under the greater obligation to serve [their] fellows. To even the lowliest of Christ's disciples it is said, *'All things are for your sakes'* " (*The Desire of Ages*, 550, emphasis added).

The principle (of love) on which Christ acted is to actuate the members of the Church, which is His body. In the kingdom of Christ, those are greatest who follow the example He has given and act as *shepherds of His flocks* (see *The Desire of Ages*, 550), working together with all their diversities unified by the principle of love. This was the spirit that pervaded the early church. After the outpouring of the Holy Spirit, "the multitude of them that believed were of one heart and of one soul; neither said any of them that ought of the things which he possessed was his own." "Neither was there among them that lacked." "And great grace was upon them all" (Acts 4:32, 34, 33; *The Desire of Ages*, 551).

Lasting Transformation

How, then, do Christians go about eliminating racism and prejudice in their individual as well as institutional life? The process shared in this chapter is a way to initiate the change process under the power of the Holy Spirit. In order to create change, one must begin transformation individually and at the institutional level, where racism, prejudice, and discrimination are embedded. A Christ-centered model of diversity is presented as a means to that end as the Church moves into the twenty-first century.

When the Church embraces change proactively, it will be prepared to meet the challenging changes and needs of the twenty-first century in ways that will impact the Church for growth and prepare it for Christ's second coming! Then we will realize the eternal charge spoken of in 1 Corinthians 15:51-54:

Listen, I tell you a mystery: We will not all sleep, but we will all be changed—in a flash, in the twinkling of an eye, at the last trumpet. For the trumpet will sound, the dead will be raised imperishable, and we will be changed. For the perishable must clothe itself with the imperishable, and the mortal with immortality. When the perishable has been clothed with the imperishable, and the mortal with immortality, then the saying that is written will come true: "Death has been swallowed up in victory" (NIV).

Ramona Perez Greek, Ph.D., is assistant director of women's ministries for the NAD. Her public roles have included: professor of mental health nursing at Auburn University and member of the Hispanic Association of Colleges and Universities. She is a writer, educator, and consultant for women's ministries. She and her husband, Jim, have one son.

Bibliography

Barna, George. *The Frog in the Kettle: What Christians Need to Know about Life in the Year 2000*. Ventura, Calif.: Regal Books, 1990.

Collins, Randall. *Theoretical Sociology*. San Diego, Calif.: Harcourt, Brace Jovanovich Publishers, 1988, 265.

Elliot, Jane. Videocassette (58 min.), *Discrimination in Education*. Iowa: Consortium of Public Television Stations, 1970.

Friedman, Leon. Quote from his report to Congress outlining a Civil Rights bill, June 19, 1963, in *The Civil Rights Reader*. New York: Walker and Company, 1967.

Hamel, G., and C. K. Prahalad. *Competing for the Future*. Boston: Harvard Business School Press.

Katz, Judith. *White Awareness: Handbook for Anti-racism Training*. Norman, Okla.: University of Oklahoma Press, 1978, 50.

Kayser, Thomas A. *Building Team Power*. New York: Irwin Professional Publishing, 1994.

Kraemer, Bernard. "Dimensions of Prejudice." *Journal of Psychology*, April 1949.

Montgomery Advertiser Journal. 21 September 1994, 1.

North American Division, Office of Human Relations. *1993 Membership* Sta-

tistics for the Multicultural Groups of the NAD of Seventh-day Adventists, 1 September 1994.

Pope and Associates (personnel diversity consultants). Statistics. Cincinnati, Ohio: Pope and Associates, Inc.

Rosado, Caleb. "Definitions for Training in Diversity." Unpublished document, 8 November 1994.

Rosado, Caleb, and Samuel Bentances. Definition with ideas adapted from Robert T. Wellman. *Portraits of White Racism*. Cambridge, 1993.

Shaefer, Richard T. *Racial and Ethnic Groups*. 4th edition. Glenview, Ill.: Scott, Foresman, and Company, 1990.

The Holy Bible. Nashville, Tenn.: Thomas Nelson Publishers. Unless otherwise noted, all scriptural passages are from the Revised Standard Version.

White, Ellen G. *Testimonies for the Church*. Volume 9. Boise, Idaho: Pacific Press Publishing Association, 1939, 190.

———. *The Desire of Ages*. Boise, Idaho: Pacific Press Publishing Association, 1940, 550.

6

Diversity and the Family Forum

Barbara A. Frye

The family is the forum for developing personal excellence, relationship skills, and a balanced worldview for children and adults. It is in the family that diversity skills and attitudes are learned and the character molded.

*M*andy and Meechi were the best of friends. At the age of three, they both enjoyed sharing their ever-expanding world with each other. They shared their dolls, their crayons, and even their food. They spent hours in the sandbox creating the most magnificent sculptures. One autumn morning as they molded their treasures of sand, I stood at the back door watching them. Mandy's silky auburn locks were a striking contrast to the softness of Meechi's dark, kinky ringlets. The girls were laughing, each stroking the other's hair. The moment was brief, and then they returned their attention to the sand. They noticed and accepted that they were different, one from the other. This acceptance was so casual, so gentle. Witnessing that tender moment, I felt a sharp jab of pain, a deep sadness for what these little girls would discover before too many more years would pass.

Soon they would discover what they did not know about each other as they sat in the sandbox—that they were the children of a nation ripped apart by racial discord, a nation with a tragic history of oppression, barriers to opportunity, and racial hatred. As I watched them playing so happily, I prayed that their innocence would be preserved, that they would be spared from hearing the cultural messages of separatism and hatred.

Value-based Diference

At a very early age, children become aware of differences, and they begin to develop categories for differences—big and little, round and square, black and white. Categorization of differences is a normal part of cognitive development. It occurs independent of assigned merit until the child is taught to place a value on difference (Derman-Sparks, 1989). Racial and ethnic hatred is rooted in the establishment of social value based on levels of difference.

Like the United States, Great Britain is a country currently experiencing much racial and ethnic discord. In a recent study of White middle-class children in Great Britain (Bennett, Dewberry & Yeeles, 1991), eight- to eleven-year-old children were tested on how they categorized other children. They were also tested for their preferences according to individual or ethnic differences. The findings were striking. The children categorized according to personality characteristics rather than ethnic or racial characteristics. They indicated preference based on individual and personality factors more strongly than on racial or ethnic factors. This British study was repeated among urban poverty-level ethnic children, and the findings were the same.

In a similar study among African American children in Arizona (Porter, 1991), the children were asked preferences of skin color ranging from light, honey-brown, dark, or very dark. Most of the children described their own skin tone as honey-brown and stated they preferred honey-brown. When asked why they preferred this skin tone, the majority of the children stated that they liked the honey-brown tone because it was their own color and the color of their friends. In other words, their preference for skin color was based upon familiar individual characteristics rather than upon assigned racial or ethnic characteristics.

Stereotyping messages shaping a child's perception of self-worth and the social value of others are learned within the context of culture (Derman-Sparks, 1989). Mandy and Meechi knew no hate or separatism on that sunny autumn day in the sandbox. They had no frame of reference for understanding the bitter struggles of their nation. They only knew that with each other they found happiness, enjoyment, and loving companionship. They had not yet learned about hatred, for it takes time to teach a child, and a child has to be taught, very carefully taught, to hate.

It Takes a Village to Raise a Child

Children do not grow up in isolation from their surrounding social and cultural world, and so it was only a matter of time before Mandy and Meechi would be confronted with the cultural messages of separatism. Children develop their understanding of how the world works from the view of the world that is presented to them. This worldview explains reality and causality.

Through an osmotic process, the culture infuses the child with messages about what is real—real food, real fun, real friendship. It frames messages about who is strong, smart, valuable, and worthy of attention. It also conveys messages about how things happen—by individual control, by fate, by spiritual forces. Having taught what is real and why things happen, the culture then goes on to shape the child through dictating behavior that fits into this worldview. As the child learns the appropriate responses, he/she becomes a mirror image of the culture. Imitation reinforces the message, rooting the child in the culture. This process takes time and constant effort. It takes everyone working together with a consistent message to make it happen. Thus the accuracy of the African proverb that says, "It takes a village to raise a child."

As the village raises the child, the child gradually incorporates cultural values and the resulting behaviors that express those values. He slowly absorbs the overt and subtle verbal and nonverbal expressions until they become automatic—so much a part of the child's fiber of being that he cannot separate himself from the roots of his culture. The child sees the world and his place of importance in that world through the prism of his culture. This prism frames his assumptions about what is real, why things happen, and who he is.

The family functions as a microcosm of the larger culture, a part of the village. The family absorbs the values of the culture but further defines them for the child in its own unique way. For example, family customs around holidays reflect a uniqueness of expression yet an adherence to the values of the larger culture. The celebration of Christmas is a global Christian holy day expressed through the giving of gifts. The origin of gift giving, the story of the Magi, is widely understood within the Christian culture. Yet this practice has unique expressions nationally, regionally, and within families. Christmas is also celebrated with special foods, turkey in the Midwest, tamales in California, and perhaps vegetarian roasts in Adventist families. The child learns that she is a member of a family but that the family belongs in the village. That cultural village may have wide boundaries of inclusiveness, or it may have tight and narrow boundaries.

The Culture of Prejudice

Narrow boundaries of inclusiveness create a rigid system highly dependent upon complex rules about who is included, who is excluded, and under what circumstances inclusion and exclusion occur. Children learn at a very young age that socially preferred skin color, language, gender, and physical ability are associated with positive social value. Derman-Sparks (1989) describes how the young child learns, through verbal and especially nonverbal messages, that these preferred characteristics are associated with privilege and power. In the book *Alike and Different: Exploring our humanity with young children* (1987), Phillips states, "It has been said that actions more often than not speak louder than words. And if this is so in the case of child-rearing, then we must be especially vigilant in our actions to shape the values children will attach as they learn about the people in their world. If we don't, they will learn by default the messages that are already prevalent out there and both we and they will contribute to perpetuating the past ideas which we do not want to replicate in our children's future" (5, 6).

Overt and Covert Messages

Some messages are expressed overtly, while others are subtle or so extremely subtle that only those deeply rooted in the culture could comprehend. One evening at twilight I was enjoying a peaceful walk with a friend around a 100-year-old churchyard. As we strolled among the blooming lilacs and admired the ancient oaks, he suggested that we explore the messages on the weathered tombstones. Among the larger stones were many tiny slabs with tender words of love for the babies than lay beneath those stones. One stone addressed to a baby named Matthew read, "We only knew you for six months but you will be forever in our hearts." Another addressed to two-year-old Sarah said, "We give you back to God."

The loss of children was such a frequent event in those early days of our country. I commented to my friend that even today, the death of infants in poor areas of the world and among the urban poor of America, especially African American babies, was not that changed.

My friend responded, "Oh, well, they expect to lose their babies, and they don't feel it like we do." I reeled with shock and disbelief as my friend, a parent who had lost a child many years before, not only ascribed feelings to another group but also assumed that their level of pain was less than his own.

Not all messages of difference are so blatant. Recently, Justin, a rapidly growing teenager, entered a barbershop. He recognized the mother of one of his friends from school. Being a friendly, outgoing teenager, Justin greeted her warmly. The adult, turning around, startled visually as she glanced into Justin's black face. It was only after Justin explained who he was that the white woman remarked, "Oh, Justin, I didn't realize it was you."

Later, Justin remarked to his mother, "Mrs. Thomas thought I was dangerous and that I was going to rob her." Halpern (1993), in writing about the experience of ethnic children, states that the key factor in affecting the child's perception of self is not what the national or overriding culture is saying about him but rather the quality of his experience at the local, everyday level. Justin received a subtle message of stereotyping and exclusion in that brief encounter in the barbershop.

The Culture of Exclusion

Drawing the boundaries of exclusion can be expressed at extremely subtle levels. It had been a busy day, and I looked forward to my twilight exercise, but the phone kept ringing, a neighbor stopped by, and my son and his teenage friends announced that they were hungry. Finally, I escaped as the sun sank behind the mountains. Darkness came quickly, and I scolded myself for not starting earlier. I hurried along on my usual course, approaching the bus stop. Out of the corner of my eye, I noticed a Black teenage male leaning on a post by the bus stop. I flinched, he smiled reassuringly, and I quickly smiled back, an encounter that lasted no more than five seconds, but represented hundreds of years of history. I felt shattered by this experience. In a brief flicker of time, I had sized up the situation, made an assumption, and communicated that assumption to him. The nameless youth understood the message and countered it with assurance that he was not one of "them" and that I was safe. I, in turn, communicated back to him that I accepted the message that he was not one of "them."

Everyone has the potential to express prejudice through derogatory remarks, and everyone is hurt by messages of exclusion. Children, especially, are hurt. Children of the dominant White culture are at risk as narrow boundaries are imposed upon them. Derman-Sparks (1989), in her book entitled *The Anti-Bias Curriculum: Tools for Empowering Young Children*, states that Caucasians who learn that they are superior based on external characteristics such as being White, male, or able-bodied have been denied their full humanity and presented with a distorted reality. They are asked to exclude before they have the opportunity to become acquainted with the person behind the face of color, the opposite gender, or the disabled body.

Ethnic minority children, conversely, learn that they are expected to feel inferior before they have been given the opportunity to fully explore and develop their God-given talents. Glancing out of the kitchen window on that long-ago autumn day, I laughed. Mandy and Meechi were gleefully pouring sand into each other's hair, the hair they had just mutually patted, acknowledging and accepting their differences without judgment. There was no show of power or superiority by either one of them, only the joy of another shared adventure—sand in the hair. Their boundaries with each other were wide and inclusive.

The Culture of Inclusiveness

The Christian worldview has a specific definition of reality and causality. God is portrayed as the ultimate reality.

Causality is explained within the framework of the great controversy. Absolutely central to the Christian message is the recognition of every individual as belonging to God, created in His image. The Christian culture shapes behavior that evolves from this view of the world—a call to servanthood toward all persons and an openness to God's leading in personal ministry toward others. The Christian worldview acknowledges the "specialness" of each person.

Recently, my son Rob had his sixteenth birthday. He and his friends had been planning the party for months. His friends were well aware of when the party was to occur. Two weeks before the big event, Rob announced that we needed to mail out the invitations. I asked why we needed to send invitations, since all his friends had known about the party for months. He replied, "Mom, I need to send invitations so everyone will feel special." The Christian culture says that everyone is special and all are invited. Christ sends the personal invitation, "Follow Me," to each person who will heed His call. His is a message of inclusiveness with wide boundaries.

Within the Christian worldview, inclusiveness is a fundamental, nonnegotiable principle. The Church, as the living body of Christ, has a great responsibility to be a vocal mediating force against the larger societal messages of prejudice and exclusion. The message of inclusion is a moral message to the larger society, but it is also a message to children, those who are a part of the Church, and those who look on at a distance. For children of dominant and ethnic minority status within the Church, the message of inclusion counterbalances the mental and spiritual health risks of superiority and disesteem that they face from the larger society.

Halpern (1993) states that cultural messages of prejudice can be buffeted by the immediate social environment when it includes protection from overt, direct prejudice and inclusion in a strong, local network. The Church has a mandate to protect its own children from the spiritual death of prejudice and to include them in the wide circle of the church family. Likewise, the church stands as a bastion against the social evil of prejudice and an example for onlooking children outside of its circle. But church begins in the family.

Cultural Inclusiveness in the Home

Our Christian conditioning is superimposed upon our social and cultural conditioning. We are, at the same time, children of the kingdom and children of our culture, no matter what our age. Like children building a tower of blocks, we build our cognitive towers that insulate "us" from "them." Frequently these towers are towers of Babel, built upon faulty assumptions, lack of knowledge, and minimal experience with "them." Through ignorance and fear, we set about to defend our towers to our own spiritual detriment and perhaps to the spiritual demise of our children. *Fear, ignorance,* and *cognitive insulation* are stumbling blocks to creating the culture of inclusiveness. It takes courage and the power of the Holy Spirit to break down the tower and build competence in inclusiveness.

How to Build Inclusiveness in the Home

So how do we build competence and comfort in inclusiveness? How do we create an environment in the home in which to nurture and act out our words of brotherhood and sisterhood? The following steps will help:

1. Recognizing Our Human Frailty

In *Intercultural Communication* (1994) Barnhund states, "Human understanding is by no means guaranteed because conversants share the same dictionary" (27). This principle applies to the Bible as well as the dictionary. Just because we share the same Holy Book and the same faith does not automatically insulate us from the strong cultural messages we have all received from early childhood. The first step in inclusiveness is recognizing that we are all part of a sinful and broken world, that we have all sinned and fallen short. Everyone clings to prejudice at some level. Recognizing and admitting prejudice can be a fearful event for a Christian who is supposed to be inclusive and free of such a mind-set. We cannot create the culture of inclusiveness in our homes if we hold onto our secret prejudices.

At one point early in my teaching career, a student of another race failed one of my courses. He had told me previously how fearful he was of the assignment, and subsequently he did not complete the assignment satisfactorily. I decided I needed to be tough with him, holding the academic line. He was most upset with his failing grade, and he asked me directly if his race had anything to do with his failure. I indignantly replied, "Of course not. You didn't do the assignment correctly." After he left, looking deflated, his words haunted me. They challenged me to go before the Lord on my knees and explore this issue. To this day, I'm still not sure if racial prejudice was a factor in my response to this student.

As I prayed and wept before the Lord about this matter, He showed me that I had been harsh, exclusive in my attitude, holding onto my knowledge rather than sharing it. He showed me that I could have helped the student more, that I could have attempted to enter into his cognitive world instead of expecting him to make all the accommodation. I called the student back, asking him to forgive me for not helping him when he expressed so much fear about the assignment. He learned how to do the assignment satisfactorily. I learned something more important—the value of inclusiveness. Until we face our spiritual stumbling blocks to inclusiveness, we cannot hope to create inclusiveness in our own homes.

2. Making the Choice for Inclusiveness

Creating an environment with wide boundaries is not a human act. It is the work of grace in our lives. But we can make the choice to work with God's grace in this matter. Making this choice involves vulnerability to hurt in new experiences. It involves willingness to build trust, to break out of the boundaries of our own safe, experiential world and test the edges of another world. It is an act of courage, a powerful example of Christian parenthood to set before our children.

Venturing out of one's own world is frequently an emotional and cultural shock. After the initial euphoria of entering a new, unmapped experience, it is common to feel irritated with unpredictable racial and cultural differences, to feel inadequate, unappreciated, and angry. Unsettling emotions and unanswered questions plague those who venture out among "them," people different from themselves. As we model this risk-taking behavior for our children, we have a model in Christ, who never feared to live close to the Samaritans, the publicans, the rich, and the poor. It was said of Him that He ate with sinners (Matthew 9:10). Can't we, as sinners, at least show our children that we are willing to "eat" with other sinners?

3. Seeking Opportunities

Inclusiveness begins by talking with our children about the problem of prejudice. The Children's Defense Fund, which publishes *The State of America's Children* (1992), advises, "Talk candidly with your children about racial fears and prejudice. Teach your children that all Americans are part of our national family and equal before God and the Constitution. Help and teach them to heal America" (xvi). Can we not also instruct our children that all children are equally a part of God's family?

If our children are to heal America, they must enter adulthood healthy and free from the malignancy of prejudice. We need to be proactive in seeking opportunities to immunize them against prejudice and to expose them to doses of interracial and crosscultural experiences. These exposures are not an end in themselves or a singling out of any particular group. Most of all, they are not a "tourist" experience. Rather, they need to be an interweaving of life in the context of the everyday experience—eating, playing, learning, worshiping.

Years after her sandbox days, my teenage daughter Mandy walked closely beside me on my voyage into the Cambodian refugee culture. I was privileged to work with the refugees within the context of the local church, in the border camps of Thailand, and in the inner-city environment of southern California. Our home was a frequent Sabbath meeting place where delicious foods from the East and the West covered the table.

In the everyday context of interacting with another race, an unfamiliar culture, a different language, the child learns that there are many ways of living, all worthy of respect, all adding zest and enjoyment to life. The child learns that differences of race and custom aren't stumbling blocks but just a normal part of everyday life. She learns to be comfortable and competent interracially and interculturally as she lives out her childhood immersed in an inclusive environment. The church, as no other institution, has the potential for providing this opportunity, but church begins in the home.

4. Building a Common Christian Unity in the Spirit

A strong sense of group identity is a powerful immunizing agent against the erosion of self-esteem that occurs among children of both the dominant culture and the ethnic minority cultures when discriminatory, prejudicial behavior is pervasive (Derman-Sparks, 1989). Further, tight group identity and unity can serve as a buffer against the negative societal messages of prejudice and low social value imposed upon ethnic minorities (Halpern, 1993).

Our children need to feel that their Christian culture is their "superculture," the culture beyond their Native American, Hispanic American, African American, Euro-American, or Asian American culture. It needs to be the culture beyond their national heritage as an American (prefix-free). This identity with their Christian heritage is not a replacement of their ethnic identity but rather an expansion of it. Their color may be Red, Yellow, Black, or White, but their enduring color is Christian, for this is their eternal culture. It is the tie that binds and will bind when all else is left behind.

Children can only develop a network of identity with each

other and a sense of unity in the Spirit when they are given the opportunity to build that sense of identity. This network starts in the home with continual verbal and nonverbal messages about the equality of each person before God. Each Christian home can be a welcoming place, a place of inclusion for all of our children. The network can be spread out to the larger community through school, church and social clubs.

Positive Interpersonal Principles

Friendship "Those who shut themselves up within themselves, who are unwilling to be drawn upon to bless others by friendly associations, lose many blessings; for by mutual contact, minds receive polish and refinement; by social intercourse, acquaintances are formed and friendships contracted which result in a unity of heart and an atmosphere of love which is pleasing in the sight of heaven" (*Testimonies for the Church*, 6:172).

Sociable "He [Jesus] carried out His teachings in His own life. He showed consistency without obstinacy, benevolence without weakness, tenderness and sympathy without sentimentalism. He was highly social, yet He possessed a reserve that discouraged any familiarity. His temperance never led to bigotry or austerity" (*Counsels to Parents, Teachers, and Students*, 262).

Affections "Social advantages are talents and are to be used for the benefit of all within reach of our influence" (*Christ's Object Lessons*, 353).

Power "The Christian home is to be an object lesson, illustrating the excellence of the true principles of life. Such an illustration will be a power for good in the world" (*The Ministry of Healing*, 352).

Injustice "The Lord would place a check upon the inordinate love of property and power. Great evils would result from the continued accumulation of wealth by one class, the poverty and degradation of another. Without some restraint, the power of the wealthy would become a monopoly, and the poor, though in every respect fully as worthy in God's sight, would be regarded and treated as inferior to their more prosperous brethren" (*Patriarchs and Prophets*, 534).

Character "It was not the purpose of God that poverty should ever leave the world. The ranks of society were never to be equalized, for the diversity of condition which characterizes our race is one of the means by which God has designed to prove and develop character" (*Testimonies for the Church*, 4:551, 552).

Equality "The religion of Christ uplifts the receiver to a higher plane of thought and action, while at the same time it presents the whole human race as alike the objects of the love of God, being purchased by the sacrifice of His Son. At the feet of Jesus the rich and the poor, the learned and the ignorant, meet together, with no thought of caste or worldly preeminence. . . . Students are to be taught the Christlikeness of exhibiting a kindly interest, a social disposition, toward those who are in the greatest need, even though these may not be their own chosen companion" (*Testimonies for the Church*, 6:172, 173).

Gracious "Let the world see that we are not selfishly absorbed in our own interests, but that we desire others to share our blessings and privileges" (*The Desire of Ages*, 152).

The Christian community is indeed a "village" that can offer a worldview of inclusiveness and a cultural buffer against societal messages of exclusion. However, it takes a consistent message from the whole "village" to make it happen. Messages of separatism and exclusion undermine this protective network. It takes a village to raise a child.

Responding to Difficult Situations

Because we live in a very imperfect world, it is inevitable that we and our children, whom we seek to protect, will hurt and be hurt by prejudice and exclusion. How we respond to these situations of hurt goes to the heart of the Christian message, which calls us to inclusiveness, acceptance, and love. Here are some ways to respond to situations of prejudice and conflict.

Ignoring the Dragon

One way of responding to the hurt of prejudice is to ignore it. This is a denial of the insidious nature of prejudice. It feeds and grows fat upon denial. The world ignored the plight of the Jews in Europe during World War II. In Germany the signs of growing prejudice were there—demeaning and slandering public images were ignored initially, then tolerated, and finally espoused. Yet the world turned its back on the Jewish population's pleas for help. It denied the possibility of a holocaust of unimaginable proportions until, in shock, it realized the danger of ignoring the dragon. Six million persons had gone to cruel and untimely deaths. Currently, similar situations of genocide exist in Europe, Africa, Asia, and in the callous disregard for infant mortality and youthful homicide among our inner-city children.

Ignoring slanderous remarks about any group of people is feeding the dragon of prejudice. Yet sometimes it seems unimportant or frightening to confront. When my children were in their early school years, they were always delighted when a beloved and benevolent older person came to visit, bearing gifts and promises of fun times. The only negative side of these visits was occasional racial slurs directed toward people of color. These comments seemed to come out of nowhere. No particular incident seemed to trigger them. My response was to wince, but not wanting to create conflict, I kept quiet, distracted the children, and hoped the comments would just disappear. I felt guilty because I didn't have the courage to speak up and stop the comments. My prior conditioning about not correcting my elders kept me in obedient silence. My behavior was no different than that of the Germans who silently watched their countrymen with yellow stars on their clothing being taken away by the Nazi secret service. It was no different than that of the South Africans who turned away from the ugly face of apartheid or those who ignore the pervasive racism that demeans our children in the inner-city ghettos of America. It was only a matter of degree.

I recognized that this kind of talk before the children had to stop and that I was responsible to stop it. I felt the need to pray for wisdom, courage, and kindness in this delicate situation. With a withering spirit, I recalled my prayer for Mandy and Meechi as they sat in the sandbox, that they would be spared from hearing the cultural messages of separatism and hatred. Yet the dragon had invaded my own home, and I was ignoring the dragon. Finally, I summoned the courage to speak privately with the person, affirming how much we all valued and loved him. I shared my hope that the children could be spared messages that other persons were less valuable than they. I asked him not to speak ill of other racial groups before the children.

I thought the issue was settled until one day I overheard him telling the children," 'Niggers' and 'beaners' are not as smart as you kids are."

This time I exploded. "Don't you ever speak like that in front of the children again!"

Later that evening as I was putting the children to bed, my daughter said, "Wow, Mom, that really made you mad, didn't it?"

I told her the story about Jesus getting angry when the temple was defiled. I explained that Jesus didn't hate the people who were defiling the temple, but He hated what was happening in the temple. I told her I didn't hate our friend, but I did hate the "hate." That evening I prayed with my children that we would all "hunger and thirst" after righteousness. That prayer has been answered over the years as I see the righteous indignation of my children when they witness prejudicial behavior. They remind me that I was a warrior in this matter, although I know in my heart that I was a fearful one. There is no room for prejudice if we are to truly live out the message of inclusiveness. The dragon cannot be ignored.

Co-existing With the Dragon

The dragon of prejudice is always with us. Sometimes it is caustic and overt. At other times it is extremely subtle and casual, communicated only with a flicker of the eyes. Frequently it is mixed up with positive, affirming messages in the way that evil works, interweaving and attaching itself to good. Recently, while having my hair cut by my Vietnamese American hairdresser, Tran, we both overheard the woman sitting in the chair to the left talking with her hairdresser, Louise. They were discussing "those" refugees who come into this country "uninvited" and "take" everything from the country. I saw the look of pain cross Tran's beautifully molded Asian face.

Here was the presence of the dragon sitting to my left in the beauty shop. I squeezed Tran's hand and commented, "It surely is a shame that Americans know so little about the world. They have such a limited understanding of other people." Louise and her customer got the point. So did the blond teenager sitting in the chair to my right. She gave me the "thumbs up" sign. Perhaps my response was confrontive, but what message would I have given Tran and the teenager if I had kept quiet?

In *The Measure of Our Success: A Letter to My Children and Yours* (1992), Marian Wright Edelman, founder of the Children's Defense Fund, advises parents, "Don't tell, laugh at, or in any way acquiesce to racial, ethnic, religious, or gender jokes or to any practices intended to demean rather than enhance another human being" (54). Co-existing with the dragon is tolerating prejudice expressed in any fashion: jokes, slurs, or innuendos—overt, subtle, or nonverbal.

Our children see the subtle forms of racism and prejudice co-existing with the gospel in our church. Each week the Cambodian refugee children faithfully came to their Sabbath School dressed in faded, clean clothes and sandals, the best clothes that they possessed at that time. One Sabbath I took them to a local church. At the end of the service, one of the elderly women whispered loudly in my ear, "Don't those people know what is proper to wear to church?" The children overheard her remark. Noticing that they understood, the woman further commented, "Oh, I didn't know that they speak English."

"They speak English perfectly," I replied, "and don't they look beautiful this morning?"

When we got back in the car, one of the children commented, "That woman didn't like us, did she?" On another occasion, the co-existence of the dragon was not tolerated by a perceptive, sensitive church member. An unruly teenager sat alone in the back of the church. She was not a regular member; no one had seen her before. Her appearance violated every Adventist "standard." Her earrings practically touched her shoulders; her short skirt was indecent; her makeup was garish. She looked pouty and angry, but she stayed for the whole service, holding her head in her hands. When the service was over, she walked out, swinging her hips amid head shaking and "tut-tut" whispered disapprovals.

Only one woman approached the teen, welcoming her warmly and engaging her in a friendly, caring conversation. Other teenagers, regular church members, observed the whole scenario. Only one woman refused to co-exist with the dragon of prejudice and exclusion directed toward the teenager. Her message was powerful. She was a part of the "village" raising the children to value inclusiveness.

Vanquishing the Dragon

Each incident of prejudice, conflict, and hurt is a potent opportunity for spiritual growth, for recognizing one's own imperfections, for showing our children our own willingness and need to receive forgiveness, for extending the gift of forgiveness when we have been hurt. On that Sabbath when the Cambodian children had been hurt, we talked about forgiveness and what Jesus would do when someone hurt His feelings. We prayed together for God to forgive the woman who had hurt their feelings. After we prayed, the children smiled. They were back in control of their lives. Forgiveness is power, the power of the Holy Spirit to overcome and vanquish the dragon. Our children need to observe us giving and receiving forgiveness. They need to participate with us in the act of forgiveness.

Rosa was a dear Hispanic friend. I felt very close to her until some of her preconceived ideas about "gringos," White North Americans, began to be imposed upon me. I was confused and hurt by her mixed messages of friendship and anger. I tried to talk with her, but she wouldn't talk about it. Finally, I walked away from the friendship. About a year later, she came to see me. With tears she related that God had given her no peace until she agreed to speak with me. She confessed her feelings of prejudice, feelings that were rooted in past injustices imposed upon her and her people by "gringos." She asked me to forgive her and accept her back as a friend. She told me how much our friendship meant to her.

My first reaction was to ignore the dragon—to pretend the problem had never really existed. Then I was flooded with a desire to excuse the problem; it really didn't matter. Finally, before I had said anything, I realized I didn't want to forgive her right then. I was angry with her, and I wanted her to suffer my anger. She had insulted me and "my" people. Is that the way of "her" people? Then God spoke to my heart and said, "Who needs the forgiveness more in this situation?" With God's grace, I gave her my forgiveness and asked for hers, for we both had fallen short. The dragon was vanquished. God had given yet another opportunity for spiritual growth and another story to share with the "village" children, at home, in Sabbath School, at the university.

Called to Inclusiveness

The Christian message is a call to inclusiveness. At the heart of this message is acceptance, love, and freedom from prejudice. Living out this message means going against the cultural norms that are loaded with messages of exclusion. These messages, both overt and subtle, not only permeate the larger society but also circumscribe our personal boundaries. Our choice of boundaries can be narrow or wide. Learning to live the Christian message of wide boundaries begins in the home, where "church" really begins.

Teaching our children to be competent in inclusiveness means recognizing and sharing our own human frailty with our children. It means making a choice to create an environment in the home that fosters inclusiveness. It means actively seeking opportunities for our children to grow in competence and to learn their Christian identity. Teaching our children inclusiveness takes courage. It means refusing to ignore or excuse prejudice. It means giving and receiving forgiveness.

By ourselves we cannot accomplish the task of inclusiveness. "For our struggle is not against flesh and blood, but against the rulers, against the authorities, against the powers of this dark world and against the spiritual forces of evil in the heavenly realms" (Ephesians 6:12). These forces may be as seemingly innocuous as a raised eyebrow or as blatantly evil as Dachau or Pol Pot's Khmer Rouge. It is only a matter of degree. Our response to exclusion and the message we give to our children about all forms of exclusion, by race, physical or mental wholeness, gender, age, language, or cultural group goes straight to the heart of the Christian message. That message is conceived in the family and nurtured by the "village," for it takes the whole "village" to raise the child in the message that God is love.

Barbara Frye, Dr.PH., is an associate professor at Loma Linda University in the School of Public Health and the School of Medicine. She teaches crosscultural communication and has traveled extensively for various organizations within the SDA Church. Her greatest joy is in her two children, Amanda and Robert.

References

Barnlund, D. "Communication in a Global Village," in L. Samovar and R. Porter, eds. *Intercultural Communication: A Reader*. Belmont, Calif.: Wadsworth Publishing Co., 1994, 26-35.

Bennett, B., D. Dewberry, and C. Yeeles. "A Reassessment of the Role of Ethnicity in Children's Social Perception." *Journal of Child Psychology and Psychiatry* 32(6) (1991):969-982.

Derman-Sparks, L. *The Anti-Bias Curriculum: Tools for Empowering Young Children*. Washington, D.C.: National Association for the Education of Young Children, 1989.

Edelman, M. The *Measure of Our Success: A Letter to My Children and Yours*. Boston, Mass.: Beacon Press, 1992.

Halpern, D. "Minorities and Mental Health." *Social Science and Medicine*, 35(5) (1993):597-607.

Porter, C. "Social Reasons for Skin Tone Preferences of Black School-age Children." *American Journal of Orthopsychiatry* 6(1) (1991):149-154.

Phillips, C. Foreword in B. Neugebauer, ed. *Alike and Different: Exploring Our Humanity With Young Children*. Redmond, Wash.: Exchange Press, 1987, 5, 6.

P.E.A.C.E.M.A.K.E.R.S.
How to Build Bridges and Resolve
Intercultural Problems

PRAY first—then figure out the what, who, when, why, how, and what of the conflict.

ENQUIRE by using the Q-A method (question and answer)—listen, then count the cost.

ACT immediately to do an attitude check—your attitude, their attitude—everyone's attitude.

CARE-FRONT the challenge—go to the source to understand—deal with issues, not individuals.

ENCOURAGE efforts toward finding a solution and affirming rather than shaming and provoking.

MASTER the pride/selfishness urge—choose humilty/selflessness through dependence on Christ.

AWAKEN and activate the principles and practice of non-blaming, affirming communcation.

KILL antagonism and animosity with the fruit of the Spirit.

EXAMINE your biblical or abiblical perception and view of the issue.

RESOLVE the issue by selecting solutions that are spiritually based—get consensus and closure.

SENSITIZE everyone involved to facilitate the needy one(s)—monitor the success of the solution.

---------------- *7* ----------------

Removing Barriers, Creating Understanding

Rosa Taylor Banks

New depths in relationships will be experienced when negative myths and stereotypes are destroyed and replaced by understanding and acceptance.

*D*efining and correcting certain misunderstandings and providing positive mental alternatives is a somewhat dangerous undertaking. There is always the possibility that some may misunderstand and misuse the points. Hopefully these insights will be accepted in the positive light in which they were intended.

In the Christian culture, we find it difficult to discuss the evils of racism. We would rather tiptoe around the subject, sweep it under the rug, or much like the proverbial ostrich who buries his head in the sand, lament, "I don't see any racism in this organization or in my world."

The truth is, the guilty may never see it, nor will one who is looking in the wrong direction. Some take the stance that one day, quite miraculously, a magic wand will be waved, and things that divide us will disappear. But *racism will not just go away*. Unless we confront it as a present barrier to the

161

development of Christian characters and the achievement of racial equality and accept that equality is a possibility, racism will continue to be the obstacle that keeps the Church divided.

There! I have actually said it. I have crossed the limits and named racism as a major problem of not only our society, but of the Christian Church. Further, unless the Church recognizes racism as the problem it is and confronts it in ways that will lead to viable solutions that bring oneness and healing, it will be impossible for the Church to model the love that will witness to the world to which God sent Jesus (see John 17:23).

This chapter will deal with breaking down barriers of racial myths and stereotypes and will focus on ways to create understanding in the context of the Christian faith in general and Adventism in particular. However, to provide for greater balance, race relationships in the larger society will also be included.

Faith and Race

The Christian doctrine of essential being affirms that "a human is not an independent being but a dependent being, owing his/her existence to God, and is held in being at every moment by God" (Kelsey, 72). *Calvin's Doctrine of Man* fleshes this belief out more succinctly: "It means, first of all, that we are creatures, that we are dust and ashes, and that in ourselves we are nothing. It means that in ourselves we have no permanence and nothing whereupon we could base our own right and our own claims, nothing that we ourselves can assert as the meaning and worth of our life" (Torrance, 26).

Kelsey believes that when humans forget this, when they fail to give thanks to God and to give Him the glory, they are, in fact, nothing. For him racism goes beyond forgetting. It is more than the religious indifference. It is idolatry. It is a decisive act of turning away from God to the creature. It is the worship of the creature instead of the Creator (Kelsey, 73). Each of the following definitions will help clarify the terms used in this chapter.

1. Race: A classification of humans, often based on an arbitrary selection of physical characteristics, as skin color, facial form, or eye shape. A human population isolated from other populations whose members share a greater degree of physical and genetic similarity with one another than with other humans. "A group of persons of, or regarded as of, common ancestry" (Simons, 244). Sometimes the term is used to refer to the entire human family, while at other times it is used to subdivide the human species into distinct racial groups.

2. Racism: A belief or doctrine that inherent differences among the various human races determine cultural or individual achievement, usually involving the idea that one's race is superior.

Roger J. Williams explains that racism involves the idea that there are superior and inferior races. "People individually have different patterns of potentialities; no person is generally inferior to another. Contradicting the view that some races hold a corner on some special virtues while others are not so generally graced, he concludes that every race is spotted with a great variety of individuals, each with a distinctive pattern of potentialities. He asks, "How could we speak of a superior race? Superior for what? Mental abilities are always spotted . . . . There are many ways in which we can be sharp or dull, and each of us has a pattern of his/her own. Each race contains individuals, each of which has his/her own distinctive characteristics" (Cory, 319).

While Williams' view is held by countless numbers of Christians, he is careful not to raise an accusatory finger at any particular race. Jesse Jackson approaches the subject more forthrightly. Cutting through the rhetoric, he directly and specifically states that racism "is an idolatry . . . a sick belief that people who are White are congenitally superior to Black people. . . . It kills Black people by locking them out of respect, making them feel inferior, and killing their spirit" (ibid.).

Some will agree with Jackson that the problem of racism has its origin in a belief of White supremacy and that it is systemic. However, others hold an opposing view. Most, however, will agree that as a result of the presence of the crippling doctrine of racism in society, there has emerged a permanent underclass that consists of hostile, resentful, and sometimes dangerous groups who are the victims. Further, it is generally agreed that this underclass is largely shut out from opportunities for legitimate success in this highly competitive society. This reality is wreaking havoc in our communities.

3. Cultural Racism: "The individual and institutional expression of the superiority of one race's cultural heritage over that of another" (Rosado, 1994).

4. Myth: A belief or set of beliefs often unproven or false, that have formed around a person, group, phenomenon, or institution. Another definition says, "Belief or a subject of belief whose truth or reality is accepted uncritically" (Stein, 882). Like fairy tales, most myths are beliefs that are based on error and ignorance and not supported by facts. While a small aspect of a myth may have validity, generally, myths are perspectives held purely by the misinformed.

5. Stereotype: "A belief or feeling that people, groups, events, or issues typify or conform to a pattern or manner, and lack any individuality" (Simons, 244). Psychologist and author Robert Baron defines stereotypes from a psychological perspective. "Stereotypes constitute society's beliefs about the traits and characteristics about a particular group." He believes that many societies attribute more favorable characteristics and behaviors to in-groups rather than out-groups. For example, characteristics that are typically attributed to males are "dominant, tough, aggressive, independent, and adventurous," while females are stereotyped as "emotional, gentle, submissive, possessive, excitable, and affectionate" (Baron, G-10). Stereotypes generally find their roots in myths that are commonly held about races. Like branches of a tree, they extend mostly in a negative direction because they are generally nourished by prejudice and an unwillingness to be informed.

6. Generalize: To form a broad or general opinion or conclusion from a few facts or cases. "To compare people against what is known (facts) about their cultural group.

Generalizations assume that not all members of a cultural group have been raised in their culture, value and accept their culture, practice their cultural skills, or even acknowledge their culture" (Pryor Report, 11).

7. Prejudice: An unfavorable opinion or feeling formed beforehand or without knowledge, thought or reason. "The act of prejudging another person or group and not changing one's mind even after evidence to the contrary, so that one continues to post-judge them in the same manner as one pre-judges them. Prejudice operates on these levels:

a. Cognitive Level—What people believe about others.

b. Emotional Level—The feelings that the "other" arouses in an individual.

c. Behavioral Level—"The tendency to engage in discriminatory behavior" (Rosado, 1994).

From the foregoing list of definitions, we shall focus on two types of negative behaviors that create problems in race relations—*Myths* and *Stereotypes*. By better understanding these problem areas and some strategies to overcome them, hopefully the reader, through cooperation with the Holy Spirit, will realize real progress.

Barriers

Myths

There are many *myths* about ethnic groups, perpetuated over many years, which are based on ignorance or error and nourished by prejudice. We will mention just a few that have been around for a long time. These will generally deal with the in-group and out-group categories. The in-group being the majority race, or the Caucasians, and the out-groups consisting of minority races. Hereby the reader will get a sense of how negative views about races, whether true or false, have a determining impact on our attitudes about those races. After reviewing them, perhaps you will want to add a few others that you have heard.

•**Whites:** In this case the myths are either perceived to be extremely positive or negative.

Positive: Whites are superior to all other races; Whites are God's chosen race; mobility is the divine right of Whites; White people are the only ones created in the image of God; Whites are more intelligent than other races.

Negative: Whites are cold and callous; Whites will do anything for money; Whites are hungry for power and control; Whites are prejudiced; Whites cannot be trusted.

Just as there are certain organizations that are racist by design (i.e., KKK, Aryan societies), some religions teach views that are deemed to be mythical too. For example, Black Muslims teach that whiteness is the naturalistic expression of imperfection. The present historical dominance of the White man is no evidence of superiority whatsoever. Rather, what the White man has done to the Black man from this position of eminence is proof that he is inferior. He is inherently beastly and oppressive. Whiteness represents evil and is doomed by Allah. Its very appearance in the order of human reality was a mistake of cosmic proportions (Kelsey, 86).

•**Blacks:** In the interest of space, Blacks, due to their history of slavery, are considered the most "out" of all ethnic groups. We shall list a few of the myths about them.

Positive: Blacks excel in sports; Blacks are great singers; all Blacks are great dancers; Blacks are good preachers, speakers; Blacks are physically strong.

Negative: Blacks are lazy; Blacks are under a curse; Blacks are always mad; Blacks are emotional; Blacks are inferior.

These two categories give an idea of what and how myths are formed around a certain group and how they are subsequently categorized.

Negative Stereotypes

Relative to race relations, myths and stereotypes are similar and can be viewed as twins. In a personal racial context, both are destructive and are unchristlike. A basic difference between myths and stereotypes is that myths generally have existed for long periods and have been embellished and elaborated over time. Stereotypes are opinions and beliefs that may develop. Stereotypes are the stuff that myths are made of.

We preface stereotypes with the term "negative" because, in a racial context, that is what stereotypes are—the worst beliefs one can have about a culture. They consist of racial slurs, innuendos, name calling, labeling, ethnic joking, and using slang expressions which are meant to depreciate the group as a whole, as well as the individuals within it. Stereotypes strongly influence social judgments that filter into every walk of life. Negative stereotyping exists for almost every race and culture.

A few selected expressions follow. Again, these are listed here to sensitize us to what we have heard (negativism) and to validate our need to correct our perceptions by obtaining relevant facts (positivism).

- African Americans are "lazy, angry, and less patriotic" (Fraser, 75)
- Chinese Americans are "passive . . . lacking in verbal skills" (Buenker and Ratner, 209).
- German Americans are "beer drinking . . . noisy singing and dancing . . . barbaric and militaristic [people]" (ibid., 65, 66).
- Italian Americans are "criminals, radicals, and buffoons" (ibid., 175).
- Jewish Americans are "money-making, sharp dealing, and professionally ambitious people" (ibid., 132).
- Mexican Americans are "hoodlums and criminals" (ibid., 223).
- Native Americans are wild, militant, and superstitious.
- Polish Americans are "big, strong, and stupid, with strong backs but weak minds" (ibid., 131).

Are Christians ever guilty of stereotyping? No human is exempt. Most of us have stereotypes about each other that have been derived from long and strongly held views. These have come from our actual dealings with people, our readings, and even the images projected on television. Many we have tucked away in our minds for later use. These images will always surround us in a society that will never be perfect. But it is truly wrong to purposely take what little we have heard about these groups and make the assumption that every member of that group behaves in that same way. Herein we greatly err. We cannot stigmatize whole races and cultures by what we know of the behavior of some members. There are the good and bad in all races.

When we stereotype, we fail to get to know individuals, their values, skills, and traditions. Kelsey makes the point that stereotypes are propositions with a purpose; they belong to the stream of culture, serving as active ingredients in shaping experience and coloring observations. He says that sociologists generally agreed that stereotypes tell us much more about the social group which uses them than about those whom they claim to be describing. Hostility toward out-races is really not the result of what out-races do. Out-races are judged to be vicious even at the moment when they do the things which the in-race honors in itself. This strange attitude is possible because the in-race in reality holds out-races to be natural enemies (Kelsey, 86).

Developing Sensitivities

First, negative characteristics of a group should not be used to describe every member of that group, because every negative trait that appears in this section can be found within some members of all cultures. No race or culture is perfect. All humans are imperfect. As all groups are spotted or tainted with human flaws and failings, the negatives should never be accentuated. Rather, we should highlight the positives and build toward improving relations within that group. Our goal should be to be informed and sensitive.

Second, since most myths and stereotypes are based on ignorance and error, it would do well for those who are misinformed to educate themselves about different ethnic groups. Some stereotypes or portions thereof can be true. According to Baron, stereotypes are "cognitive frameworks that include beliefs about members of various social groups, suggesting that they all share certain characteristics" (Baron, G-10). But therein is the great danger. Some things can be true about some people some of the time for whatever sociological factors.

Still, one must resist the tendency to generalize and form myths and stereotypes. Myths and stereotypes, whether containing a grain of truth or a barrel of error, if believed, result in the formation of attitudes about specific ethnic groups that take whole lifetimes to correct. Attitudes are "lasting evaluations of people, groups, objects, or issues—in fact, of virtually any aspect of the social or physical world" (Baron, G-11).

The New Message

The message that must be preached, at least in the spiritual community, to counteract the damage that myths and stereotypes cause is not that there is a kernel of truth in them but a barrel of error and subjectivity. The Christian who is striving to live as Christ lived and love as Christ loved will resonate with George Fraser, who made the following observation, underscoring our need to deal with the problem. "I don't care what color you are—a constant feeding of those kinds of images and words and you would believe them also. . . . The impact on us is both subtle and not so subtle . . . .While this negativism has impacted our professional upward mobility and our ability to develop entrepreneurially, the worst thing it has done is "impacted our children and how they see themselves and who they select as their heroes" (Fraser, 75).

Myths and stereotypes about ethnic groups frustrate attempts to improve race relations both inside and outside the Church. Whether or not there is an underlying fact or two that undergirds the attitudes that we hold about each other, most myths are based on ignorance or error and are supported or nourished by self-interest and prejudice. In this age of multiculturalism and managing diversity, it is imperative that these negative attitudes be changed if we are to succeed in this world and make it into the world to come.

Of course, individuals cannot always be blamed for the views which they hold or the acts which follow from those beliefs. But as Christians, we have a duty to dispel ignorance by providing the correct information and facts. We who know better also have a duty to assist those who do not, especially those who have a desire to learn and grow.

Faith and Equality

Christians accept the gospel commission as expressed by Christ in Matthew 28:16-19 as the mission of His Church on this earth. This means that Christians must preach the good news to every nation, kindred, tongue, and people. The universality of Christianity affirms that all races are loved by and are equal before God.

On this matter of equality of all races, when we speak of equality in the Christian faith, we refer to the action and purpose of God. God has created all peoples in His own image and called all to the same destiny. The decision as to whether or not races are equal cannot be made by looking at the different races and cultures. One must look at God, as God alone is the source of human dignity. All peoples are equal because God has created them in His own image. Herein lies their dignity. Human dignity is not an achievement, nor is it an intrinsic quality; it is a gift, a bestowal. Christian faith asserts that all humans are equally human; all are creatures and all are potentially children of God. Variations in the talents and skills of culture rest upon this fundamental humanness. The Christian faith affirms the unity of human-kind (Kelsey, 86, 87).

The fact that races are different from each other means they are dependent on each other. If they were all the same, they would all have the same characteristics and gifts, and therefore not be dependent upon each other. In the Christian community, members must be willing to serve each other in their mutual dependence (Galatians 5:13). The one recognizes its dependence upon the other, no matter how lowly the occupation of the other may be in the eyes of the world. There are so many respects in which one member may be superior or inferior to another that there is probably no person who is superior or inferior to another in every respect. The unity of humankind is made the more manifest by the inequalities which have their basis in individuality.

Kelsey persuasively states that the Christian idea of the unity of humankind finds concrete expression in societies of mutual cooperation and helpfulness. Differences of function create of necessity variations in status and role in institutional structures. But role and status in these institutions are assigned on the strength of real individual differences (Kelsey, 88-90).

The Value of Training

A helpful tool that can assist the Church in making improvements in race relations is the creation of diversity training programs at all levels of the organization. It must be recognized that for diversity programs to succeed, they must include key components such as race and nationality, age, value systems and beliefs, gender, physical condition, culture, traditions, occupation and work experiences, educational experiences, economic status, social class, family background, ethnic background, culture, and their relationships to people (Dickens, 394). Naturally in the Christian context, all of these components must be viewed from a spiritual perspective and filtered by the Bible, the Spirit of Prophecy, and other available counsel.

Stereotyping and to an extent, generalizing, will continue to occur when we fail to deal with division within the Church. Diversity is not an evil in our Church; it is a gift of God. Evidently God must love diversity; otherwise, He would not have made us all different, and He would not have sent us into the world to bring diverse peoples into the fold. Diversity programs help us deal with our differentness, helping us learn how to celebrate it instead of fear it.

Diversity programs "help us counteract racism and ethnic prejudice. They help us affirm the cultural values, traditions, and skills handed down from one generation to another in particular groups . . . that an employee from a strong cultural heritage may bring . . . extra qualities to the workplace" (Pryor Report, 11). "The management of diversity," Dickens and Dickens assert, "teaches cultural pride, high self-esteem, the value of utilization of other cultures, and national unity. . . . It rejects the concept of the melting pot by promoting the view that all groups came to this country bringing their own uniqueness" (Dickens, 400-402). It teaches us to value our differences and use them for the benefit of the Church.

Generalizations vs. Stereotypes

What role, if any, can generalizations versus stereotypes play in a diversity program of the Seventh-day Adventist Church? Dickens and Dickens explain the difference between the two. "Stereotyping gives one a fixed picture of a group representing an oversimplified opinion, an affective attitude, or a judgment. They are almost always negative pictures of individuals in the target group. Generalizations do not imply a fixed pattern. Rather, it says that groups of people have observable behaviors and habits and that people belonging to the same group will have similar habits, behaviors, attitudes, and value systems."

Further, Dickens and Dickens explain: "We can make some generalization about that group based upon what we think we see and know, but when we interact with and get to know an individual from the group about which we have generalizations, then we must relinquish our generalizations in favor of the specific data we have about that individual as a specific personality" (Dickens, 400-402).

Unlike stereotypes which are generally negative, generalizations tend to be neutral or positive. How, then, can the Seventh-day Adventist Church make use of generalizations in its diversity programs? *It can emphasize the fact that we are*

*all different, that it is all right to be different, and that because
of our differentness, we have a uniqueness that we can bring
to the Church.*

Celebrating Diversity

There are extra qualities and added values that are unique
among selected ethnic groups, all of which are included in the
membership of the SDA Church. This information (adapted
from Dickens, 404-407) can be useful as an alternative to
negative myths and stereotypes. While there may be many
things that can be added or subtracted from this list, these
insights can be helpful to the Church as it contemplates its
diversity program. The authors warn us to be aware of
individual differences within groups and take the time to
learn about an individual before you assume that he or she
has a particular value or cultural skill. Additionally: *Be
careful about turning these generalizations into stereotypes:*

1. *Irish.* Generally, the Irish are verbal people who are
given to eloquence in speech and to humor. Many an Irishman
or Irishwoman can break the tensest of moments with an
appropriate quip or humorous story. The Irish tend to teach
neighborhood involvement and a sense of obligation to neighbors. In the work environment, they would tend to want to
pull their work force into a community, with people helping
people. They tend to be loyal to what they believe in and like.

2. *English.* Most of us are familiar with the English culture, on which much of how we do business and run our
government is based. English added value tends to be a part
of our daily lives: our judicial system, social services, legisla-
ture, and punctuality. The English are known for their "stiff
upper lip"—their perseverance against the odds. Here are
people who will tend to charge ahead for their organization no
matter what. We get a lot of our concepts of the rugged
individual from the English.

3. *German.* Germans tend to be very strong-willed and
determined. Once a decision is made, you can count on them

to see it through—for themselves and the organization. Self-discipline is highly valued among Germans. As hardworking people, Germans seek precision. In their creativity, they will tend to be very methodical and thorough.

4. *Black*. Blacks are relationship-oriented. The institution of slavery made them learn how to quickly size up people and rapidly formulate strategic responses. Having excellent people-assessment skills and being able to think quickly on their feet makes Blacks valuable in dealing with people issues in the organization. Because of a tradition of having limited resources with which to work, Blacks have learned how to be exceptionally good at creating something out of almost nothing. Blacks will automatically focus on how to stretch a resource or make do without it. Blacks have learned how to move easily across socioeconomic lines and how to successfully live and negotiate in multicultural environments.

5. *Jewish*. Jews have learned to love debate and the knowledge gained from questioning and seeking answers. Jews can push an organization to clarify its visions and goals in such a way that people can understand its mission. Through the process of learning their religion, Jewish people have developed highly refined negotiating skills. The Jewish sense of duty is legendary. Because Jews have historically been the victims of oppression and slavery, they have learned tolerance of others and have compassion and empathy for others who are oppressed.

6. *Mexican*. Mexican people have a passion for many things, and they are not shy about showing it. The energy they bring to a job can be a great motivator for an organization in tackling its toughest jobs. Mexican attitudes are often rooted in the "now." Mexicans tend to focus on the most pressing issues at hand. They have little patience with dragging issues out; instead, they will want to very quickly compress long lists to the most essential items. A valuable skill within the Mexican culture is that of building interpersonal relationships. The ability to be personable—even with strangers—give respect, and to behave with honor is looked upon with great favor.

7. *Chinese*. The Chinese, although resilient, will seek

harmony and conflict resolution first. They have a love of harmony and order, and organizations can rely on Chinese employees to seek resolutions designed to leave people in win-win situations. Chinese are probably best known for their patience. They are most often willing to work hard and wait for rewards. They are even-tempered and wait out the opponent. Chinese employees bring a strong sense of relationships, structure, and organization. They tend to be focused, with a fine eye for detail.

8. *Dutch.* The Dutch are known to be frugal. They avoid waste and value saving and investing their money. The Dutch bring the value of taking care of what we have and better using what we gain. Many of Dutch extraction find themselves drawn to areas of finance. Dutch are persistent in their tasks, are generally slow to anger, and often have a calming influence in chaotic situations.

The Church's diversity program must not encourage members to ignore diversity or their own cultures. We cannot ignore our racial and ethnic differences, nor should we view every one in the same way. The wonderful heritages that all cultures bring to the membership and workforce are added values that equip and enhance the Church. Negative stereotyping, racial slurs, ethnic jokes, and innuendos militate against improving race relations among diverse groups. Diversity programs are designed to educate the membership to be sensitive to constantly bear in mind that what they think and do does make a difference.

Love, the Prescription

The mission of the Seventh-day Adventist Church contains the three elements of proclaiming, nurturing, and serving—all essentials of a relational church. Undergirding these three elements is love, a love of the Triune God and our brothers and sisters in Christ—regardless of their ethnicity. Because "the devil is wroth with the woman and is making war with her seed" (Revelation 12:17), the Church has not achieved the state of oneness that it is possible to achieve. Some believe that one reason for this is that we speak with many voices instead of one. Others share the conclusion that Bishop Tutu made of the church in South Africa: "The real reason is that our dividedness undermines the gospel of Jesus Christ. He came to bring reconciliation, He broke down the middle wall of partition. How can we, the Church of God, say to a sadly divided world that we have the remedy for your animosities, your hatreds, your separateness when we are ourselves so sinfully divided? Surely the world will retort, 'Physician heal thyself' " (Tutu, 117).

Love is the prescription that the "physician must use to heal itself." The relationship that love has to the accomplishment of the mission of the Church and the unity of the brethren is clarified in 1 Corinthians 13. This passage stresses the point that love makes it easier to create and sustain human relationships. If we have *"love for the brethren,"* the accomplishment will be possible and real. If we don't have love, then we will have hate, the opposite of love. Hatred impairs and destroys relationships. Hatred is not always shown overtly, such as in acts of violence. A covert expression of hatred exists in acts of perpetuating myths and stereotypes and other negative behavior, which are apparent in the world and in the Church.

Clearly, one of the marks of the true Church of God is that it not only *proclaims* the gospel to every nation but also *practices* racial equality as taught by Jesus Christ Himself. SDAs believe that the gospel must be preached to all the world. In this regard the church has had good success. As a result of responding to the gospel commission, the Church has grown to more than eight million members worldwide and over eight hundred thousand within the North American Division. Further, the Church believes that racial equality must be practiced within the body of Christ. In this division alone, the membership consists of five major cultures and over forty ethnic and language groups. But the challenge to "love" remains.

The Church's policy on Human Relations (NAD Policy C-50) affirms that "all members in good and regular standing will be given full and equal opportunity" for service. An examination of the components of this seven-statement policy before the Church's Human Relations Advisory confirmed that institutionally, the Church is making progress in the area of celebrating its diversity. In an effort to apply Christ's prayer for oneness and unity, where policies are felt to promote division and inequality, they are being addressed. Additionally, perspectives, policies, programs, personnel, and practices of the Church relative to race relations are continuing to be addressed in ways that seek to make the goal of heaven (Revelation 7:9) a reality.

The proclamation of the gospel in all the world by SDAs is expected to produce a sense of oneness and unity, since the gospel transcends the barriers of language, race, color, and culture (Galatians 3:26-28).

For a diversity program to be effective, each entity must secure leadership support and identify the right persons to direct it as well as set aside adequate resources to implement goals and objectives. Also, diversity training programs must be ongoing, not one-time activities. Delgado, in his chapter on "Strategies for Improving Race Relations," underscores this view. He states the following: "The history of efforts to alter race relations in organizations and communities throughout America is replete with rhetoric and goodwill seldom translated into new behavioral patterns and organizational outcomes" (Delgado, 182).

New Directions

Obviously, to create a humane, compassionate environment that celebrates diversity by eliminating division will mean that the Church must develop a new paradigm or way of thinking and doing business to accomplish this goal. In relating to this need in the Seventh-day Adventist Church in North America, a special Multicultural Relationship Model Commission was established to aid it in strategizing for the improvement of race relations.

In further addressing the needs of diversity, we agree with Delgado that "improved race relations do not mean simply increasing interracial civility or even social interaction" (ibid., 202). They mean incorporating what Caleb Rosado, consultant and commission member, has termed the five 'Ps,' referred to earlier (Perspectives, Policies, Programs, Personnel, and Practices), into its total organizational system. Where needed, it means creating policies and practices that result in more equal opportunities for service and outcomes for all people, regardless of their race and ethnicity.

Delgado makes this statement, which I shall use to conclude this chapter. "Such changes are clearly compatible with efficiency and high levels of production; indeed, they represent the most efficient and humane use of a full range of human resources. Just as the 'normal' way of doing things often has had racist consequences, the 'new' way of doing things, once institutionalized, should have different and more just consequences" (Delgado, 202).

In order for the kind of change to take place that will result in greatly improved race relations in the Church in North America, and in order for the Church to experience the oneness that will truly make it the witness to the world, this change *must* begin with someone, somewhere, and sometime.

If our song of unity could be, "Let there be oneness in the Church, / And let it begin with me," and every member who sang it not only meant it but practiced it, the Church could experience in this generation the kind of oneness in the fellowship that Christ prayed for His Church. As a result, we can realize the oneness of spirit, oneness in rights and privileges, and oneness in the blessedness of the future world. We would realize that each one of us can make a difference!

Rosa Taylor Banks, Ed.D., is associate secretary and director of the Office of Human Relations for the NAD. She is an author, a speaker, and an educator. She regularly conducts workshops and seminars on diversity, on conflict resolution, and on a variety of issues related to women. She and her husband, Halsey, have three children.

Selected Bibliography

Baron, Robert A. *Psychology*. Second Edition. Boston, Mass.: Allyn and Bacon Publishing Company, 1992.

Buenker, John D., et al. *Multiculturalism in the United States: A Comparative Guide to Acculturation and Ethnicity*. New York: Greenwood Press, 1992.

Chester, Mark, and Hector Delgado. "Race Relations Training and Organizational Change." *Strategies for Improving Race Relations*. England: Manchester University Press, 1987.

Cory, Lloyd. "Racism." *Quotable Quotations*. Wheaton, Ill.: Victor Books, 1985.

Dickens, Floyd, and Jacqueline Dickens. *The Black Manager*. New York:American Management Association, 1991.

Fraser, George C. "Excellence, Education, and Perceptions: An African-American Crisis." *Vital Speeches*. South Carolina: City News Publishing Company, 1991.

Kelsey, George D. "Equality and Inequality." *Racism and the Christian Understanding of Man*. New York, N.Y.: Charles Scribner's Sons, 1965.

"Managing Diversity: Cultural Diversity Adds to the Workplace." *The Pryor Report*. South Carolina: Image, Inc., 1994.

Rosado, Caleb. From a list of definitions on diversity training prepared for the Multicultural Relationship Model Commission in Silver Spring, Maryland, 1993 and 1994.

Simons, et al. *Transcultural Leadership: Empowering the Diverse Workforce*. Houston, Tex.: Gulf Publishing Company, 1993.

Stein, Jess. Editor in Chief. *The Random House College Dictionary*. Revised Edition. New York, N.Y.: Random House, Incorporated, 1980.

Torrance, T. F. *Calvin's Doctrine of Man*. New Edition. Grand Rapids, Mich., 1957.

Tutu, Desmond Bishop. *Crying in the Wilderness*. Grand Rapids, Mich.: William B. Eerdmans Publishers, 1982.

SOME THINGS CHANGE AGENTS
NEED TO KNOW

Change agents are people who "adopt a brand of 'realism' that accepts the uncertainties and ambivalences of the comtemporary situation, while trying to maximize the hopes inherent in it."[*]

Change Agents Need to Know:

1. the organization—its formal and informal rules, its methods of support and resistance, and its decision-making processes;
2. systems thinking—the BIG picture;
3. the assumptions on which change is based;
4. change processes are extremely intentional—great effort must be spent to plan what we want to have happen;
5. their personal and institutional power—what they have power to do;
6. themselves and their style—their "preferred intervention strategy";[*]
7. the hills they are willing to die on;
8. "the nature of [his] influence on and relationship to various parts of the . . . system";[*]
9. how to form ally relationships; and
10. what sort of roles they want to play and when, e.g., catalyst, lightning rod, helper, stirrer-upper.

"One person trying to change an organization is suicide,
Two people trying to change an organization
is jumping off lovers' leap,
Five or more make a cadre."
Peter Senge

*Quotes from *The Planning of Change*, 3rd ed.

8

Diversity Needs to Include Everybody

Monte Sahlin

The issues of diversity and relationship building have to include the majority group as well as minority groups. God's plan for diversity will only be realized when love is the standard and every group values and unites with each other.

Over three generations, almost everything has changed in the way the White, Anglo majority culture of the United States experiences the realities of ethnicity. The experience of my own family is instructive. My father attended Enterprise Academy in Kansas at the beginning of World War II, and the student body included no minorities. When I attended Glendale Academy in the 1960s, the Civil Rights movement was a topic of discussion, and there were a handful of African Americans, Hispanics, and Asians among the students. In 1990, my daughter attended Takoma Academy, where she, as a Caucasian, was a minority.

The Seventh-day Adventist Church is ahead of the trends that are advancing slowly in the demographics of America.

White Americans are already a minority in the North American Division. When African Americans, Hispanics, Asians, Native Americans, Canadians, and Bermudians are subtracted from the total membership, less than 50 percent remains. By the end of this decade, people of color will make up the majority of the membership across the division. (See Figure 1.) This creates the unique and difficult category of the majority minority; a major challenge for the Adventist Church in the years ahead.

Figure 1
Ethnic Background of Members
Seventh-day Adventist Church in North America

	1990	2000
Anglo, Caucasian	65%	49%
African American	25%	33%
Hispanic	7%	12%
Asian/Pacific Islander	3%	5%
Others	1%	1%

Source: NAD Office of Information & Research

A Crisis of Faith

Prejudice, based in part on lack of experience and information and in part on the tendency of the sinful heart to divide the world up into "them" and "Us," is basic to human nature. Fear exacerbates prejudice. When a person is threatened by complex social and economic changes, when pillars of the predictable and stable are taken away from them, it is easy for this fear and prejudice to fasten on "them" as the enemy. When popular culture and politicians manipulate these fears and prejudices for reasons of profit and power, then an even more dangerous mix results. The dominant precedent for what can happen is forever written in the history of Western

Civilization in the blood and horror of the Europe of the 1930s and 1940s.

The Church is a source of eternal truth and rock-solid nurture that people of faith turn to in times of turmoil and change. When they find that the Church, too, is convulsed with the same kind of change from which they flee in the outside world, it can be a cause of great disappointment and anger. It can initiate a crisis of faith, even for mature believers. It requires of the shepherds of the flock not only a strong relationship with God and an abiding faith in Christ's leadership in His Church, but also extraordinary sensitivity, awareness, knowledge, and compassion.

The majority of Adventists in North America have the luxury of being shielded from these issues at present. Most congregations are made up almost entirely of one or another major ethnic group. At the same time, a growing number of congregations and almost all denominational institutions, especially those located near major metropolitan areas on the two coasts, are thrust into the middle of this volatile situation. Pastors, lay elders, and church board members increasingly report that they feel ill-prepared to deal with the issues.

Much of what is written on the topic of diversity focuses on the dynamics and issues associated with one or more minority groups and their relationship with the dominant culture (this book being an exception). My objective is to review the issues of diversity and relationship building from the perspective of a White male. What are the unique needs and attitudes of the Caucasian male in a world that was once the absolute domain of his kind but is now increasingly populated by women and people of color? How can the contribution and value of the White male be included in the diversity of today's (and tomorrow's) workplace, community, and church? How can he be included without the role of dominance?

Dealing With Displacement

I will never forget the anguished tone of voice; "Can he be here without being in charge?" I was asked by a female of color in the midst of one situation a few years ago, referring to a White male co-worker. It has come to symbolize for me one of the fundamental issues for the present transitional period of diversity in America. I would like to rephrase it a bit to capture all the nuances. Does he know how to be something other than "the man"; does he know how to deal with the feelings of displacement and loss without resentment?

The extent to which the White male became dominant in American society was unjust, but it was not the result of social change. For the vast majority of previous generations, it was simply the natural order which they inherited. One of the oft repeated arguments against the extension of equal rights and opportunities to people of color and to women has been some variation of "it's unnatural." Although the net effect of the argument is to continue the oppression of others, it must be recognized that this is also an honest expression of reality for many White men. When Christ quoted the Pharisee who prayed, "Thank God that I was not born a Gentile or a woman," the man betrayed himself innocently.

The most difficult kind of oppression to remove is the kind that is not intentional, but unconscious. The Victorian White man was secure in his world, a benevolent dictator. He exercised ownership of his spouse and household not only for his own comfort, but also because he believed it was his duty. He maintained proprietorship in his occupation not only for his own benefit, but because he believed it was his calling. He held to himself the reigns of authority in government not only for his own empowerment, but also because he believed he had a manifest destiny. He extended colonial systems among "the heathen" not only for his own profit, but also because he believed he was exporting to them the benefits of Western, "Christian" civilization. "The White man's burden" was to rule, to prevail, to civilize.

The majority of White males born since 1945 in America no longer want to be the Victorian White man, but he is a part of the furniture in their minds. His hat and coat hang in their closet. His cologne wafts on the air. His fire burns on their hearth. They simply do not have a dominant paradigm for how to be something else. "The sensitive male" is a butt of jokes. The quest for "the new man" has died with the profound and absolute failure of Marxism. Except for John F. Kennedy and Martin Luther King, the major male figures of the post-war period are all throwbacks, reassuring because they re-package the Victorian White male as a 1950s television myth, or reactionary or flawed and weak. Much intellectual activity has focused on placing the figures of prior generations under the microscope of historiography, seemingly in an effort to prove that they were all just as flawed as Harry Truman or Richard Nixon. No new White male paradigm has emerged. John and Martin were shot. If the alternative is oblivion, the most sensitive, progressive, and just White man of the 1990s will hold onto his mental image of his Victorian great-grandfather.

Facing the Fear

For the White male today, the world is filled with fear. Competition is greater. Secure jobs are fewer. The economy is less predictable. Institutions are convulsed with change. Schools and neighborhoods are threatened by the dangers of AIDS, drugs, and violence. It does not appear that he will be able to pass on to his children a better life than he has. And the baby boomer White male has the tinge of guilt that he helped open Pandora's Box, setting loose the forces of change in the 1960s and 1970s.

It is easy for this fear to be fastened on the face of a Black man or an immigrant or a woman. Politicians are not above manipulating these powerful emotions for their own ends. But beyond the talk-show cults, the racist religions, the neoNazi men's clubs, and the reactionary political move-ments, there is a palpable fear in the heart and an empty place in the mind of every American White male. The fear of the White male requires as much attention from the students and managers of diversity as do the unique needs and contri-butions of other groups.

The core question that must be answered for the White male in any diverse work group, community, or institution is this: "Can I have integrity, make a contribution, be at ease, and have fun without being 'the man' or 'the runt'?" A friend once told me that his entire high school career was misery because his older brother had been a football hero on the campus. His older brother had been large for his age and fast with his temper and fists. He had been a "glory hog," and by the time he graduated, the younger students who did not leave with his class were glad to see him go. When they discovered his younger brother among the incoming freshmen, they vowed that he would never achieve the dominance of his older brother. For three years they went out of their way to see that he was controlled, blocked, humiliated, and put down, and by the time he got to his senior year, all of his classmates were habituated in keeping him in the role of "runt."

It is the fear of the White male today that he will be assigned a role in our diverse society that is essentially a reaction to the role of his Victorian great-grandfather. Another friend explained to me once, "I still remember when I was in fifth grade that a boy named Jack had been put at the head of the line going to the cafeteria every day for the first several weeks of school, and some of the kids complained to the teacher that they were always last. The teacher announced that the line would be rotated and innocently said, 'Jack, you've had all of your times at the head of the line this year. You will have to go last from here on.' It was a long year for Jack." It can be argued that this is an irrational fear, but that does not banish it. Most fear is irrational, nonetheless, real and powerful.

Need for New Skills

"Quotas" and "affirmative action" have become red flags because of this fear of being moved to the back of the line. Of course, the most fanatic of the anti-quota rhetoric is likely generated by those who do not want to give up a privileged position, but it resonates with millions of men who only want to avoid being stigmatized. "Reverse discrimination" has only been proven to exist in a handful of court cases, but it represents the fear of the majority of White males in America today. It is a fear they may not wish to admit, even to themselves. It is a fear that must be managed if a permanent and sound diversity is to be established in any community, work group, or institution.

A new set of relational skills must be taught the next generation of Americans; one that includes inter-group conflict management and the crosscultural relations. New rules already prevail in business and institutions, but many people, especially the White male, find that they do not know or understand these rules. Confusion about the ground rules adds to the fear of being placed at the back of the line, the fear of making unnecessary, foolish mistakes. This is the underlying emotion that results in all of the jokes about "PC—politically correct." This is why the political manipulators among the reactionary have invented the "PC" myth and made so much of it.

"I'm not quite sure any more, do I open the door for a woman or not? What word do I use to refer to another race that will not offend anyone? Every time I use a new term that I've learned, I get a lecture from someone, and I begin to think it is a conspiracy to make me feel stupid." These are all recent quotes from White males attempting to cope with the changing world which diversity is thrusting upon them. They reflect the uncertainty and frustration of men who (for good or bad reasons) do not want to insult their professional colleagues, nor do they want to be labeled "PC" by reactionaries among their peers. This kind of confusion can only be cleared up with a careful investment in education.

The Majority Minority

White, Anglo people constitute the cultural majority in America. For better or worse, the history of the American nation has been shaped largely by the White male, and

Caucasians will continue to be the majority into the coming century. Yet within a few years, Adventist Church members from that majority culture will constitute a minority within their national denomination. In a number of local conferences and church-related institutions this is already true.

When minorities become the majority in the Church, it has historically hampered church growth among the majority population. England has become a case study of this phenomena. No one really knows whether this is true because of a racist reaction among Caucasian members or because the new majority takes insufficient interest in winning Whites. It is likely that this kind of finger-pointing is unproductive and that the truth has more to do with the prevailing attitudes outside the Church. It represents a new problem for which denominational strategy has yet to establish a proven response, yet it is clear that the mission of the Adventist Church cannot be accomplished in any nation or community in which outreach among the majority population is ignored or underfunded.

One solution that has been proposed is the Brotherhood or All Nations Church. These "rainbow congregations" have set out to build an identity around their most obvious fact; that they include a wide range of ethnic backgrounds, and in their midst everyone is a minority. The record of these experiments is mixed. In south Florida and Hawaii, they have been successful in an un-self-conscious way. In cities further north where there have been more publicly defined attempts with the same approach, the "rainbow congregations" have, in most cases, not successfully stayed multicultural. It proved to be a transitional phase, not a permanent solution.

Problem Needing a Solution

The American Adventist Church must find a solution to this issue if it is to stay true to its mission to reach everyone with the remnant message. As the majority becomes another minority, a new crosscultural awareness must emerge on the part of leaders in minority groups within the Church. Where once they focused on progress for their own people, they must now focus on progress among all peoples. The established dynamic of minority demands and majority concessions breaks down when there is no majority. It creates a dysfunctional process to continue these precedents.

A new vision for a global mission that will reach all people groups must become the new paradigm for the Church in North America. "From everywhere to everywhere," is the term used by missiologists today to describe the fact that missionaries in the World Church no longer leave only North America and Europe and arrive only in Southern Hemisphere nations. A similar pattern of evangelistic and pastoral concern and planning is needed among the leaders of each ethnic community within the Church in North America.

Diversity, Inclusiveness, and an Evangelistic Response

Ultimately, the fact of the majority minority in the Seventh-day Adventist Church in North America means that "brotherhood"—inclusive fellowship—becomes a "testing truth" for Adventists today. The concept of a "testing truth" is a core element of Adventist heritage and faith. It means a fundamental teaching or doctrine of the Church that places the believer at odds with the larger culture. Many of the Bible truths that Adventists teach in evangelism are widely shared among Christian denominations or require only a change of opinion, not a change in behavior. A testing truth demands not only change of behavior on the part of the convert, but an unpopular change that goes against the grain of common life patterns and values.

Testing Truth

During most of the last 150 years, the Sabbath has been the most significant testing truth for Adventist converts. Until recent decades, most jobs required that a person work on Saturdays at least part of the time. To become a Sabbath keeper meant losing one's job. When prospective members come to this point in a series of Bible studies, their faith is tested. Will they choose to follow Christ in taking a stand that is unpopular, even opposed by society? Or will they give in to the social pressure, the price to be paid? This kind of situation can become what missiologists call a "power encounter"—a public confrontation between the power of Christ and the power of evil. Stories of Christ's power sustaining a family when the new-convert breadwinner has lost his job, and then has found a better job eventually, are repeated again and again. These faith-building, encouraging stories are part of our soul-winning heritage.

In the context of today's society, it is becoming increasingly true that for a White Anglo person to become a Seventh-day Adventist means to leave a world in which the person is part of the majority and enter a community in which the person is part of a minority. The difficulty of making that adjustment cannot be underestimated. The teaching that "in Christ . . . there is neither Jew nor Greek, slave nor free, male nor female" (Galatians 3:28) becomes a testing truth.

The baptismal vows that each member takes as they join the Adventist Church includes the affirmation that they desire to be part of a "fellowship . . . that people of every nation, race, and language are invited and accepted into." The statement of Fundamental Beliefs includes the assertion, "In Christ we are a new creation; distinctions of race, culture, learning, and nationality, and differences between high and low, rich and poor, male and female, must not be divisive among us. We are all equal in Christ. . . . We are to serve and be served without partiality or reservation."

Prayer for Oneness

The time has come to place this Bible teaching higher on the preaching agenda of Adventist evangelists. We can no longer assume that this issue will take care of itself. We must carefully build the biblical case for joining the remnant that includes "a great multitude . . . from every nation, tribe, people and language" (Revelation 7:9) and has a specific message to proclaim "to every nation, tribe, language and people" (Revelation 14:6). We must help each convert and long-term member understand that Christ's prayer for "oneness" among His believers is "so that the world may believe" (John 17:21).

As a practical matter, if we clearly present this testing truth and take the time to build a biblical basis for its importance, then it becomes easier for people to deal with it. They are not surprised when they discover the reality of the majority minority. They have a spiritual and theological preparation for the transition they must make from a world in which they are part of the majority to a community in which they are a minority. This sometimes difficult social reality has a divine purpose; it is given meaning and scriptural support.

The issues of diversity in the Adventist Church are not limited to ethnicity. Because Adventism is an evangelistic movement, members come from diverse religious backgrounds and carry with them many differences—gender issues, physical conditioning, class, different tastes in music, worship, and the organizational process. Many converts come from among immigrants, the poor, and others with little education, and because of the Adventist commitment to Christian education, the majority of those born into Adventist families have attained higher education. No denomination in America is more widely spread among all demographic categories. Inevitably, many differences result.

Love: Mission Accomplished

Pastoral leadership in this context demands regular attention to the biblical values of inclusiveness, caring for one another, and practical demonstration of the compassion of Christ. The Sabbath School, small group ministries, midweek meetings, and leadership seminars must be used to teach the practical skills of diversity. Christian fellowship will mean the practice of love, acceptance, and forgiveness.

As the Church moves into the new realities, it will increasingly become apparent that, as Ellen White has written, "love to man is the earthward manifestation of the love of God. It was to implant this love, to make us children of one family, that the King of glory became one with us. And when His parting words are fulfilled, 'Love one another, as I have loved you' (John 15:12); when we love the world as He has loved it, then for us His mission is accomplished" (*The Desire of Ages,* 641).

Simply achieving ethnic inter-group justice or gender equality is not enough. Christ's vision for His remnant body is one in which there is a palpable sense of acceptance and hospitality extended to all kinds of people, a texture of compassion touching all kinds of needs, an actual reproduction of the unselfish character of the God who is willing to die for our sins.

Monte Sahlin is assistant to the president of the NAD. He has served as a pastor for many years. He is an author, researcher, and consultant for church growth. He regularly does training workshops and seminars. He and his wife, Norma, have two daughters.

SECTION THREE

RELATING

9

Building Bridges
Through Communication

George Atiga

*Communicating across cultural lines is challenging,
but rewarding. One can be successful at building
cross-cultural relationships by practicing time-tested
communication principles that work.*

*B*efore the bombing of
Hiroshima and Nagasaki, the Allied forces sent a message to
Japan urging them to surrender. The very slight chance that
remained of preventing a catastrophic holocaust was ruined
when the key word *Mokusatsu* in Japan's reply was
mistranslated by the Allied forces as "reject." Hence the
bombing went on, which caused the annihilation and suffering of millions of lives. Properly translated, *Mokusatsu* means
"reserving an answer until a decision is reached."[1]

If more serious study and effort were given to improving
cross-cultural communication, many problems arising out of
inter-group and international interactions could be avoided.
At least the violence generated by racial and ethnic groups in
conflict would be minimized. Infighting would be averted,
and a more lasting peace and harmony would exist both in the

nation and in the family of God on earth.[2]

Human diversity has given rise to a dynamic multicultural society. It therefore provides a more compelling rationale for designing programs that improve and enhance cross-cultural communication inside and outside the Church.

More than thirty years ago, it was widely assumed that direct and sustained contact between groups of different cultures would result in a decrease in differences between them. It was believed that improved relations would ultimately lead to the disappearance of the various minority cultures. Hence America was called the "Melting Pot." Yet, in their now famous study of ethnic groups in New York City, N. Glazer and D. P. Moynihan (1963) noted that the "Melting Pot" did not happen. Despite changes brought about by processes of acculturation, the ethnic groups maintained their identities and will doubtless continue to do so.

Since the revival of racial and ethnic pride in the sixties and seventies and with the unabated flow of immigrants and refugees in the eighties and nineties, the prevailing trend in the U.S.A. is toward a multicultural society. We are more like a "salad bowl" with the various vegetables remaining individually distinct but flavored by a common dressing.

The very idea of a multicultural society is disturbing to those who would subscribe to an assimilationist perspective. People who hold this view are committed to a mind-set that would break down the distinctiveness of cultural groups. However, a more realistic position is one that accepts the reality that the multicultural society is here to stay. The challenge, then, is to deal with its inherent diversity and to cultivate the idea that cultural diversity is desirable and work toward the elimination of superior/inferior relationships based on membership in a particular ethnic group, culture, or religion.

In order to be effective, an understanding of intercultural communication must be rooted in a multiculturalist framework that promotes toleration and respect for the views, traditions, and values of other cultures. This chapter will develop the subject of intercultural communication as a skill that is helpful and obtainable for Christians as well as society in general.

Dynamics of Communication

The word *communicate* comes from the Latin word *communicatus,* which means "to share" or to make common, The goal of cross-cultural communication is just that—to share or make common a message from a person of one culture group to a person from another. It is easily said but more difficult to do. Another approach defines cross-cultural communication as the social interaction between cultures resulting in an exchange of meaning through words or sets of symbols or actions that have an agreed upon meaning.[3]

The act of communication is dynamic, not static. It involves a *communicator* (sender), a *message,* and a *receptor* (receiver). But the communicator of the message usually wants to know if the message has been received. So, the receptor usually sends *feedback* in the form of a message to the communicator.

Smooth interaction between cultural groups is experienced when a sincere effort is made to be sensitive to needs of the receiver and the sender. Further, it helps for everyone involved in the communication process to be aware of the rules underlying communication and social interaction of both cultures involved in the process. Problems arise when there is interference (or noise) that interrupts the message or feedback. This is caused by attitudes, actions, or words that send the wrong message. As a result, the process may bog down or stop. The ultimate objective of a person communicating cross-culturally is to achieve intercultural communication competence. One will know if they have achieved this goal by the overall ability of an individual to deal with unfamiliarity, manage cultural differences, and other interferences that may come up in the communication process.

The Bible has a lot to say about communication that is relevant to the subject of diversity and cross-cultural communication. One of the most direct and helpful texts was written by the apostle Paul to the Ephesians. He identifies a successful communication approach. "But speaking the truth in love, may grow up into Him in all things, which is the head, even Christ" (4:15). This text identifies three helpful elements for the Christian involved in the intercultural communication process. First, the person must *speak* (communicate or talk). Second, they must speak the *truth* (according to verified facts). Third, they must speak the truth in *love* (with the spirit of Christ).[4]

This series of principles separates regular communication from Christian communication. It infers that the Christian communicator must be vulnerable (speak), honest (truth), and spiritual (love). Here is the difference with Christians involved in intercultural communication: they use the principles of Christ found in the Word of God. (See also Ephesians 5:4 and James 3:5; 4:11.)

Aims for Cross-Cultural Communication

The main aim in cross-cultural communication is for the message to be correctly understood and appropriately responded to by the receptors. This aim is better achieved when the communicator has a high degree of credibility with those with whom interaction is made. Credibility is defined as "offering reasonable grounds for being believed." Whether we like it or not, our attitudes, habits, views, and expressions (verbal or nonverbal) are all closely observed. When any of these behavioral patterns impacts negatively on observers, the credibility of the speaker is lessened or cut off, and one's ability to effectively communicate with others is hampered. Ralph Waldo Emerson said, "What you do sounds so loud I can't hear what you are saying."

On the other hand, when one's credibility is high, the believability and acceptability of one's communicational interaction is also high. The answer is Yes to questions such as "Can I trust this person to even give consideration to what he is telling me?" Because of one's positive relational interaction to others, it's more likely that his communication will be acceptable. Edgar Guest also said, "I'd rather see a sermon than hear one any day."

One of the most effective means of building credibility is to build positive relationship, and some of the simple rules in building relationships are: (1) be sympathetic to others; (2) put forth sincere effort to be of help to others; and (3) as much as possible, be involved in what happens in the lives of others. This is the method Christ employed in dealing with people in His day. Ellen G. White said, "Christ's method alone will give true success in reaching the people. The Saviour mingled with men as one who desired their good. He showed His sympathy for them, ministered to their needs, and won their confidence. Then He bade them, 'Follow Me.' "[5]

Seek Understanding

In cross-cultural communication the communicator and receptor are not of the same frame of reference. Their meaning, culture, and language may be different, hence they may have differences in their worldview and ways of thinking. Therefore, adjustment, must be made by both the communicator and receptor. The following suggestions may increase understanding when cross-cultural communication takes place:

• State your message in a simple and clear manner. By enunciating carefully in an intercultural setting, you will increase the effectiveness of your message. Don't try to say too much at once. Break it up into smaller parts. Then verify to see that the listener understood. Just because they act as though they got the message doesn't mean they really did. Check and recheck.

• Seek to refer to items familiar to the listener when conversing with him or her. You will be appreciated and respected for doing so. It requires sincere effort to understand your receptor's experiential frames. Any word or action that shows your interest in your receptor's culture or language will open up many avenues of better understanding. Communication becomes virtually impossible when there is no common experience. The greater the overlap in common interest and experience, the easier it will be to communicate.[6]

The following are samples of usual greetings for different language groups in America. It is amazing to watch the appreciation that people will have for you when they see you've taken the time to learn a few words of greeting from their language:

Arabic	—ELSSALAMO ALEIKOM	—Peace be unto you!
	—MARHABA	—Hello!
Cambodian	—NGIEM CHUM RIP SYOR	—Hello, how are you?
Chinese	—PING ANG	—Peace be unto you!
	—NIHOU	—How are you?
Filipino	—KOMUSTA PO KAYO	—How are you?
	MABUHAY	—Long live!
French	—BON JOUR	—Good day!
	—COMMENT ALLEZ-VOUS?	—How are you?
German	—GUTAN TAG	—Good day!
Hawaiian	—ALOHA	—Welcome and blessings to you!
Hungarian	—SZER BUSZ	—Hi!
Indonesian	—SELAMAT SIANG	—Good day!
	—APA KABAR?	—How are you?
Hebrew	—SHALOM	—Peace be unto you!
Japanese	—KONICHIWA	—Good afternoon!
	—DODESKA	—How are you?
Korean	—ANYUNG HA SHIPNIKA	—How are you?
Lao	—SABAYDEE	—Greetings!
Portuguese	—ALÔ, COMO ESTÁ VOCÊ?	—Hello, how are you?
Romanian	—ZIUA BUNÂ	—Greetings!
Russian	—DO BRIY DYEHM	—Good day!
Samoan	—TALOFA	—Greetings, blessings to you!
Spanish	—HOLA, ¿COMO ESTA?	—Hello, how are you?
Swahili (African)	—JAMBO	—Hello
Thai	—SAWADDEE CROP (For Men)	—Greetings, how are you?
	—SAWADDEE KHA (For Women)	—Greetings, how are you?
Vietnamese	—CHÀO MÙNG ÔNG BÀ	—Greetings to you!
Yugoslavian	—ZDRAVO	—Good Health!

You will find that these are great conversation openers. Try them.[7] Christ is the great example of using the language of the masses. He used the unpolished, unimpressive, but communicative "Koine" Greek. We may not be able to fluently learn the language of our neighbors, but at least we can show interest in it.

Christ did not come to this planet Earth only as the Word. He also exemplified His sincerity by becoming a man. Thus He had a relational interaction with the human beings whom He sought to save. He involved Himself in the life, joys, sufferings, and death of humanity. While Christ's involvement with human beings is a mystery, He was the most effective communicator that the world has ever seen.

Be Simple

Instead of saying, "You can't have your cake and eat it too," why not just simply say, "You can't have it both ways"? Instead of saying, "Hang loose," why not just simply say, "Have a relaxed attitude"? Instead of saying, "Meet your Waterloo," why not just simply say, "Suffer a severe defeat"? Instead of saying, "Pull yourself up by the bootstraps," why not just simply say, "Raise or improve your position or standing, socially, economically, or culturally without help"?[8] These and thousands of other American clichés may not be readily understood when used in a conversation with people not of American background.

Get Feedback

If the communicator feels that the message received varies from the intended meaning, he should reframe the message, and send it again. Repeat the question or statement until she or he understands it. This is to make sure that the response or feedback is in harmony with the question. It should be kept in mind that those whose mother tongue is not English, though they be fluently bilingual, think in reference of their major language. Thus it may take them longer to respond or even understand.

Aim to Build Bridges

As Christian communicators, we should aim to communicate in the most effective manner possible. Few things will help you cope with diversity and building relations better than loving communication. The following ten aims are ways to improve your cross-cultural communication skills.

1. Aim to reflect a loving, caring attitude

First Corinthians 13:8 says: "Love never faileth." I take this to mean that love as a method never fails. When a loving style of communication is employed, many of the cultural gaps are overlooked. First Peter 4:8 also says: "And above all things have fervent charity (love) among yourselves: for charity shall cover the multitude of sins." How is a loving attitude in communication reflected?

2. Aim to modulate the pitch and tone of your voice

Studies indicate that 38 percent of what we verbally communicate come from the pitch and tone of the voice.[9] The first real clue you convey about your message and mood when you communicate is in your voice. Through your voice, the receptor can detect whether you are communicative with a

---

Tips for Intercultural Negotiations

The following is advice offered by David Seltz and Alfred Modica in *Negotiate Your Way to Success*. Negotiating skills are especially vital when dealing in an intercultural setting:

1. **Research:** Amass insightful factual information that is relevant.
2. **Preparatory work:** Think like the other person. Likes? Dislikes? Flexible? Narrow-minded?
3. **Self-evaluation:** What are your strengths and weaknesses?
4. **Plan your strategy:** What will happen if you get what you want? When, where, and how will the negotiations be scheduled?
5. **Practice:** Actually rehearse the negotiations, using another person as a devil's advocate.

loving attitude or you are authoritative and arrogant. Usually a loving conversational attitude is spoken in a low, slow paced voice and usually ends with a question.

While moving into my rented home in the Austin area of Chicago, a woman next door bent over the fence and shouted at me, saying, "Why don't you go back to your yellow country?" She evidently was not so pleased to have an Asian as her neighbor.

Not wanting to "render evil for evil," I answered in a low, slow-paced voice. I said, "Ma'am, don't you think you should give me the joy of being the neighbor of a sweet woman like you and let me prove what kind of neighbor I am?"

She must have discerned a loving attitude in my answer and voice. She finally said, "Wait a minute while I go to the house and get something." I thought she would come down with a gun, but when she returned, she was holding a big glass jar filled with money. While handing the coin-filled jar out to me, she said, "Here, buy yourself a lawn mower and make your lawn look nice." I lavished her with much praise, and I became her good friend throughout my family's stay in Chicago.

3. Aim to control your facial expressions

Ralph Waldo Emerson wrote, "The eyes of men converse as much as their tongues, with the advantage that the ocular dialect needs no dictionary, but is understood the world over." Studies have shown that 55 percent of what people communicate comes from the facial expression.[10] Usually when one expresses a loving attitude through facial expression, the eyes reflect a sympathetic look. While these facial expressions vary from person to person or from culture to culture, whatever facial expression you have that reflects a loving and caring attitude will greatly enhance your communicational relationship.

Let us learn from the communicative practice of Jesus Christ our Saviour. Ellen White said:

> Jesus did not suppress one word of truth, but He uttered it always in love. He exercised the greatest

tact and thoughtful, kind attention in His intercourse with people. He was never rude, never needlessly spoke a severe word, never gave needless pain to a sensitive soul. He did not censure human weakness, He spoke the truth, but always in love. He denounced hypocrisy, unbelief, and iniquity; but tears were in is voice as He uttered His soothing rebukes. He went over Jerusalem, the city He loved, which refused to receive Him, the way, the truth, and the life. They had rejected Him, the Saviour, but He regarded them with pitying tenderness. His life was one of self-denial and thoughtful care for others. Every soul was precious in His eyes. While He ever bore Himself with divine dignity, He bowed with the tenderest regard to every member of the family of God. In all men He saw fallen souls whom it was His mission to save.[11]

4. Aim to reflect a humble attitude

There is no greater hindrance to cross-cultural communication than a proud and haughty attitude, especially as it relates to, or because of, one's racial or cultural framework. The portrayal of ethnocentrism (the tendency of each group to take for granted the superiority of its own culture) during a conversational event, blocks out the interest of a receptor to listen to or accept the message. Whether you are a communicator or a receptor, a humble attitude must be reflected. The apostle Paul said, "Let nothing be done through strife or vainglory; but in lowliness of mind let each esteem other better than themselves" (Philippians 2:3, KJV).

5. Aim to be considerate

To be considerate is to practice a thoughtful and sympathetic regard to the rights, values, practices, and feelings of others. This is an important aspect in cross-cultural communication where worldviews (ways of perceiving the world), cognitive processes (ways of thinking), linguistic forums (ways of expressing ideas), behavioral patterns (ways of acting), social structure (ways of interacting), media influences (ways of channelling the message), and motivational resources (ways of deciding) vary from culture to culture.[12]

6. Aim to express yourself logically and persuasively.

For example, in American rhetoric the speaker tends to view himself or herself as an agent of change, persuading his or her listeners in a confrontational setting. The speaker is a transmitter of information, ideas, and opinions, while the audience is a receiver of these speech messages. To communicate well means, for the American speaker, to express himself or herself logically and persuasively. Focus on the expressive is a hallmark of American rhetoric.

However, in most Asian rhetoric, especially Japanese, the emphasis is on the importance of the receptor rather than on the speaker or communicator. The Japanese people, in a sense, are excellent perceivers, capable of accurately tuning in to the faintest of signals. There is not a clear differentiation, but rather an integration of roles between the speaker and the audience. The speaker, therefore, always attempts to adjust himself or herself to his or her listeners.

In a culture of *sasshi* or *omoiyari* (both words mean "considerateness"), to communicate well for the Japanese speaker is to understand and perceive the explicit message even to the point of deciphering the faintest nuances of nonverbal communications. *Sasshi ga ii*, or "being a good mind reader" and *Omoiyari ga aru*, or "being considerate about other's feelings" are both considered virtues in Japanese culture.[13] It is not my intention to define which rhetoric is preferred, but when one's practice is different from yours, loving consideration must be exercised.

7. Aim to be considerate of other cultures using English.

People from other cultures, although fluent in English, may have a more elaborate meaning to a word or sentence than what you usually believe or understand. For example, the Arabic expression for our English "Thank you" is "May Allah increase your well-being." The Arabic for "Get well soon" is "May there be upon you nothing but health, if Allah wills." For "We missed you," it is "You made us desolate."[14]

The pronunciation of English words may vary from culture to culture. Some pronounce the consonant R as L; others pronounce L as R. Some pronounce V as F. I have a friend who says, "I life in San Dimas" instead of "I live in San Dimas." Some cultures pronounce P for F. I attended a Sabbath School program where the superintendent announced the opening song as hymn number pipty-pive instead of fifty-five. Some stress the R in a word so much that it really roars.

When inter-cultural interaction does occur, close attention should be given to the trend of thought rather than on individual words, and be considerate to those of us whose mother tongue is other than English. After all, even those born in this country do not all pronounce and speak the English language in the same way. Southerners sound different from those in the rest of the country. And much more, the British English and Australian English sound different from the American English. So, let us be considerate to one another while we are doing all we can to be as perfect as possible as we communicate interculturally.

8. Aim to be sensitive of the nonverbal interactions

Like spoken language, body language varies from culture to culture. Those visiting a foreign country should heed the words of one expert. "Watch where people stand when they talk to you. And don't back up if they stand close. You will feel funny doing this. But it's amazing the difference it makes in people's attitudes." North Americans like to stand about two to three feet apart during conversation. If people get too close, they tend to back up. We feel they are being pushy and aggressive, breathing down our necks and into our faces.[15]

Eye movements, too, vary from one culture to another. The normal American eye contact lasts about one second. In some countries, people gaze intently into each other's eyes while talking. In England, a fixed stare and an occasional eye blink are normal attentive listener patterns. In many Asian cultures, it is considered rude to place your hands on your hips while talking with people.[16]

9. Aim to be conscious of the culture's language of color

The language of color is not the same with every culture. In the United States, black is the color of mourning, but in China and Korea, white, not black, is the color for mourning. In the United States, red stands for danger or radicalism. But in Russia, red stands for beauty and life. In the U.S., green means envy ("Go" for traffic lights), but in France, to be "green" to someone means not to bear a grudge. And to be depressed is "to have a black humor." In the U.S. you are yellow if you are afraid, but in Italy and Germany you are yellow with envy.[17] These are just a few examples to show that the language of color is not international.

10. Aim to be sensitive, kind, and loving

That is, aim to be Christlike in all you do and say. As Proverbs 15:1 says, "A soft answer turneth away wrath, but grievous words stir up anger."

Proposals to Enhance More Effective Cross-Cultural Communication

Finally, we end this chapter by sharing some practical suggestions on how to build bridges among other Christians or Adventists who are of a different culture. These are just a few. Make your own list and then in the Spirit of Christ work toward making them happen.

• **Exchange pulpits**

We could learn from each other by listening to sermons of pastors other than those of our own culture. If pastors of different language groups within the conference would arrange so they could exchange pulpits from time to time, our church members would learn to appreciate other cultures.

• **Foster more cross-cultural interactions**

It is observed that where there are Adventist gatherings, members of the same culture interact together. Encouragement should be given to all members to seek the company and interaction of other cultures so as to learn from each other.

• **Put on or attend cultural festivals**

Encourage our members to attend festivals of different cultural groups like *Cinco de Mayo*, Black History programs, the Chinese New Year, or Filipino *Barrio Fiesta*. You will learn a lot from those cultures.

• **Write articles in church papers describing the different cultures in the church**

Encourage the editors of our union papers or the *Review* to print a series of articles on cultural backgrounds. We should all be more informed about each other.

• **Develop multicultural curricula on high-school, college, and university levels**

Our denominational educators should be encouraged to develop multicultural curricula for our schools. Cross-cultural communication should be taught and encouraged.

• **Reflect more ethnic diversity in school faculty and staff and church hierarchy**

This will be perceived by church members as a sign of sincerity on the part of church leaders to foster love, unity, and understanding among the diverse membership of the Church today.

• **Pray and work to bring about true unity in the Church**

Love and unity are signs of the Holy Spirit's presence, and they are a witness to the world. Progress in this area will help to usher in the soon coming of Jesus Christ.

My Hope and Prayer

It is my hope and prayer that as we strive to apply the principles, aims, and proposals shared here, there will be a greater understanding of each other, more loving communication, and better relationships with our brothers and sisters from other cultures and that there will be a true revival of positive cross-cultural communication.

George Atiga, D.Min., is director of Asian/Pacific ministries at the Pacific Union Conference and associate director of multilingual ministries at the NAD. He is a second-generation minister and has a deep interest in evangelism. He is involved in cross-cultural ministry and training. He and his wife, Caroline, have three children.

Endnotes

1. Clarence L. Ver Steeg, *World Cultures* (Glenview, Ill.: Scott, Foresman and Company, 1977), 324.

2. Bangele Alsaybar, Jr., *Intercultural Communication* (Unpublished article, 1994), 2.

3. Caleb Rosado, "Ministry in a Multicultural Society," *The Challenge of Cross-Cultural Communication* (California), n.d., n.p.

4. Delbert Baker, ed., "How to Bridge Cultural Differences," *Message Magazine Supplement* (Hagerstown, Md.: Review and Herald Publishing Association, 1987).

5. Ellen G. White, *The Ministry of Healing* (Boise, Idaho: Pacific Press Publishing Association, 1909), 143.

6. Shirley Burton, *Communication and Ethnic Unity* (Westlake Village, Calif.: Pacific Union Minority Groups Committee, 1982), 4.

7. Thanks to the ethnic Seventh-day Adventist pastors within the Pacific Union Conference for furnishing these greetings from their respective cultures.

8. James Rogers, *Dictionary of American Clichés* (New York: Ballantine Books, 1989).

9. Burton, loc. cit., 1.

10. Ibid.

11. Ellen G. White, *Steps to Christ* (Boise, Idaho: Pacific Press Publishing Association, 1950), 12.

12. Rosado, loc. cit.

13. Roichi Okabe, *Cultural Assumptions of East and West, Japan and the United States* (Beverly Hills: Sage Publications, 1983), 21.

14. Ver Steeg, loc. cit., 326.

15. Ibid.

16. Ibid.

17. Ibid.

—————— *10* ——————

The Art of Solving Cultural Conflicts

Donald G. King

Understanding and meaningful relationships will take the place of fights and rivalry when the spirit of love and the tools of diversity are used to prevent and resolve conflicts. It all starts with you.

*T*he entire world community is the territory of the SDA Church. No country is too distant, no community is too remote, no class of people is too removed. The task, the divine mandate, is to take the good news, the everlasting gospel of Christ, to all the world. Incredibly, with a world membership of more than eight million, relatively small in comparison with a global population of approximately five and a half billion, the SDA Church has penetrated most of the world's countries with its presence and mission.

It is precisely because of the international characteristics of the Church that discussions surrounding cultural diversity cannot be ignored. The SDA Church in North America, in the process of supplying a rich supply of missionaries from various cultural and racial backgrounds to other countries, has become a diverse mixture of cultures, nationalities, and races. In light of this phenomenon, the challenge facing North America SDA members is to go beyond tolerance. We must actively and intentionally seek to understand and love each other (John 15:12).

In order to realize continual success in fulfilling the gospel commission here and abroad, SDAs must become more broad in our understanding of our diversity and more accepting in our love. We must come to the point where we can spiritually and skilfully resolve cultural conflicts. Further, we need to be able to prevent conflicts even before they occur.

Understanding Cultural Conflict

Global diversity is no longer a catch phrase. It is a reality. According to George Simons, author of *Transcultural Leadership,* the work force in North America is shrinking. Without the entrance of large numbers of people, mostly women, immigrants, and visible minorities, this decline would be even more severe. Traditional areas of employment are also diminishing as new sectors open. According to Joel Dreyfuss, writing for the *Atlantic Monthly*, "The shrinking workforce gives the diversity issue a level of urgency that affirmative action never had."

Furthermore, while women will continue to increase as a proportion of the work force (predicted to be a hefty 47 percent by the end of 1990s), the Bureau of Labor Statistics points out that White males, the traditional source of labor in the United States, will drop to 39.4 percent of the labor force by the end of the decade.

By the year 2000, it is predicted that at least 10 percent of the U.S. work force will be foreign born and will account for more than 20 percent of the work force's net growth. By the end of the next century, a full 50 percent of workers will likely be immigrants or descendants of immigrants arrived after 1980 (Simons, 1993). These changes not only affect secular society, but they dramatically impact the Church and its way of doing business.

Widespread Change

Changes in North America are so sweeping today that it is not desirable, necessary, or possible to eliminate the cultural diversity of mainstream society. The old melting pot mentality that assumes that cultural diversity is a temporary nuisance that will go away; the belief that if we just put enough different people to work, give them fair wages, promotions, and in general, blind ourselves to their differences, is passe.

North America will have a new culture. But it will not be like the past which is based on assimilation when individuals fully adopt the culture and values of another culture to the total exclusion of their own. Instead, the new culture will be based upon acculturation, which is the process of learning to survive and become comfortable in a different environment while retaining one's own cultural identity. This process is the road to empowerment.

Assimilation is unrealistic, a dead-end street. Acculturation is empowering, the road to success. The reality applies in the secular and spiritual realms. One writer wisely observed that equity is not the main problem of diversity. However, the lack of equity is a manifestation of the inability to properly manage diversity.

Accepting that diversity is the right emphasis today, it still needs to be clarified, understood, and managed. Affirmative Action and Equal Opportunity (known as Employment Equity in Canada) made a difference for many disenfranchised people. Now, however, a different kind of effort is required, an effort given focus through empowerment. It is the revolutionary twenty-first century alternative to the melting pot mentality. What is the new focus? It is an empowering diversity mentality. For the Christian it means being motivated by love to respect, appreciate, and include all people in the body of Christ.

Managing Diversity

In order to manage diversity, one must have a sense for the global picture. In fact, diversity and globalism are two sides of the same coin. It is the new world currency unit of thinking. Leaders (including North American church leaders) must be able to think globally, yet at the same time act locally. They must be more cosmopolitan and less provincial in both thought and action.

The necessity for diversity maturity in church leadership, however, presents a real challenge. Today's leaders themselves are caught up in the transition to the new work culture mentality. Church administrators, employees, and church members are experiencing a new kind of culture shock similar to what Alvin Toffler, more than a decade ago, called "future shock."

We all land as immigrants, as it were, on the doorstep of the twenty-first century. We are living in that future today. We are affected by its culture, but hardly acculturated to it. We are eager to take advantage of this new culture, but ill-equipped to utilize the full range of benefits that this new diversity offers. We may be filled with enthusiasm for the new wave of thinking, but still hold on to the old. This dilemma often creates stress, especially for those who try to assimilate. We tend to forget our own culture and with it, sometimes, our own self-esteem.

On the other hand, to acculturate sometimes means living in two worlds—biculturally and often simultaneously. It sometimes means dividing life into separate compartments, creating personal and professional discomfort. For example, it may mean having one view of authority at work and another at home and sometimes not feeling confident with either. For most leaders, this will mean making a shift from assimilation-melting-pot thinking to acculturating themselves to the new work force and helping others to do so as well.

Culture: What Is It?

Before we examine cultural breakdowns and how to manage them, lets attempt to define culture. One author says, culture is a way of life. It is developed and communicated by a group of people consciously or unconsciously to subsequent generations. It consists of ideas, habits, attitudes, customs, and traditions that help to create standards for people to coexist. It is what makes a group of people unique.

Another says, culture is a set of mental formulas for survival and success where a particular group of people has developed. Still another way of putting it is that in its most basic and fundamental sense, culture is a set of inner understandings and rules developed by a group or organization for survival and success. *Essentially, culture determines how people think, what they value, and how they behave and communicate with each other.* (In this chapter, culture refers to any racial, ethnic, language, gender, or cultural minority group.)

When people of different cultures come together in the Church, work place, or in any setting, there is a certain acculturation journey that we pass through. First, when we enter the new situation, naturally there is some *excitement, surprise, caution,* and even enthusiasm that takes place between the different cultures. When things turn out to be different than we expected, *frustration and anger sets in*—sometimes even depression. From this level we emerge into trying to *acknowledge the real differences* on a practical everyday level. Finally, we try to work out *agreements* in order to *collaborate* and produce new results in our newfound situation.

Acculturation, then, is not a one-time journey. People and organizations will experience it repeatedly. It will happen when people of diverse cultural backgrounds first meet, when the environments change in the church, work, or school setting. It will happen when we begin new tasks and share new ideas together. Acculturation is more manageable when we understand the predictable stages that we pass through. It helps when we are able to recognize the stage that we are in and how we tend to act or react when we are experiencing it. The Christian has the added advantage of prayer and the help of the Holy Spirit to help negotiate these changes. Nevertheless, one shouldn't expect the process to be easy or necessarily pleasant.

In time, with practice and a spirit of acceptance and

humility, these cultural challenges may become easier to accept and resolve. Instead of becoming sources of barriers and frustration, our differences will become interesting and useful. How? Because when people of diverse cultures begin to value their differences, we have moved from the stage of acculturation to empowerment, and the positive results which follow are phenomenal in their impact.

Intercultural Breakdowns

Good leaders—whether pastors, teachers, administrators, local church leaders—should strive to become experts at diversity troubleshooting. They can, if they work at it, prevent, resolve, and successfully handle breakdowns in communications and relationships. When these breakdowns occur because of racial, ethnic, or cultural differences, there are certain factors that one needs to be aware of in order to handle these delicate situations. It will take observation/action; sensitivity/resolution, and management/follow-through.

Observation/Action: It is important to pay attention to the surrounding circumstances, sometimes overlooked when a disruption occurs in the normal work flow. The breakdown may take the form of a personal conflict, a heated verbal exchange, or a group confrontation. In some cases the cultural hints are close to the surface. For example, a woman may complain of sexual harassment; instructions are misunderstood or not carried out by someone whose English is not clear; a prejudicial or racial slur is made; and someone is offended by another group's attitude, appearance, or behavior.

Whatever the reason, a breakdown in the system occurs, emotional discomforts develop, and/or an all out dispute erupts. If this happens several times in a cultural context, this is indication that there are cultural underpinnings. To apply surface solutions will only complicate the problem. The cultural differences must be addressed prayerfully and sensitively. They must also be addressed directly.

Sensitivity/Resolution: As soon as the interruptions take

place, we experience negative and emotional fallout. What is needed, then, is a safe forum in which cultural factors can be viewed and calmly discussed by all parties involved. In some cases, to begin the process, it might necessitate resourcing someone with cultural-diversity skills to initiate and interpret the needs of the different cultures involved and to negotiate a win-win situation.

Those involved in the resolution meeting need to come to a common understanding of the problem, an agreement about what needs to be done, and a commitment to follow through on which steps will produce the right results. Such collaboration will create synergy of mutual cooperation for goal accomplishment. Such collaboration will enable the organization to resolve the problem and to help prevent similar problems in the future.

Management/Follow-Through: If this stage is not managed properly, it can badly damage an organization with far-reaching repercussions. Sometimes breakdowns become blow-ups as people personally attack each other instead of the problem. Wise leaders will see that follow-through takes place. They will seek to implement or facilitate the agreed upon course of action.

It should be kept in mind that in order to understand the needs of the organization and its people, those involved, including the leaders, must first accept the differences of each other's culture, language, definitions, and values. So, it is helpful to keep in mind that not all fallouts are totally negative. If managed with discretion, situations like this can help people grow and be more proactive and sensitive to the needs of others. They can help us to better bear one another's burdens (Galatians 6:1, 2).

Steps to Resolving Cultural Conflict

When a problem occurs, the following proactive steps can be helpful in guiding the parties toward a successful resolution.

1. *Be open* to different ideas and ways of doing things. It has been said that what may be perfectly obvious to a person of one paradigm may be quite literally invisible to another person with a different paradigm. Our ethnocentrism naively assumes that other people are just like us, should be, or, at least, they should understand our position. Leaders must learn to be open to ways of viewing situations from a different perspective than that of their own ethnocentric worldview.

2. *Use the 80/20 rule.* Be able to distinguish systemic problems from personal issues. When breakdowns occur and reoccur between people of different cultures, you can safely assume that 80 percent of the problem is systemic with cultural roots and 20 percent of the problem is personal. It is important to focus on the 80 percent in order to create the most productive changes in the environment.

3. *Avoid perception pitfalls.* Leaders should strive to make judgments grounded on factual observations of individuals. This approach is preferred rather than acting on personal impressions and perceptions which may result in skewed thinking.

Monitoring our own feelings and looking carefully at what others are actually doing or saying will help to compensate or balance our tendency to impose personal or cultural perceptions. For example, if you sense someone is projecting their feelings on you, empathize with them, but be clear about what is true for you ("I can understand how you feel right now, but . . ."). Be sure that your assumptions have a basis in fact. Try to imagine explanations other than what you have assumed.

4. *Become knowledgeable about cultural values.* When two nonnegotiable, absolute, or diametrically opposed cultural values are brought to bear on the same issue, the resulting fallout creates a deadlock, putting both sides in a double bind. Both sides will feel that they have betrayed themselves and their group if they give in to the other side. This has been called the "Rushdie Dilemma."

The transcultural church leader has to act proactively to

avoid such situations in which compromise no longer seems possible. Such a leader must first make every effort to become knowledgeable about the principal cultural values of the different people in the environment. He must keep his ear to the ground which means paying attention to even small discomforts in the organization, keeping the lines of communication open and dealing with complaints without dismissing them as trivial. It is important that he or she respectfully and regularly inquire about what is not working for people in order to avoid igniting the potential internal bomb.

5. *Factor in the historical context.* The bomb inside (cultural disruption) is often based on one's own historical or cultural memory. "Remember what they did to us when . . ." For example, a little more than two decades ago, U.S. Blacks were discriminated against in public facilities, denied basic constitutional rights, and even barred from participation in religious services with Whites. In light of this history, the subject of racial discrimination is a sensitive one.

So a consciousness of history and context should be factored into one's thinking when dealing with race in cross-cultural settings in the Church. Some examples of triggers that can set off disruption include even physical factors such as "They look strange and different," "They're not like us," "They talk boisterously or act funny," "They always remain in the church foyer chatting long after the service is over." Understanding these internal bombs and the external triggers which can set them off is a key characteristic of transcultural leaders.

Get Understanding

The Bible gives us excellent counsel when it says, "Get wisdom and with all thy getting, get understanding" (Proverbs 4:7). Groups must intentionally attempt to understand the context in which other groups operate. On one hand, some cultures operate in a context where vast amounts of information can be taken for granted. Much is assumed to be known and left unsaid without interfering with communication. In other cultures, everything must be specific, detailed, and carefully articulated. Everything must be explained and spelled out to ensure that others get the message.

In other words, some groups come from a "more tightly knit" background where much information is already understood, where group members "read between the lines," and instructions are minimal. In a "more loosely knit" culture, specific details are valued. Nothing is taken for granted, and everything must be described and explained. Each time interaction occurs, questions and answers are more direct. When persons or groups of different cultural "knit" try to communicate without an understanding of cultural context, suddenly a goldmine for misunderstanding presents itself. A commitment to understanding will motivate people to always seek to understand.

Seeking to get people to dispel their own cultural context and buy into the North American way—*assimilation*—is a thing of the past. What is needed is *acculturation.* Thereby people's cultural context is not ignored or eliminated, but a new context is created in the church and work setting where everyone's cultural heritage is valued. The goal of the Christian is to glorify God (1 Corinthians 10:31), and that can be done through the diversity of cultures, styles, and approaches. The balance for managing diversity is found in the next verse (verse 32) of 1 Corinthians 10 when we are told to seek to avoid giving offense or to cause others to stumble. Therefore, all diversity activities must be balanced by the Spirit of Christ and love (1 John 4:7, 8).

Breakdowns in a multicultural environment can actually help people to become acculturated to one another. Breakdowns can be used to educate and reveal things we don't know about each other. As sharing occurs, churches and organizations of diverse people can start weaving a new basket of contexts to carry forward the work of the Church.

Strategizing to Prevent Cultural Conflict

The following five strategies will help the motivated Christian to not only solve cultural conflicts, but it will help him/her to prevent unnecessary cultural conflicts.

Strategy 1: Understand the unspoken language of culture.

People are different; therefore, they need to communicate. When communicating across cultures, bear in mind that the message that counts is the one the other person gets or perceives, not what we think we have sent. We understand by listening, because listening is culture at work.

Strategy 2: Remember Dos and Don'ts for preventing breakdowns.

• *Do* anticipate cultural differences in new environments, and anticipate possible breakdowns.

Don't allow yourself to be distracted by differences that appear on the surface such as accent, physical or personal appearance, tone of voice, style, etc. Try to evaluate the merit of what people say and do.

• *Do* have a positive and open attitude to appreciate other cultures without losing a healthy pride in your own cultural identity.

Don't make assumptions about people you don't understand. Seek alternatives to assumptions and prejudices that tend to show up without thinking.

• *Do* try to learn about the expectations, values, and communication styles of people from other cultural backgrounds.

Don't stereotype or pigeonhole cultures or people. In every culture, there are those who depart from that culture's norm.

• *Do* avoid explosive blunders such as ethnic jokes, inappropriate touching, sexualized expressions, etc.

Don't be afraid to ask yourself "stupid" yet valuable questions such as, "What's going on here?" "What are the issues and needs in this situation?" They may be very important to survival in a new environment.

• *Do* seek win-win and dignity-saving resolutions to problems and conflicts.

Don't embarrass or highlight a person's faults during or after a conflict.

Strategy 3: Value diversity.

A set of values is an important ingredient of most successful organizations and their leadership today. It plays a vital role, consciously or unconsciously, in organizational decision making. Diversity is a part of individual or institutional values. It means that we respect the values of others even when they conflict with our own.

If I'm from a more loosely knit culture such as Whites from the United States or Canada, I may not value staying around in the foyer of my church after the service is over and "fellowshiping with the saints" in the same way someone from a more tightly woven culture such as an African American or West Indian would do. But I can accept that he or she values that practice in that way. Hopefully, I can then consciously include that particular value into how I work and communicate with people from that culture.

Here are some points in the process of valuing diversity:

• Make a conscious effort to discover the other person's values by observing patterns that are consistent.
• Try to identify which values are at work in a given situation in order to pinpoint potential problems and to be able to effectively relate to the specific problem.
• Look for the positive side to other people's values. Just because there is a conflict doesn't mean the other person's values are wrong or of no use. This means being able to see not only how a particular value operates beneficially in another's culture, but how that same value could be applied to your own culture or to the organization for which you both work.
• When you have identified the positive side of the value, apply it to the issue at hand in order to manage differences.

Strategy 4: Intentionally manage diversity in times of stress.

When stress is high and the conflict intense, it is hard to see positive possibilities. We so focus on survival that we often become prone to fight or flight. Under stress, we instinctively resort to what we were brought up to do. We think less of what we are trained or learn to do in order to get along with others. Everything tends to become right or wrong.

When the economy is booming and expertise is in short supply, employing ethnic minority workers seems like the necessary and affirmative thing to do. However, when recession sets in, these same people who were so needed are now seen as different, as a part of the problem, and are accused of stealing jobs from "our own." Therefore, we respond in ways that are more racial, more male, or more female, etc.

It is when times are tough and stressful that transcultural church leaders must rise to the occasion and exercise self-control, thereby diffusing suspicion and resentment. This is the time to facilitate clarification and interpretation, so both sides can better see what is taking place in the organization.

There are several guidelines that can help during these intense periods:

• Increase your awareness and others' of how stress affects people's thinking and behavior. This could make the difference in catching oneself before doing or saying something for which one will later be remorseful.
• Remember to practice using the 80/20 rule (explained earlier) to mediate conflict between individuals or groups.
• Be a "mind shifter." That is, to say to yourself "Stop!" when you hear yourself thinking old stereotypes and automatic negative judgments about others. Instead, ask yourself, "What alternative, positive ways can I think about this?" or "What other possible solutions can I see?"
• Don't personalize what *you* consider to be an emotional response. This may be a natural way of speaking for that person *or* for people from that culture.
• Don't confuse race with ethnic identity. For example, there are many from African American, Hispanic, West Indian, and African ethnic orientation who may look similar (race) but who come from very different backgrounds (ethnicity).

• Make friends. Take time to converse and become acquainted with the people in your environment. This is one of the best ways to increase understanding and to build relationships.

• Nip in the bud all whispering campaigns, wild rumors, and inappropriate humor that is done in the name of easing tension or letting off steam. Often such communication can do damage that is virtually irreparable.

• Always keep communication lines open. Share information. Let people know what is happening. Take the time to inform others who may not be part of the organizational mainstream.

When the chips are down, the leader or organization that continues to demonstrate that it values all its people is the organization that will have the morale and teamwork to survive difficult times and will be ready to seize new opportunities.

Steps in Dealing With an Intercultural Breakdown

These steps are suggested for follow-through on a breakdown due to a cross-cultural dispute. The fallout stage of the breakdown is the critical part. But it can be managed successfully if attention is paid to the cultural information it yields and if perception pitfalls are avoided. Think of a recent incident that you had or are now having, and use the steps below when seeking to bring about resolution.

1. **The Interruption**
   Describe what happened/how the breakdown occurred.
   a. What really took place? Give an objective step-by-step description of who did/said what.
   b. With whom did it happen?
   c. When did it happen?
   d. Where did it happen? Who else was present?
2. **The Fallout**
   a. What thoughts came to your mind when the incident occurred?
   b. How did you judge the situation?
   c. Can you think of other possible interpretations to this scenario?
   d. What different cultural contexts and values are present in

this situation? What differences (both your own and the other person's) surfaced in this case?

3. **The Resolution**
   a. To what resolution are you committed in trying to salvage the situation?
   b. Who can you involve or what resources can you use to realize the desired resolution?
   c. How would you handle this situation face to face, using both listening/transcultural skills?

Strategy 5: Practice empowerment 2000

Acculturation, not assimilation is the superhighway to empowerment as we near year 2000 and the twenty-first century. Assimilation says, "You must become like us." An attitude of empowerment says, "Together we can." As the Seventh-day Adventist Church continues to fulfill its mission and therefore becomes more diverse with people of all colors, races, nationalities, and languages, an attitude of empowerment will help to drive out fear, because fear is one of the great adversaries to progress in the area of diversity.

Empowerment produces visionary members and leaders who can collaborate together to make their best contribution of service to the Church and society. Such leadership gives the organization of the future the greatest possibility of balanced budgets, high morale, and a satisfied employee and lay work force. It will provide the Church with growing members who will make a powerful witness by loving God and people. These people will not only be prepared for the world to come, they will be prepared to function effectively in the world that now is.

Watch out, however, for obstacles to empowerment within the Church or organization. One is the matter of change. Because the Church and organizations may have to change their structure and management style and then train people to use these changes to the greatest advantage, empowerment can come to be resisted. For example, a church administrator may be reluctant to let a subordinate make his own decision for fear that things might get out of control. But if empowerment is to be successful, there must be a willingness on the part of leadership to trust workers (and members). There must be a willingness to deal with a varied work force with its different perceptions of authority and communication styles.

One of the communication styles that has been deeply entrenched in our thinking is hierarchial thinking. However, like assimilation, it is on its way out. As consultant Erica Henser writes, "Bureaucracy is high, hierarchies are complex, workers are told what to do and then hammered to improve. Most managers think that the way to run a company is for the executives to make the decisions and the employees to execute them. Workers are asked to check their brains at the door when they come in." The "together we can" mentality of acculturation and empowerment will help to change this hierarchical type of thinking that has been the standard in the past. The new kind of leader appearing on the scene today, the leader needed today in North America and around the world, will empower people to reach their potential, to be all that they can be!

Triumphing Over Cultural Conflict

Seventh-day Adventists believe they have a mandate for the global proclamation of the gospel—a gospel that produces a sense of oneness, unity, and dignity (Galatians 3:26-28). This gospel must therefore transcend all barriers of gender, language, race, skin color, or culture. According to Sakae Kubo, in his book, *The God of Relationships,* "We need to remember that we do not belong to the First, Second, or Third World, but to a new world, a new race, the Fourth World, where members from the First, Second, and Third Worlds worship as equal members."

The apostle Paul, obliged to deal with the racial conflict between the Jews and the Gentiles, admonished us that Christ is our peace. "In His flesh He has made both groups into one and has broken down the dividing wall, that is, the hostility between us." Indeed he has made "in himself one new humanity in place of the two, thus making peace" (Ephesians 2:14, 15, NRSV).

As Adventists, who love God and people, we should not only believe in preaching the gospel to every nation, kindred, tongue, and people, we must practice and live the gospel among all peoples.

After all, if the new earth will be populated by the redeemed from all the diverse peoples and cultures of the earth, aren't we simply rehearsing now for the bigger event which John the revelator wrote about? He said, "I looked, and there was a great multitude that no one could count, from every nation, from all tribes and peoples and languages, standing before the throne and before the Lamb, robed in white" (Revelation 7:9, NRSV). What tremendous unity and dignity amidst diversity!

Donald G. King, Dr.PH., is executive secretary and human relations director of the Alberta Conference, Canada. He also serves on the Multicultural Commission of the NAD. He and his wife, Lois, regularly conduct seminars and serve as consultants on health and family relations. The Kings have two sons.

Bibliography

Burton, John. *Conflict: Resolution and Prevention*. New York: St. Martin's Press, 1990.

Davis, James H., and Woodie W. White. *Racial Transition in the Church*. Nashville, Tenn.: Abingdon, 1980.

Elashmawi, Farid, and Philip R. Harris. *Multicultural Management: New Skills for Global Success*. Houston, Tex.: Gulf Publishing Company, 1993.

Harris, Philip R., and Robert T. Moran. *Managing Cultural Differences*. 3rd edition. Houston, Tex.: Gulf Publishing Company, 1991.

Kubo, Sakae. *The God of Relationships*. Hagerstown, Md.: Review and Herald Publishing Association, 1993.

Simons, George F., Carmen Vazquez, and Philip R. Harris. *Transcultural Leadership: Empowering the Diverse Workforce*. Houston, Tex.: Gulf Publishing Company, 1993.

———————————11———————————

Celebrating Our
International Roots

D. Robert Kennedy

If we appreciate the international origins of the neighbors of North America, we can better respect, support, and build productive relationships with diverse groups. This area has opportunity for ministry and witness.

*T*he students were anxious to share their varied cultural experiences as they participated in a chapel exercise on human relations. They had been asked to present their perspectives on a unique aspect of their culture and how they identified with the Adventist family in North America. Several descriptions were given, but the one that called for an intense emotional response was by a Cambodian student. This profoundly sensitized us to the acute tensions felt by a person who has to live in somebody else's country. The remarks went as follows.

Atheist to Adventist
"We came from different backgrounds, different understandings, different races, different socioeconomic contexts,

and different languages. The way we accepted the Adventist message is also different. Some of us were born Adventist, some were converted to Adventism. As for me, I was converted from an atheist to an Adventist. That happened in a refugee camp on the Cambodian-Thai border almost 10 years ago.

"July, 27, 1984, I fled from Cambodia to the Cambodian-Thai border camp. The journey was very dangerous. After crossing 22 miles of mine fields and the bandits, I finally reached the camp. Life was extremely difficult, and I lived in fear of being drafted to fight with the Vietnamese-installed Cambodian government. I didn't want to kill my fellow countrymen. I saw enough killing in my life. One morning, approximately one week after I arrived at the refugee camp, I walked around the camp. I came upon a small, bamboo church from which music and songs were coming. I was curious to know what was going on, so I drew closer until above my head there was a sign written 'Nong Sameth SDA.' I never heard about Seventh-day Adventist or Christianity before. I wondered what they looked like so I went to the back and quietly listened to the song.

"I still remember the very first Christian song that I learned to sing 'Onward Christian Soldiers.' Whenever I hear this song, I always remember the refugee camp and the day I gave my life to Christ. I still remember the young preacher who came to greet me and invite me to join his congregation. I was so thrilled to learn about God, to learn that despite all the suffering and torments in the past, I could still find people to trust. Since the day (May/1985) I was baptized in Khao-I-Dang refugee camp in Thailand, I remain faithful to my God and my Church.

"On September 1, 1988, I came to America. My fantasies about America, streets paved with gold, or chasing the rainbow to find a pot of gold did not come true. Instead I experienced what we call 'cultural shock.' I did not know how to speak English properly. I didn't know how to dress appropriately. I didn't know how to eat American foods. I never saw computers, microwaves, VCRs or even calculators. Whenever I walked away from home, I got lost. I was terrified of the busy traffic. I dared not even cross the road myself. Wherever I went, people stared at me as if I was an alien."

Culture Shock

"How was I suppose to know about this modern society? I was just a refugee who spent most of my life in concentration camps, refugee camps and a communist country. In all of my confusion, my greatest desire was to find an SDA church. I prayed that God would help me find such a church. One day, I met an Adventist Rumanian family who invited me to their church one Sabbath morning. When I went the pastor of the church came to say 'hello' to me at once. One other gentleman, an Asian from Indonesia, came to greet and talk to me. Everyone else seemed to ignore me. I was quite disappointed. I knew I didn't dress properly. I had no suit or sport jacket like everyone else. I came with a T-shirt and an old pair of pants from the refugee camp. However, I did not let that feeling ruin my relationship with God. I felt that people would let me down, but God wouldn't. I knew that I should love God, and regardless of what happened to me, I should always fix my eyes on God, and God alone.

"In describing a little of the uniqueness of my culture, I note that there are many traditions different from American culture. For example, in my country, old people are considered to be the head of the family. Their advice must be taken seriously. It is inappropriate to look at them straight in the eyes. It is a curse to cross one's legs while talking to older people. It is important not to call them by name. When speaking to them one always uses addresses such as aunt, uncle, mister, miss, brother or sister.

"In my culture any physical contact, except between very close friends, is considered impolite. People greet each other with a specific form called 'wye.' There is no public dating or any public romantic relationship between the sexes. Romance between young people is considered scandalous and punishable. Marriages take place only with the approval of parents. Normally marriages are arranged by the parents, and that is acceptable and appropriate for the young people.

"In America, if you see a beautiful girl, you can say, 'Wow! you are beautiful!' and she generally responds politely, 'Thank you.' If you say 'Oh, you are ugly,' she might slap you. But in Cambodia, either compliment or insult is nonacceptable. A young lady will become angry and slap you. The message is straight and clear, 'Keep your eyes off me and leave me alone.' No comment is needed. It is safer to ignore.

"If people go to the beach in Cambodia they always cover themselves from the neck to the ankles. No body part can be seen. Also one never touches or pats a man's head. If such is done, it is a sign of confrontation and an invasion of privacy.

"These are only a few of the unique things that make my country different from America. And these differences can isolate us individually. But I have found that we can make great relationships if we find common ground in Jesus."[1]

Alone and Lonely

This student's stories are repeated every day. They typify the experience of countless persons in this country in and out

---

Seven Basics of Intercultural Understanding

The following points are adapted from Roger Axtell's bestselling book *Do's and Taboo's Around the World* (a guide to international behavior).

1. **Exchange of Names.** This is the first transaction between even ordinary citizens—and the first chance to make an impression for better or worse. In America, there's usually not very much to get wrong with a name. Not so elsewhere. Especially in the Eastern Hemisphere, where names frequently denote social rank or family status, a mistake can be an outright insult. "What would you like me to call you?" is the best approach. It is even "better to ask several times than to get it wrong."

2. **Your Best Behavior.** In the world of cultural behavior, the only truly safe generalization is don't generalize. So it goes. One would do well to learn some general rules about each region and each nation, even though there may be exceptions.

3. **Eating and Drinking.** Away from home, eating is more than just a way to keep your clothes from falling off. It is a language all its own. Clearly, mealtime is not time for a thanks-but-no-thanks response. Acceptance of what is on your plate is tantamount to acceptance of host, country, and company. So eat if you can.

4. **Cuddly Personal Ethnocentrics.** It should come as no surprise that

of the Seventh-day Adventist Church. Too often their stories are full of pain, loneliness, and ostracism.

The following poem, written by another Asian immigrant, further bears out the depth of the tension and ostracism felt by people new to this country.

> What is it like to be an outsider?
>
> What is it like to sit in the class where everyone has blond hair and you have black hair?
>
> What is it like when the teacher says, "Whoever wasn't born here raise your hand."
>
> And you are the only one.
>
> Then, when you raise your hand, everybody looks at you and makes fun of you.
>
> You have to live in somebody else's country to understand.
>
> What is it like when the teacher treats you like you've been here all your life?
>
> What is it like when the teacher speaks too fast and

---

people surrounded by oceans rather than by other peoples end up ethnocentric. Even our biggest fans admit that Americans often strike the rest of the world as often well-meaning but spoiled, wanting desperately to please but not paying too much attention to how it is done.

5. **Clothes Can Unmake.** Wherever you are, what you wear among strangers should not look strange to them. Which does not mean "When in Morocco, wear djellabas," etc. It means, wear what you look natural in—and know how to wear what you wear—that also fits with your surroundings.

6. **Watch Your Words.** It is nice to be born free. But we should be just as grateful that we are born speaking the language most people speak besides their own. It is when we try to talk in other tongues that the most dramatic failure of communication seems to occur. If you use another language, know it reasonably well.

7. **Religion and Sex.** If discussing politics is like playing with matches, transgressions in the areas of religion and sex are like playing with live hand grenades. Still, neither area can be ignored. Religion is often an important part of a culture (e.g., the Middle East) and therefore an unavoidable adjunct to business or tourist travel. For Westerners, who are usually Christian-oriented, a respectful—repeat, respectful—conversation about some of the other great religions of the world can be both illuminating and ingratiating.

you are the only one who can't understand what he or she is saying, and you try to tell him or her to slow down.

Then when you do, everybody says, "If you don't understand, go to a lower class or get lost."

You have to live in somebody else's country to understand.

What is it like when you are an opposite?

When you wear the clothes of your country and they think you are crazy to wear these clothes and you think they are pretty.

What is it like when somebody bothers you when you do nothing to them?

You tell them to stop but they tell you that they didn't do anything to you.

Then, when they keep doing it until you can't stand it any longer, you go up to the teacher and tell him or her to tell them to stop bothering you.

They say that they didn't do anything to bother you.

Then the teacher asks the person sitting next to you.

He says, "Yes, she didn't do anything to her" and you have no witness to turn to.

So the teacher thinks you are a liar.

You have to live in somebody else's country to understand.

What is it like when you try to talk and you don't pronounce the words right?

They don't understand you.

They laugh at you but you don't know that they are laughing at you, and you start to laugh with them.

They say, "Are you crazy, laughing at yourself? Go get lost, girl."

You have to live in somebody else's country without a language to understand.

What is it like when you walk in the street and everybody turns around to look at you and you don't know that they are looking at you.

Then, when you find out, you want to hide your face but you don't know where to hide because they are everywhere.

You have to live in somebody else's country to feel it.[2]

These two vignettes comprise a plea for each of us to be sensitive and caring. But first, we need a historical overview to better understand the plight and challenge of being an immigrant in North America.

The Multicultural Roots of North America

The story of North America can be rightly called a history of immigrants and immigration. Both the United States and Canada are populated by people from around the world. Of all of the countries that could relate to the trials and experiences of immigrants and foreigners, the United States and Canada should be foremost. Unfortunately, this is often not the case.

United States (U.S.): Social scientists tell us, the United States (U.S.) is peopled by individuals from all nations. With the exception of descendants of Native Americans, a few Blacks who were here when the age of exploration began (1492), and the Africans who were brought here unwillingly in the 1600s, the rest of the population is primarily comprised of descendants of people who left their countries *voluntarily* to settle here and start a new life.

Such individuals, knowingly or unknowingly, are participants in the creation of a new and diverse culture. For Richard T. Schafer, the diversity of the American people is unmistakable evidence of the variety of places immigrants came from.[3] However, the different immigrating groups have not always welcomed one another. Instead, they nursed jealousies and rivalries, which have set in motion attitudes of intolerance, disrespect, and distrust. As diversity increases, so do the tensions.

The British and Spanish were not the only ones in the 1600s to come as colonists to the Americas. In 1624, the Dutch came and settled in New York, Connecticut, Delaware, and later, Pennsylvania. The Swedes and Germans also came and settled along the Atlantic Coast. Soon, these people became Anglicized in their language and practices. The eighteenth century followed with a steady flow of immigrants. The largest groups during the 1840s and 1850s were mainly from Northern and Western Europe, the Irish, the Germans, the Norwegians, the Swedes, and the Dutch. As people settled into the new country, the cultural conflict was severe.

In the late 1800s to early 1900s, another heavy contingency of immigrants—Jews, Poles, Slavs, Italians, and others—commonly known as "new immigrants"—came from Southern and Eastern Europe. They, too, suffered disdain. They settled in the cities and found low paying jobs in factories. Gradually they set up new communities for those who were beginning to turn away from the stress of the cities. In this same wave of immigration, Asians were allowed into the U.S. The Chinese were the first to come, and then the Japanese following 1890. For the Asians the glamour of coming to the U.S. was short-lived because soon they were restricted and circumscribed by the government. Anti-Oriental prejudice and the competition with American workers led to anti-Chinese riots (1877) in San Francisco, then to the Chinese Exclusion Act of 1882, which banned Chinese immigration for ten years. In 1943, a new law extended citizenship rights and permitted an annual immigration of 105 Chinese. The quota was abolished in 1965.

Following the Asian immigration, there was a steady influx of settlers who came from Latin America, the Caribbean, and other islands of the seas. They experienced deep hostility from many of the older immigrants. This hostility eventually led to a quota system. In 1976, the quota system was repealed, making way for more outsiders to come in. Preference was given to people who were highly skilled, well educated, and who had close relatives residing in the U.S. In this same decade, the political conditions of the world had changed, and a new form of immigrant-refugees were granted opportunity to enter American shores. Large numbers came from the Soviet Union, Cuba, Vietnam, Cambodia, and other regions where repressive governments made it difficult for people to live.[4]

According to demographic experts, the fastest growing ethnic group of the 1980s was neither Black nor White, but people of Asian and Pacific Islander ancestry. They increased seven times faster than the overall population. They account for 80 percent of this new group of immigrants and account for over 90 percent of its growth. The nine million Asians are currently under 4 percent of all Americans.

In the last decade the growth of minorities has been phenomenal. America's twenty-one million Hispanics grew at four times the national rate during the 1980s. If the Hispanic population continues to grow as quickly as it did in the 1980s, it will outnumber the Black population in the twenty-first century. At 12 percent of the total population, America's thirty million Blacks are still the nation's largest minority.

During the 1980s, Blacks gained less than one percentage point as a share of the total U.S. population. Meanwhile, the White population slipped from 86 percent of the total to 84 percent. In 2030 America's minorities will account for one-third of the entire population. Within ten years, one-third of the population under age eighteen will belong to a minority group.[5]

These rapidly changing demographics are what is fueling the new interest in diversity. Conditions are changing. Lifestyles and business are not what they used to be. People, all people of every ethnic group, are having to re-evaluate and reassess their role in the larger national and global family. The Church is not immune to this national introspection. However, in order to fulfill its mission, there must be denominational introspection as well.

Canada: What has been said of the United States can be resonated when describing Canada. According to *Statistics*

Canada, while nearly three-quarters of a million Canadians report some aboriginal origin, Canadian society has been built up, as successive waves of immigration have come to the Canadian shores. The census of 1911 to 1931 recorded that immigrants comprised 22 percent of the country's population. Before 1961, 87 percent of the immigrants who went to Canada were from Europe, 7 percent from the United States, 3 percent from Asia, and 3 percent came from the Caribbean, South and Central America, Africa, and Oceania (includes Australia, New Zealand, and the Pacific Islands). From 1981-1986, however, of the new immigrants to Canada, 43 percent came from Asia, 29 percent from Europe, 7 percent from the United States, and over 20 percent came from the Caribbean, Africa, and Oceania, collectively.

In effect, immigrant population in Canada has faced some of the same challenges being faced by immigrant population in the U.S., though perhaps to a lesser degree. One of the most interesting features of Canada's response to its immigration is its recognition of multiculturalism as fundamental in its constitution. Two languages have legal status—English and French. In 1986, more than four million Canadians reported that they could conduct a conversation in both English and French. Bilingual individuals represented more than 16 percent of the population. Quebec and New Brunswick recorded the highest rates of bilingualism at 34.5 percent and 29.1 percent, respectively. All Canadians, then, are grouped as English, French, or Allophones.[6] Like the U.S., Canada is having to adjust to the challenges of diversity.

A Rationale for Sensitivity

It is helpful to understand something of the immigration background of the two great neighbors of North America because it helps to emphasize that cultural and racial diversity have existed in North America long before the sixteenth century, when the first European settlers arrived to join the aboriginal peoples. Today we hear a lot about multiculturalism—multicultural education, multicultural evangelism, and multicultural families, etc. However, the aboriginal society has always been multicultural. What we are experiencing is a renewed interest in diversity and multiculturalism because of the rapidity with which the demographics are changing, the new sense of freedom and self-empowerment experienced by all people, and the imperative of cooperation and interdependence of all people.

The question is not "Can we all get along?" We must. Rather, we should more specifically ask "How can we all get along?" Therefore, the major question which we must answer, especially as a Church community, is "How can we develop sensitivity for the new and different peoples that now comprise our communities?" The challenge of every wave of immigration has always been "How can diverse populations live together in harmony and respect?"

The public strategies of pluralism and multiculturalism are secular conceptions which are intended to seek the harmony of all immigrants to the United States and Canada. As concepts, they mean that diverse groups and communities are free to retain their respective identities, while joining one another as equal partners in the building of the two North American nations. While it may not be widely known, "multiculturalism" is a Canadian creation. It is believed by some social scientists that within the next century, multiculturalism will become a successful Canadian export, as other nations adopt Canadian-style policies to achieve social harmony within their borders. Increasingly, the Canadian public is coming to recognize—as others already have—the importance and value of "the Canadian way" of nation building.

In an eloquent Canada Day essay published in the July 1, 1987, edition of *The Toronto Star*, Alla Gower, who taught English as a second language at an Etobicoke school observed: "All Canadians of whatever creed, background or colour have a destiny—a destiny to build a country." He also insisted that if Canadians can live in harmony and in peace, they could prove their country to be not only a land of freedom, but a land of justice and hope for those who follow, and the rest of the world will come to ask the Canadian secret.[7]

Unfortunately, Canada has not had a very great show of multiculturalism nor has the United States had a good demonstration of diversity. So with all the discussions of multiculturalism, diversity will doubtless continue for many years to come. This does not say, however, that we should not be learning strategies to increase how to appreciate and get along with people of different cultures. We should. However, as we look to the future, we must be more careful to clarify and refine our perceptions with people of other cultures. Further, from our faith and church perspective, we have much to model and teach the world about unity in diversity.

Journeying Toward Unity

A key question to ask is "what is the impact of diversity and multiculturalism on the unity and upbuilding of the Church?" We must also ask in a general way, "What are some of the pressing challenges created by diversity and multiculturalism for human relations?" It needs to be stated that no scientific data can lay out for Christians what the formula for successful relationship building is. Nor can the sciences cause us to make it the priority that it should be. Only the Holy Spirit and the Word of God can guide us in that process. As a result of this guidance, we have effective principles regarding commitment to loving, caring, and unity building that will help us in our relationship building. The following seven guidelines can help us in our journey to cross over the bridge of divisiveness to experience unity in diversity.

1. Crossing the friendship barriers. In a complex society, we discover that making friends across cultures is not always easy. But friendship building is possible if we learn how to welcome people, be warm enough to them, ask the right kinds of questions, and be sensitive to their answers. Two phrases that are useful and powerful are *"be informed"* and *"be gentle and respectful."* I have discovered that people are tolerant when they know I am respectful to them, even if they sense that I do not fully understand them. Generally they will go out of their way to provide necessary information to understand them. Once the ice is broken, it becomes easier to build understanding. People who have left the warmth and security of their country to enter another often feel lonely. The Church has a unique opportunity to be the first zone of comfort to help such people in their time of need. The Seventh-day Adventist teachings are ideally suited to speak to people in their need and to offer them new hope and vision.

2. Crossing language barriers. A conference president from a southern city and I were discussing the issue of multiculturalism. He told me that there were thirty-four ethnic groups in one of his congregations. The church was once Anglo, but now *only* the main worship is conducted in English. He further shared that he needed to find new ways of meeting several language needs, since on any given worship day one can hear several languages being spoken in the vestibule at the end of services. Listening to that president reminded me of the reality of diversity and its impact on the Church. There is much more diversity than Black and White, Anglo and Hispanic, Québécois and English. The current situation involves people from different language groups, gender, physical condition, age, and more. As a result, in order to look deeper than the traditional purposes, we have to look at the future of human relations from a linguistic point of view. The same challenges which caused many church leaders in the seventeenth and eighteenth centuries to learn new languages are here again. Even with a second Pentecost, the problems of multilingual relations will not go away. As the social situations change, we have to change. That means that learning a second language should not be considered an option. For by learning about the language and culture of our new arrivals, we can help to break down "high walls" of separation and misunderstanding and make way for meaningful relationship and witnessing opportunities.

When I went to Quebec in the 1970s as a student and pastor, language diversity was one of my first challenges.

Quebec is a different world, not because it is French but
because one is always "between two worlds"—French and
English. Whatever is being done for the churches in general
must always be adapted to a French *and* English mind-set.
Even in a small conference of churches, one also needs to pay
attention to Spanish, which is a vibrant part of the membership. In a workshop I conducted a few years ago, the language
difference was a facilitator because I was able to break out the
participants into language-area working groups. They were
able to look at their indigenous challenges and make appropriate recommendations. It was interesting to note that even
though languages might be different in a multicultural context, human needs and dreams remain essentially the same.
The working groups echoed the same needs. Potential for
conflict will always be present in language diversity because
language is the greatest tool for misunderstanding. But that
need not dissuade us. We can look at every challenge as an
opportunity for learning new ways of relating to one another.

Language diversity offers us creative possibilities. In our
church worship experience, we can give opportunities to our
new neighbors to pray, sing, and/or read a scripture in their
own language. Parker Palmer was right when he said, "If the
Church could become . . . a community—a place where people
confront the stranger in each other and in themselves, and
still know that they are members one of another—it would
help people enter the public sphere."[8]

3. Crossing competing cultural styles in worship. As
great as the high wall of language is, there are other things
that deserve attention in order to increase sensitivity in our
church culture for our new neighbors. Principal among those
needing attention is the worship liturgy. Discussions about
celebration worship is reflective of what some persons perceive as a shift from what is considered "normative" worship.
Since a "quiet" and more "cerebral" worship was thought to be
"normative," for some churches, any shift toward the direction of what was considered to be emotional has been resisted
by some members. New worship styles often lead to tension.

While this has been discussed at length in other contexts, I only state here that multicultural worship will challenge congregations to ask hard questions—"What worship style shall we use?" etc., etc.

It is not a matter of raising questions in order to exclude others. There must be a sincere desire to challenge our ways of doing things. It has to do with allowing ourselves to experiment with forms of worship which open our community to our new neighbors. These are difficult areas to work through. They take sensitivity, an understanding of the Bible principles of worship, and a willingness to balance *flexibility* to try new things with *commitment* to defined standards. But it can be an exciting search, and God will help us in our quest.

4. Crossing cultural chauvinism. Cultural chauvinism, like ethnocentrism, is an attitude of superiority that says my culture is better than yours, and I will protect it from you. In congregations it is usually produced by groups of people who are in positions of power and who fear being overtaken by an incoming group. Cultural chauvinism highlights the need for self preservation and the desire to maintain a homogenous community. It is a real challenge for those who call themselves third- and fourth-generation *natives*. Powerful people who have dominant roles may deny that they have power, yet they are easily threatened if they feel that their power is being usurped. Having worked closely with immigrant populations from Eastern and Western cultures, it is fascinating to me when I hear the complaints from the *natives* that the newcomers are aggressive. Inquiry often reveals that what is thought to be aggression is often frustration and desperation seeking acceptance.

When enough people of a different culture enter into a stable culture congregation, those members of the older tradition are not always ready to welcome them. It is believed that they have come "to take over." Andrew Hacker, in his groundbreaking book *Two Nations,* has shown that if Black arrivals in a community do not exceed 8 percent, Whites will stay. Once the Black proportion passes the 8 percent point, Whites begin to leave.[9]

The point can be replicated in many other ways. Cultural chauvinism is not created so much by "fear" as it is created by prejudice. Prejudice is pre-judgment. Prejudice is ignorance. And there is no one who can be judged more easily than the new neighbors we do not know. The lack of knowing, "ignorance" and "arrogance," leads to misunderstanding, misrepresentation, and fear.

When one person thinks his/her culture is superior, then he/she treats others as an "inferior" by acting in paternalistic ways. It is this superiority syndrome which says, "My customs, mores, and behavior are better than yours. You accept my ways and dictates. Learn from me, for I make the world." It is within this cultural chauvinistic attitude that the subordination and "putting down" of others develops.

When new people come into a community, often prejudices which remained hidden for generations begin to surface. People who fear the coming of others tend to react to them violently. When people feel strongly about differences of any kind (cultural, linguistic, or religious), they tend to accentuate these differences by emphasizing "the difference." Although we talk about difference, it is encouraging to note we have many similarities. Though we need not fear our differences, as Adventists we should highlight the similarities that are found in Christ as members of His body.

Let us remember we are all humans—homo sapiens—who have the same emotions of love, joy, sorrow, aspiration, and anguish. We need to give more attention to these matters as part of the training for cross-cultural life. As Paul, in Philippians states, let us emphasize the positive whenever possible (see Philippians 4:8). By so doing, we will begin to dismantle the structure of culture chauvinism.

5. Crossing the social problem of racism. Racism runs too profoundly in our culture. Unfortunately, the Church is not isolated from its effects. It is sometimes difficult to discern where personal racism ends and institutional racism begins. Both are difficult problems even in the Adventist Church. "Race," as

Elaine Pinderhughes insists, "takes on a cultural significance as a result of the social processes that sustain majority-minority status." The subordinate status assigned to persons with given physical traits (racial) and the projections made about them are used to justify exclusion or inclusion within the society. Obviously, this is wrong and unchristian.

The responses of both those who are dominant and therefore included, and the victims who are subordinate and therefore excluded, must be heard and responded to in the process of cultural adaptation.[10] In order to successfully cross this barrier, we need people to courageously stand for truth and justice (see Luke 4:16 ff).

In the U.S., society is confronted on all sides. On one hand, the rights of minorities still have to be met. Then there are the charges of reverse racism. There are appeals of the new neighbors for the visible involvement in leadership. All the concepts have elements that deserve attention. It is easy to become disheartened about our efforts for social equity. It should be remembered that the demands for power-sharing might seem difficult, but this, too, is a challenge to our hospitableness.

The most comfortable approach to protect our isolationism is simply to say, "Our new neighbors are just not qualified" or "the concerns are not legitimate." While that position is clearly not biblical, it also indicates that we need to examine our own motives. Why? Because power interactions between people determine whether their motives are characterized by dominance, subordination, or equality.

The willingness to create opportunities for our new neighbors and those in need is what love and Christianity is all about. It is part of our sensitivity to their divine personhood and to the reality of their right to exist. For the Christian, it speaks to their legitimate place in God's family.[11]

6. Crossing the world of labeling. When we discuss and relate to cultures different from our own, often unpleasant truth emerges. When we examine our perceptions of others, we often realize images inside us that are embarrassingly narrow. This is known as labeling. It is that practice that tends to treat our neighbors as a group without trying to know them as persons. Such labeling is carefully worked out. It works well in our antisocial world.

When we see African Americans, Anglos, Native Americans, Asians, Latinos-Hispanics, and others, labels cause us to fail to see them as people. Thus we fail to know the truth about their existence. That is, we fail to recognize the deceptive, irrational fears or misperceptions we have of other groups.

Each of us is compelled to acknowledge that it's not just "them" who are guilty of labeling but "we," too, are participants in this destructive way of thinking. It is important for us to pray for clear understanding of God, others, and ourselves so we can better relate to our neighbors. Like Clara Scott (1841-97), we can pray:

> Open my eyes, That I may see
> Glimpses of Truth thou hast for me;
> Place in my hands the wonderful key
> That shall unclasp and set me free.
>
> Open my ears, that I may hear;
> Voices of truth Thou sendest clear;
> And while the wave notes fall on my ear
> Everything false will disappear.
>
> Silently now I wait for thee,
> Ready my God, Thy will to see;
> Open my eyes, Illumine me,
> Spirit Divine.

These verses call us to truth. Truth that unmasks all falsehood, lying, and artificiality in our relationships. The challenge to Christians is to so identify ourselves with our neighbors that they might know they are appreciated—not as labels but as sons and daughters of God. This is the essence of celebrating diversity and building relationships.

7. Crossing the information resource barrier. We

should help those in need to adjust and make a success of their experience in the U.S. We need to inform our new neighbors about available resources and services. A significant, but overlooked, challenge facing the Church in North America today is how to make resources and services available and accessible to its new neighbors. For example, at a Resource Workshop I recently attended, I heard the plaintive concerns of people who are not able to obtain materials in their own language or ethnocultural framework. Even when materials are available, people don't seem to know how to obtain them at reasonable costs.

Resource control is an important question not only for Québécois, Haitians, Asians, and Native Americans, but for other disadvantaged groups. The need for helping people, therefore, to access these resources may be demanding, but it is a necessary part of helping our neighbors adjust and feel that we really care. This is a viable area for individual Adventists and conferences and institutions to become active in. Just as you did it to one of the least of these who are members of My family, you did it to Me (Matthew 25:40, NRSV). So Christ gives us our marching orders.

No Longer Strangers

Having presented what I believe are sensitive and effectual guidelines on how Adventists can cross over and help the international neighbors in our midst, we finally need to implement a new mental paradigm about our new neighbors. The future of the Church will be brighter—if we think of our new neighbors who are Adventists as neighbors for eternity and if we think of all our new neighbors who are non-Adventists as potential members.

As Bruce Larson counsels us that when we meet and minister to people with Christlike love, we make them no longer strangers but friends![12] George Barna said it another way; namely, that the Church in America has promulgated Christianity as a White man's faith for many decades. However, if the Church hopes to stem its current decline in numbers and influence, it must embrace minorities not only as equals, but as a key to future impact in ministry.

Obligation of Love

The importance of attending to the spiritual life of immigrant groups, our new neighbors, is underscored by surveys which show that Asians and Hispanics are more likely than native-born Whites and Blacks, to accept Christ as their Lord and Saviour.[13] This offers exciting possibilities for ministry (see Revelation 14).

We can move beyond talk and learn from the biblical injunctions on how new neighbors are to be treated. We have an obligation of love to them. Here are some ways we can better work with them:

• **Understand them:** You shall neither mistreat a stranger, nor oppress him; for you were strangers in the Land of Egypt (Exodus 22:21, NKJV).

• **Facilitate them:** You shall not oppress a stranger for you know the heart of a stranger, because you were strangers in the Land of Egypt (Exodus 23:9, NKJV).

• **Love them:** The stranger who dwells among you shall be to you as one born among you, and you shall love him as yourself; for you were strangers in the land of Egypt: I am the Lord your God (Leviticus 19:34, NKJV).

• **Empathize with them:** Therefore love the stranger; for you were strangers in the land of Egypt (Deuteronomy 10:19, NKJV).

• **Protect them:** The Lord watches over the strangers; he upholds the orphan and the widow, but the way of the wicked he brings to ruin (Psalms 146:9, NRSV).

• **Cooperate with them:** Foreigners shall build up your walls, and their kings shall minister to you; for in my wrath I struck you down, but in my favor I have had mercy on you (Isaiah 60:10, NRSV).

• **Share with them:** You will divide it by lot for an

inheritance for yourselves, and for the strangers who sojourn among you. . . . They shall be unto you as native born among the children of Israel; they shall have an inheritance (Ezekiel 47:22, NKJV).

• **Witness to them:** So then you are no longer strangers and aliens, but you are citizens with the saints and also members of the household of God (Ephesians 2:19, NRSV).

• **Assist them:** Do not neglect to show hospitality to strangers, for by doing that some have entertained angels without knowing it (Hebrews 13:2, NRSV).

• **Befriend them:** Beloved, you do faithfully whatever you do for the friends, even though they are strangers to you; they have testified to your love before the church (3 John 5:6, NRSV).

Understanding these injunctions is fundamental in a relationship with Christ (1 John 2) and of the Gospel Commission (Matthew 28:19, 20). Jesus showed in the story of "The Good Samaritan" (Luke 10:25-37) that community "upbuilding" and "growth" cannot be our only interest for sacrificial love.

Our attitude should not be what can I *get* but what can I *give*. Ellen White beautifully sums it up when she said: "The fact that we are under so great obligation to Christ places us under the most sacred obligation to those whom He died to redeem. We are to manifest toward them the same sympathy, the same tender compassion and the unselfish love, which Christ has manifested toward us. Selfish ambition, desire for supremacy, will die when Christ takes possession of the affections."[14]

The greatest biblical injunction on relationship building is to "love God with all our soul and mind and strength and our neighbor as ourselves." Nowhere is this more genuinely tested than in the context of new neighbors. They are lonely and waiting for people who will befriend them. They are frightened and waiting for people who will calm their fears. They are hurting and waiting for people who will listen, understand, accept them. This then is the true test of a neighbor. Brian Wren (1976) said it well:

As Christ breaks bread for us to share
Each proud division ends.
That love that made us makes us one,
And strangers now are friends,
And strangers now are friends.

D. Robert Kennedy, Ed.D., is an associate professor of religion at Atlantic Union College. He is a writer, speaker, and workshop facilitator. He has done ministry and training in a variety of multicultural settings. He and his wife Selsie have three sons.

Endnotes

1. The person who gave this description of his cultural pilgrimage is Chann Touch, a Cambodian student at Atlantic Union College. He is now in his final year of nursing and is very conscious about building community across cultures.

2. By Noy Chou, taken from *A World of Difference: Teacher-Student Resource Guide: Anti Defamation League of B' nai B'rith* (1986), Lesson 15, 93.

3. Richard T. Schafer, *Racial and Ethnic Groups*, 113.

4. Barton J. Berstein and Allen J. Matusow (eds.), *Twentieth Century America: Recent Interpretations* (New York: Harcourt Brace Jovanovich, Inc. 1972), 136-166; Melvin Schwartz and John O'Connor, *Exploring American History* (New York: Glove Book Company, Inc., 1986), 276-281; 368-371.

5. Judith Waldrop and Thomas Exter, "The Legacy of the 90s," *American Demographics*, March 1991, 32-38.

6. *Statistics Canada*, 1990; cf. Canadian: Current Issues in *Multiculturalism Review*, Library of Parlimament, 1988 (ed). For a clear understanding of how multiculturalism developed in Canada, contact The Research Branch of the Library of Parliament or any Canadian Public Library. Their bibliography on the theme is extensive.

7. Alla Gower, *Toronto Star*, 1 July 1987.

8. Parker Palmer, *The Company of Strangers: Christians and the Renewal of America's Public Life* (New York: Crossroad, 1981).

9. Andrew Hacker, *Two Nations* (New York: McGraw-Hill, 1983), 59-64.

10. Elaine Pinderhughes, *Understanding Race, Ethnicity, and Power* (New York: The Free Press, 1989), 21

11. Elaine Pinderhughes, *Understanding Race, Ethnicity, and Power* (New York: The Free Press, 1989), 9.

12. Bruce Larson, *No Longer Strangers* (Waco, Tex.: Word, 1971).

13. George Barna, *The Frog in the Kettle: What Christians Need to Know About Life in the Year 2000* (Ventura, Calif.: Regal Books, 1990).

14. Ellen White, *Testimonies for the Church*, (Boise, Idaho: Pacific Press Publishing Association, 1948), 5:170.

―――――――――――――*12*―――――――――――――

Resources for Diversity: Inspired Counsel

Delbert W. Baker

The principles from the Bible and Ellen White's writings on how to achieve unity in diversity are as relevant now as when first written. The counsel supersedes the best literature in the area of diversity in that it practically incorporates spiritual and relational principles.

*D*iversity and multiculturalism didn't exist as such in Ellen White's day. However, in principle she provided counsel on diversity, building relationships and multiculturalism via her counsel on the work in the South, White-Black race relations and leadership issues. Though Ellen White didn't specifically speak on diversity and multiculturalism we have a rich source of counsel to draw from. While the principles may not always be obvious they can be discovered through prayer and study.

Principle-Centered Approach

When a person desires to apply Ellen White's counsel to a modern situation, it is helpful to use what can be called a "principle-centered approach" (PCA). A principle is a fundamental truth, law or axiom. It is an unchanging truth that may be applied with success to different situations. The principle-centered approach means that a person reads the Spirit of Prophecy, the writings of Ellen White, with a deliberate sensitivity for applicable principles for today.

The PCA builds on the basics of successful Spirit of Prophecy study. For example, when one studies the writings of Ellen White a primary goal should be *understanding*. The first question one should ask is "what was Ellen White's original and fundamental message." Often the point or purpose of the passage is obvious from the beginning. However, if the original intent is not clear, effort should be made to discover the context in which the statement was made. This may take time and study but the results are well worth the effort. Throughout the process, the PCA will cause one to be on the lookout for the underlying rule or principle in the reading.

You will find that if you invest the time and energy you will come away with a helpful principle(s). When commenting on how to use her writings, Ellen White said "Regarding the testimonies, nothing is to be ignored; nothing is cast aside; but time and place must be considered" (Selected Messages, 1:57).

The steps are straightforward. *First*, expose yourself to the broad counsel that she has given on a topic. *Second*, value everything written. *Third*, carefully note the *time* (the period in history when the counsel was given) and *place* (the motivating situation or circumstances) that provided the context for her counsel. *Fourth*, apply the principle to an appropriate modern-day situation unless the specifics of time or place invalidate a broader application of her counsel. *Fifth*, the final check should be to seek to verify that the principle is consistent with the wider counsel in the Bible and Spirit of Prophecy.

When we follow this approach, we can rest on the promise that "circumstances and emergencies will arise for which the

Lord must give special instruction. But if we begin to work, depending wholly upon the Lord, watching, praying, and walking in harmony with the light He sends us, we shall not be left to walk in darkness" (Letter 192, 1906).

The problems and challenges faced in the area of diversity are often difficult to deal with. Many problems occur due to selfishness, misunderstanding, human nature, and an unwillingness to followBible principles. Therefore the ultimate solution to diversity issues and relational problems must be spiritual. Though there is room for a plethora of approaches and applications, the real and lasting answer to relationships and diversity challenges is found in Christ. It is here Ellen White makes a major contribution to the literature on diversity and relationship building. Programs, methods, techniques, as well as workshops, seminars and interactive encounters are helpful and in many cases should be encouraged. However, it should be foremost to a Christian that the real and lasting solution is found in Christ and His Word. The reader will find Ellen White's counsel practical, sensitive and spiritual. It speaks to the heart as well as to the mind.

Consistent with the PCA the following quotations have been selected from Ellen White's writings. Each quotation speaks in principle to different aspects of diversity, and relationship building, and leadership in the SDA Church. The counsel is divided into several categories. The first category is a compilation of some *Selected Scriptures* Ellen White used in relation to topics having to do with race relations, relationship building and diversity topics. The references are listed for convenience and study. The second category provides counsel relative to *Enabling Attitudes* that Christians can nurture in order to build successful relationships with diverse members in the body of Christ. The last category describes specific *Effective Actions* that a Christian can take to build relationships and prevent or resolve diversity problems. Each quotation is introduced with a lead sentence that highlights an inherent principle.

Selected Scriptures

Old Testament

Text	Topic
Exodus 12	Freedom
Exodus 20:8-11; 23:12	Equity
Deuteronomy 6	Word of God
Deuteronomy 10:19	Strangers
Deuteronomy 15:7-11	Poor
1 Samuel 20	Friendship
Psalms 119	Guidance
Psalms 121	Providence
Proverbs 3	Wisdom
Proverbs 24:17	Graciousness
Proverbs 25:21-22	Enemies
Isaiah 56:1-8	Inclusiveness
Isaiah 58	Service
Isaiah 61:1-3	Liberation
Micah 6:8	Expectations

New Testament

Matthew 5, 6, 7	Lifestyle
Matthew 18:15-20	Resolution
Matthew 22:37-40	Model
Matthew 28:16-20	Commission
Mark 11:25-26	Condition
Luke 4:16-21	Deliverance
Luke 6:27-35	Retaliation
Luke 6:35-38	Forgiveness
Luke 10:30-37	Neighbors
John 4	Spirituality
John 13	Humility
John 15	Fruit
John 15:1-5	Strength
John 17	Love
Acts 10	Multiculturalism
Acts 15:36-40; 2 Timothy 4:11	Reconciliation
Acts 17:26	Origins
Romans 12	Relationships
Romans 13:11	Fulfillment
Romans 14	Brotherhood
1 Corinthians 12	Cooperation

1 Corinthians 13	Love
Galatians 2:11-14	Discrimination
Galatians 5:14	Preeminent
Galatians 5:22-26	Virtues
Galatians 6	Helper
Ephesians 2:12-22	Believers
Ephesians 4	Unity
Philippians 4	Attitudes
James 2:1-9	Favoritism
James 3	Communication
James 5:1-6	Justice
2 Peter 1	Development
1 John	Relationships
Revelation 14	Diversity

Enabling Attitudes. . .

Attitudes Toward One's Self

"Finally, brothers, whatever is true, whatever is noble, whatever is right, whatever is pure, whatever is lovely, whatever is admirable—if anything is excellent or praiseworthy—think about such things" (Philippians 4:8, NIV).

1. Increasing diversity sensitivity and relationship building begins in the heart. "When the Spirit of God takes possession of the heart, it transforms the life. Sinful thoughts are put away, evil deeds are renounced; love, humility, and peace take the place of anger, envy, and strife. Joy takes the place of sadness, and the countenance reflects the light of heaven" (*The Desire of Ages*, 173).

2. A healthy self-image (how we see ourselves) and self-esteem (how we feel about ourselves) is found in a personal relationship with Christ. "None have fallen so low, none are so vile, but that they can find deliverance in Christ... No cry from a soul in need, though it fail of utterance in words, will be unheeded. Those who will consent to enter into covenant relation with the God of heaven are not left to the power of Satan or to the infirmity of their own nature" (*The Desire of Ages*, 258, 259).

3. Personal potential and value are discovered through faith in the providence of God regardless of race, culture, gender, appearance, status, economics and physical condition. "Man is of value with God in proportion as he permits the divine image to be retraced upon his soul. However misshapen has been his character, although he may have been counted as an outcast among men, the man who permits the grace of Christ to enter his soul will be reformed in character and will be raised up from the condition of his guilt, degradation, and wretchedness. God has made every provision in order that the lost one may become His child. The frailest human being may be elevated, ennobled, refined, and sanctified by the grace of God. . . . Whatever may be the nationality or color, whatever may be the social condition. . . . No one is to be looked upon with indifference or to be regarded as unimportant, for every soul has been purchased with an infinite price" (*The Southern Work,* 31).

4. Godliness and cultural sensitivity requires self-examination. "I call upon every church in our land to look well to your own soul. 'Examine yourselves whether ye be in the faith; prove your own selves. Know ye not your own selves, how that Jesus Christ is in you, except ye be reprobates?' God makes no distinction between the North and the South. Whatever may be your prejudices, your wonderful prudence, do not lose sight of this fact, that unless you put on Christ, and His Spirit dwells in you, you are slaves of sin and Satan. Many who claim to be children of God are children of the wicked one, and have his passions, his prejudices, his evil spirit, his unlovely traits of character. But the soul that is indeed transformed will not despise any one whom Christ has purchased with His own blood" (*The Southern Work,* 13).

5. Love is more powerful than prejudice. "The walls of sectarianism and caste and race will fall down when the true missionary spirit enters the hearts of men. Prejudice is melted away by the love of God" (*The Southern Work*, 55).

Attitudes Toward Others

"I am the true vine, and my Father is the gardener. He cuts off every branch in me that bears no fruit, while every branch that does bear fruit he prunes so that it will be even more fruitful. You are already clean because of the word I have spoken to you. Remain in me, and I will remain in you. No branch can bear fruit by itself; it must remain in the vine. Neither can you bear fruit unless you remain in me. I am the vine; you are the branches. If a man remains in me and I in him, he will bear much fruit; apart from me you can do nothing" (John 15:1-5, NIV).

1. Divine assistance for relationship problems will come if we cooperate. "If we surrender our lives to His service, we can never by placed in a position for which God has not made provision. Whatever may be our situation, we have a Guide to direct our way; whatever our perplexities, we have a sure Counselor; whatever our sorrow, bereavement, or loneliness, we have a sympathizing Friend. If in our ignorance we make missteps, Christ does not leave us. His voice, clear and distinct, is heard saying, 'I am the Way, the Truth, and the Life'" (*Christ's Object Lessons,* 173).

2. Character development happens when we handle difficult people and problems in a spiritual manner. "If we encounter difficulties, and in Christ's strength overcome them; if we meet enemies, and in Christ's strength put them to flight; if we accept responsibilities, and in Christ's strength discharge them faithfully, we are gaining a precious experience. We learn, as we could not otherwise have learned, that our Savior is a present help in every time of need" (*Testimonies for the Church,* 5:34).

3. Racial problems are instigated by Satan and will probably remain a challenge. "The powers of hell are working with all their ingenuity to prevent the proclamation of the last message of mercy among the colored people. Satan is working to make it most difficult for the gospel minister and teacher to ignore the prejudice that exists between the white and the colored people." "The relation of the two races has been a matter hard to deal with, and I fear that it will ever remain a most perplexing problem" (*Testimonies for the Church*, 9:208; *The Southern Work*, 83).

4. Racial deeds or misdeeds that are done are as done to Christ Himself. "Those who slight a brother because of his color are slighting Christ." "God weighs actions, and every one who has been unfaithful in his stewardship, who has failed to remedy evils which it was in his power to remedy, will be of no esteem in the courts of heaven. Those who are indifferent to the wants of the needy will be counted as unfaithful stewards, and will be registered as enemies of God and man. Those who misappropriate the means that God has entrusted to them to help the very ones who need their help, prove that they have no connection with Christ, because they fail to manifest the tenderness of Christ toward those who are less fortunate than themselves. As Christians, we are to manifest to the world the character of Christ in all the affairs of life. To be a Christian means to act in Christ's stead, to represent Christ. We are not to get rid of the responsibilities that connect us with our fellow men" (*The Southern Worker*, 13, 38).

5. Unity and equality are the outworking of a relationship with Christ. "Christ recognized no distinction of nationality or rank or creed. . . . Christ came to break down every wall of partition. He came to show that His gift of mercy and love is as unconfined as the air, the light, or the showers of rain that refresh the earth. The life of Christ established a religion in which there is no caste, a religion by which Jew and Gentile, free and bond, are linked in a common brotherhood, equal before God. No question of policy influenced His movements. He made no difference between neighbors and strangers, friends and enemies. That which appealed to His heart was a soul thirsting for the waters of life. . . . He sought to inspire with hope the roughest and most unpromising, setting before them the assurance that they might become blameless and harmless, attaining such a character as would make them manifest as the children of God" (*The Ministry of Healing*, 25, 26).

Attitudes Toward the Church

"For through him we both have access to the Father by one Spirit. Consequently, you are no longer foreigners and aliens, but fellow citizens with God's people and members of God's household, built on the foundation of the apostles and prophets, with Christ Jesus himself as the chief cornerstone. In him the whole building is joined together and rises to become a holy temple in the Lord. And in him you too are being built together to become a dwelling in which God lives by his Spirit" (Ephesians 2:18-22, NIV)

1. The Church is one. "The life of Christ established a religion in which there is no caste, a religion by which Jew and Gentile, free and bond, as linked in a brotherhood, equal before God" "In calling God our Father, we recognize all His children as our brethren. We are all a part of the great web of humanity, all members of one family" (*Gospel Workers*, 46; *Sons and Daughters of God*, 267).

2. Diversity synergy (the combined action/function of all parts) is found in the Christ bond. "Christ came to this earth with a message of mercy and forgiveness. He laid the foundation for a religion by which Jew and Gentile, black and white, free and bond, are linked together in one common brotherhood, recognized as equal in the sight of God. The Savior has a boundless love for every human being. In each one He sees capacity for improvement. With divine energy and hope He greets those for whom He has given His life. In His strength they can live a life rich in good works, filled with the power of the Spirit" (*Selected Messages*, 2:485, 486).

3. In racial as in other matters the Christian is challenged to be gracious rather than petty. "When the Holy Spirit moves upon human minds, all petty complaints and accusations between man and his fellow man will be put away. The bright beams of the Sun of Righteousness will shine into the chambers of the mind and heart. In our worship of God there will be no distinction between rich and poor, white and black. All prejudice will be melted away. When we approach God, it will be as one brotherhood. We are pilgrims and strangers, bound for a better country, even a heavenly. There all pride, all accusation, all self-deception, will forever have an end. Every mask will be laid aside, and we shall 'see Him as He is.' There our songs will catch the inspiring theme, and praise and thanksgiving will go up to God" (*Review and Herald*, 24 Oct. 1899).

4. The Bible is the essential resource for principles for diversity and relational issues. "The Bible is a precious treasure. It should be in every home, not to be laid away or put upon a shelf, but to be diligently studied. The Bible is the hope of both the white and the colored race. . . . The Bible is the poor man's book, and all classes of people are to search the Scriptures for themselves. God has given reasoning powers to men, and by bringing our mental faculties into connection with the Word of God, the spiritual powers are awakened, and common people, as well as teachers and clergymen, may understand the will of God." "The Lord has given us light concerning all such matters. There are principles laid down in His Word that should guide us in dealing with these perplexing questions [racial issues]. The Lord Jesus came to our world to save men and women of all nationalities." "Christ's teaching, like His sympathies, embraced the world. Never can there be a circumstance of life, a crisis in human experience, which has not been anticipated in His teaching, and for which its principles have not a lesson" (*The Southern Work*, 46; 9; *Education*, 81, 82).

5. The remnant will triumph over every obstacle in diversity and race relations. "When the Holy Spirit is poured out, there will be a triumph of humanity over prejudice in seeking the salvation of the souls of human beings. God will control minds. Human hearts will love as Christ loved. And the color line will be regarded by many very differently from the way in which it is now regarded. To love as Christ loves lifts the mind into a pure, heavenly, unselfish atmosphere" (*Testimonies for the Church*, 9:209).

Attitudes Toward God

"I lift up my eyes to the hills— where does my help come from? My help comes from the Lord, the Maker of heaven and earth. He will not let your foot slip— he who watches over you will not slumber; indeed, he who watches over Israel will neither slumber nor sleep. The LORD watches over you— the LORD is your shade at your right hand; the sun will not harm you by day, nor the moon by night. The LORD will keep you from all harm— he will watch over your life; the LORD will watch over your coming and going both now and forevermore" (Psalm 121, NIV).

1. Adam and God, the Creator, objectify our origins and similarities. "The genealogy of our race, as given by inspiration, traces back its origin, not to a line of developing germs, mollusks, and quadrupeds, but to the great Creator. Though formed from the dust, Adam was the 'son of God' " (*Patriarchs and Prophets*, 45).

2. Christ came to provide salvation for all people— persons of all races and ethnicities have equal access to His grace and providence. "No distinction on account of nationality, race, or caste, is recognized by God. He is the Maker of all mankind. All men are of one family by creation, and all are one through redemption. Christ came to demolish every wall of partition, to throw open every compartment of the temple, that every soul may have free access to God. . . . In Christ there is neither Jew nor Greek, bond nor free. All are brought nigh by His precious blood" (*Christ's Object Lessons*, 386).

3. God has special pity and assistance for people who have greater burdens to bear than others. "The Lord's eye is upon all His creatures; He loves them all, and makes no difference between black and white, except that He has a special pity for those who are called to bear a greater burden than others. Those who love God and believe on Christ as their Redeemer, while they must meet the trials and difficulties that lie in their path, should yet with a cheerful spirit accept their life as it is, considering that God above regards these things, and for all that the world neglects to bestow, He will Himself make up to them in the best of favors" (*The Southern Work*, 12).

4. God identifies with the oppressed and acts to deliver them through His providence and followers. "When the Hebrew people were suffering cruel oppression under the hand of their task masters, the Lord looked upon them, and He called Israel His son. . . . God cares no less for the souls of the African race that may be won to serve Him than He cared for Israel." "The Lord God of Israel has looked upon the vast number of human beings who were held in slavery in the United States of America. The United States has been a refuge for the oppressed. It has been spoken of as the bulwark of religious liberty. God has done more for this country than for any other country upon which the sun shines. It has been marvelously preserved from war and bloodshed. God saw the foul blot of slavery upon this land, he marked the sufferings that were endured by the colored people. He moved upon the hearts of men to work in behalf of those who were so cruelly oppressed. . . . God spoke concerning the captivity of the colored people as verily as he did concerning the Hebrew captives, and said: 'I have surely seen the affliction of my people . . . , and have heard their cry by reason of their taskmasters; for I know their sorrows; and I am come down to deliver them.' The Lord wrought in freeing the Southern slaves; but he designed to work still further for them as he did for the children of Israel, whom he took forth to educate, to refine, and ennoble. . . . The condition of the colored people is no more helpless than was the condition of the Hebrew slave" (*The Southern Work*, 14, 42, 43).

5. Salvation and sanctification is God's solution to problems and challenges of race and diversity. "When the sinner is converted he receives the Holy Spirit, that makes him a child of God, and fits him for the society of the redeemed and the angelic host. He is made a joint heir with Christ. Whoever of the human family give themselves to Christ, whoever hear the truth and obey it, become children of one family. The ignorant and the wise, the rich and the poor, the heathen and the slave, white or black—Jesus paid the purchase money for their souls. If they believe on Him,

His cleansing blood is applied to them. The black man's name is written in the book of life beside the white man's. All are one in Christ. Birth, station, nationality, or color cannot elevate or degrade men. The character makes the man. If a red man, a Chinese, or an African give his heart to God, in obedience and faith, Jesus loves him none the less for this color. He calls him His well-beloved brother. . . . The day is coming when the kings and the lordly men of the earth would be glad to exchange places with the humblest African who has laid hold on the hope of the gospel" (*The Southern Work*, 12, 13).

Effective Actions . . .

Actions Toward Self

"Through these he has given us his very great and precious promises, so that through them you may participate in the divine nature and escape the corruption in the world caused by evil desires. For this very reason, make every effort to add to your faith goodness; and to goodness, knowledge; and to knowledge, self-control; and to self-control, perseverance; and to perseverance, godliness; and to godliness, brotherly kindness; and to brotherly kindness, love. For if you possess these qualities in increasing measure, they will keep you from being ineffective and unproductive in your knowledge of our Lord Jesus Christ" (2 Peter 1:4-8, NIV).

1. Learn about each other, study how best to support each other and work together. "There are no two leaves of a tree precisely alike; neither do all minds run in the same direction. But while this is so, there may be unity in diversity. . . . Look at the flowers in a carpet, and notice the different colored threads. All are not pink, all are not green, all are not blue. A variety of colors are woven together to perfect the pattern. So it is in the design of God. He has a purpose in placing us where we must learn to live as individuals" (*Review and Herald*, 4 July 1899).

2. Monitor your emotions and perceptions. "We sustain a most solemn relation one to another. Our influence is always either for or against the salvation of souls. . . . There are thoughts and feelings suggested and aroused by Satan that annoy even the best of men; but if they are not cherished, if they are repulsed as hateful, the soul is not contaminated with guilt, and no other is defiled by their influence" (*Review and Herald*, 27 March 1888).

3. Through the help of Christ and personal effort determine to overcome every prejudice and negative attitude. "Men may have both hereditary and cultivated prejudices, but when the love of Jesus fills the heart, and they become one with Christ, they will have the same spirit that He had. If a colored brother sits by their side, they will not be offended or despise him. They are journeying to the same heaven, and will be seated at the same table to eat bread in the kingdom of God. If Jesus is abiding in our hearts we cannot despise the colored man who has the same Savior abiding in his heart" (*The Southern Work*, 14).

4. Deliberately view every person as a neighbor and facilitate the maturation as your grow in respect, inclusion and compassion. "Christ tears away the wall of partition, the self-love, the dividing prejudice of nationality, and teaches a love for all the human family. He lifts men from the narrow circle that their selfishness prescribes; He abolishes all territorial lines and artificial distinctions of society. He makes no difference between neighbors and strangers, friends and enemies. He teaches us to look upon every needy soul as our neighbor and the world as our field" (*Thoughts From the Mount of Blessing*, 42).

5. Practice the abundance-assistance rule—where much is given much is required—and where you have much and others have little, help them. "Those who have been favored with opportunities of education and culture, who have had every advantage and religious influence, will be expected of God to possess pure and holy characters in accordance with the gifts bestowed. But have they rightly improved their advantages? We know they have not. Let these privileged ones make the most of their blessings, and realize that they are thus placed under greater obligation to labor for the good of others" (*The Southern Work*, 16).

Actions Toward Others

"You were taught, with regard to your former way of life, to put off your old self, which is being corrupted by its deceitful desires; to be made new in the attitude of your minds; and to put on the new self, created to be like God in true righteousness and holiness. Therefore each of you must put off falsehood and speak truthfully to his neighbor, for we are all members of one body. 'In your anger do not sin' : Do not let the sun go down while you are still angry, and do not give the devil a foothold. He who has been stealing must steal no longer, but must work, doing something useful with his own hands, that he may have something to share with those in need. Do not let any unwholesome talk come out of your mouths, but only what is helpful for building others up according to their needs, that it may benefit those who listen. And do not grieve the Holy Spirit of God, with whom you were sealed for the day of redemption. Get rid of all bitterness, rage and anger, brawling and slander, along with every form of malice. Be kind and compassionate to one another, forgiving each other, just as in Christ God forgave you" (Ephesians 4:23-32, NIV).

1. Create diverse teams where all can learn from the other—collaborate, share and grow together. "In the Lord's plan human beings have been made necessary to one another. If all would do their utmost to help those who need their help, their unselfish sympathy and love, what a blessed work might be done. To everyone God has entrusted talents. These talents we are to use to help one another to walk in the narrow path. In this work each one is connected with the others, and all are united with Christ. It is by unselfish service that we improve and increase our talent" (*Mind, Character, and Personality*, 2:431).

2. Practice turning to Christ in the midst of interpersonal problems—He will help you resolve and deal with any problem. "If we encounter difficulties, and in Christ's strength overcome them; if we meet enemies, and in Christ's strength put them to flight; if we accept responsibilities, and in Christ's strength discharge them faithfully, we are gaining a precious experience. We learn, as we could not otherwise have learned, that our Savior is a present help in every time of need" (*Testimonies for the Church*, 5:34).

3. Remember that unity in diversity is an indisputable argument in favor of the gospel. "We seldom find two persons exactly alike. Among human beings as well as among the things of the natural world, there is diversity. Unity in diversity among God's children, the manifestation of love and forebearance in spite of disposition, this is the testimony that God sent His Son into the world to save sinners" (*Sons and Daughters of God*, 286).

4. Use positional power, influence and wealth in a judicial and balanced manner. "The high-handed power that has been developed, as though positions had made men gods, makes me afraid, and ought to cause fear. It is a curse wherever, and by whomsoever it is exercised. This lording it over God's heritage will create such a disgust of man's jurisdiction that a state of insubordination will result. The people are learning that men in high positions of responsibility cannot be trusted to mold and fashion other men's minds and characters. The result will be a loss of confidence even in the management of faithful men" (Letter 55, 1895).

5. Honor and respect each member and group for the part they play in the body of Christ. "Each one is to stand in his lot and in his place, doing his work. Every individual among you must before God do a work for these last days that is great and sacred and grand. Every one must bear his weight of responsibility. The Lord is preparing each one to do his appointed work, and each one is to be respected and honored as a brother chosen of God, and precious in His sight. One man is not to be selected to whom all plans and methods shall be confided, while the others are left out. If this is done, errors will be made; wrong moves will be taken. Harm, rather than good will be done. No one of you needs to be afraid of the other" (Letter 49, 1897).

Actions Toward the Church

"The body is a unit, though it is made up of many parts; and though all its parts are many, they form one body. So it is with Christ. For we were all baptized by one Spirit into one body—whether Jews or Greeks, slave or free—and we were all given the one Spirit to drink. Now the body is not made up of one part but of many. If the foot should say, 'Because I am not a hand, I do not belong to the body,' it would not for that reason cease to be part of the body. And if the ear should say, 'Because I am not an eye, I do not belong to the body,' it would not for that reason cease to be part of the body. If the whole body were an eye, where would the sense of hearing be? If the whole body were an ear, where would the sense of smell be? But in fact God has arranged the parts in the body, every one of them, just as he wanted them to be. If they were all one part, where would the body be? As it is, there are many parts, but one body. The eye cannot say to the hand, 'I don't need you!' And the head cannot say to the feet, 'I don't need you!' On the contrary, those parts of the body that seem to be weaker are indispensable, and the parts that we think are less honorable we treat with special honor. And the parts that are unpresentable are treated with special modesty, while our presentable parts need no special treatment. But God has combined the members of the body and has given greater honor to the parts that lacked it, so that there should be no division in the body, but that its parts should have equal concern for each other. If one part suffers, every part suffers with it; if one part is honored, every part rejoices with it. Now you are the body of Christ, and each one of you is a part of it" (1 Corinthians 12:12-27, NIV).

1. Actively support unity and diversity in the Church—talk it, act it, be it. "Thus Christ sought to teach the disciples the truth that in God's kingdom there are no territorial lines, no caste, no aristocracy; that they must go to all nations, bearing to them the message of a Saviour's love" (*The Acts of the Apostles*, 20).

2. Join together and consult with each other for the accomplishment of the work. "As brethren located where you must be more or less connected, you must draw closer together in your councils, in your associations, in spirit, and in all your works. One man among you is not to be made the counselor for all" (Letter 49, 1897).

3. Share leadership, responsibilities, decision making, and resources among diverse groups in the Church. "God has not set any kingly power in the Seventh-day Adventist Church to control the whole body, or to control any branch of the work. He has not provided that the burden of leadership shall rest upon a few men. Responsibilities are distributed among a large number of competent men" (*Testimonies for the Church*, 8:236).

4. Help obstinate or difficult believers to cooperate with each other and broader counsel. "Obstinacy is a barrier to all improvement. An obstinate man will not be readily convinced of anything which his sight cannot take in. He does not know what it means to walk by faith. He adheres to his own plans and opinions, be they right or wrong, because he has already adopted this line of thought. He may have abundant reason to see that he is wrong; his brethren may raise their voices against his opinions and his methods for making a success of the work; but he cherishes an almost immovable bar against conviction" (Manuscript 159, 1898).

5. Diversity and relationship building are "effortful"— they take timing, flexibility, and understanding— strength, solutions, and security result from such efforts. "In different places and under varying circumstances, the subject will need to be handled differently." "We are not to be in haste to define the exact course to be pursued in the future." "Let them understand that this plan is to be followed until the Lord shows us a better way." "I have heard the angel voice saying, 'Press together, press together, press together. Do not let Satan cast his hellish shadow between brethren. Press together; in unity there is strength" (*Testimonies for the Church*, 9:2, 13, 209, 207; *Selected Messages*, 2:374).

Actions Toward Goals

"Brothers, I do not consider myself yet to have taken hold of it. But one thing I do: Forgetting what is behind and straining toward what is ahead, I press on toward the goal to win the prize for which God has called me heavenward in Christ Jesus" (Philippians 3:13, 14, NIV).

1. Activate love to disarm prejudice. "Walls of separation have been built up between the whites and the blacks. These walls of prejudice will tumble down of themselves as did the walls of Jericho, when Christians obey the Word of God, which enjoins on them supreme love to their Maker and impartial love to their neighbors" (*The Southern Work*, 43).

2. Resolve relationship problems with kindness. "We may never know until the judgment the influence of a kind, considerate course of action to the inconsistent, the unreasonable, and unworthy. If after a course of provocation and injustice on their part, you treat them as you would an innocent person, you even take pains to show them special acts of kindness, then you have acted the part of a Christian; and they become surprised and ashamed, and see their course of action and meanness more clearly than if you plainly stated their aggravated acts to rebuke them" (*Medical Ministry*, 209, 210).

3. Be lovable. "Let Christ be seen in all that you do. Let all see that you are living epistles of Jesus Christ. . . . Be lovable. Let your life win the hearts of all who are brought in contact with you. There is too little done at the present time to render the truth attractive to others" (*Mind, Character, and Personality*, 2:433).

4. Solve difficulties. "If pride and selfishness were laid aside, five minutes would remove most difficulties" (*Early Writings*, 119).

5. Respond to confrontation with kindness. "We may never know until the judgment the influence of a kind, considerate course of action to the inconsistent, the unreasonable, and unworthy. If after a course of provocation and injustice on their part, you treat them as you would an innocent person, you even take the pains to show them special acts of kindnesses, then you have acted the part of a Christian, and they become surprised and ashamed and see their course of action and meanness more clearly than if you plainly stated their aggravated acts to rebuke them" (*Medical Ministry*, 209, 210).

6. Stop negativism whenever and wherever it may appear. "Caviling, ridicule, and misrepresentation can be indulged in only at the expense of the debasement of your own souls. The use of such weapons does not gain precious victories for you, but rather cheapens the mind, and separates the soul from God. Sacred things are brought down to the level of the common, and a condition of things is created that pleases the prince of darkness, and grieves away the Spirit of God" (*Life Sketches*, 325).

7. Focus on the big picture, avoid minor points when possible. "In our business meetings, it is important that precious time should not be consumed in debating points that are of small consequence. The habit of petty criticism should not be indulged; for it perplexes and confuses minds, and shrouds in mystery the things that are most plain and simple" (*Gospel Workers*, 447).

8. Always work toward resolution in diversity and relational areas, never give up. "It will be impossible to adjust all matters regarding the color question in accordance with the Lord's order until those who believe the truth are so closely united with Christ that they are one with Him. Both the white and the colored members of our churches need to be converted. There are some of both classes who are unreasonable, and when the color question is agitated, they manifest unsanctified, unconverted traits of character. Quarrelsome elements are easily aroused in those who, because they have never learned to wear the yoke of Christ, are opinionated and obstinate. In such, self clamors with an unsanctified determination for the supremacy" (Letter 105, 1904).

9. Be a blessing to yourself, others, and God. "In the

creation it was His purpose that the earth be inhabited by beings whose existence should be a blessing to themselves and to one another, and an honor to their Creator. All who will may identify themselves with this purpose" (*Education*, 174).

10. Do multicultural sharing. "There is no person, no nation, that is perfect in every habit and thought. One must learn of another. Therefore God wants the different nationalities to mingle together, to be one in judgment, one in purpose. Then the union that there is in Christ will be exemplified" (*Historical Sketches of the Foreign Missions of the Seventh-day Adventists*, 137).

11. Seek out and help those who are disadvantaged. "Many are in obscurity. They have lost their bearings. They know not what course to pursue. Let the perplexed ones search out others who are in perplexity and speak to them words of hope and encouragement. When they begin to do this work, the light of heaven will reveal to them the path that they must follow. By their words of consolation to the afflicted they themselves will be consoled. By helping others, they themselves will be helped out of their difficulties" (*Mind, Character, and Personality*, 2:431, 432).

12. Enrich your personal atmosphere. "It is of the greatest importance to us that we surround the soul with the atmosphere of faith. Every day we are deciding our own eternal destiny in harmony with the atmosphere that surrounds the soul. We are individually accountable for the influence that we exert, and consequences that we do not see will result from our words and actions" (*Mind, Character, and Personality*, 2:433, 434).

Delbert W. Baker, Ph.D., is special assistant to the president and director of diversity at Loma Linda University in Loma Linda, California. He is a professor on the faculty of religion and also teaches in the schools of public health and of medicine. He has been a pastor, teacher, editor, and administrator. He is the author of four books and does organizational and human relations training internationally. He and his wife, Susan, have three sons.

Epilogue

Love,
the Last Word

Calvin B. Rock

"And so abideth diversity, individuality and love, but the greatest of these is love."

*T*his book comes at a good time. It covers the gamut in terms of diversity and developing relationships with brothers and sisters of all ethnicities in the body of Christ. It comes at a good time because the SDA Church is at a crossroads in its history.

This year our Church is celebrating its 150th anniversary. It has experienced the special blessings of God in growth, vitality, and expansion. Our structures are imposing, and our influence is gowing. But how is it with our love for each other? How is it with our interpersonal interaction as we live out the gospel imperative to love one another? Love and oneness or unity in Christ is the real test of the genuineness of our experience.

Where are we on the road to the oneness that is found in a love relationship with Christ and with His followers? The Church is, by definition, one—"one Lord, one faith, one baptism" (Ephesians 4:5, KJV); one in truth, one in faith, and one in love. Richard Neuhaus, in his book *Freedom for Ministry*, says, "God is one, and all who are God's are one. The church is a communal articulation of that truth." But *where are we* individually and institutionally on the journey to oneness?

Yes, it is true that we don't just arrive at a state of oneness. It is a journey, rather than an event. But are we seeing progress toward oneness in our personal lives, our institutions, our churches, our conferences, our unions, our divisions? And what about our General Conference headquarters? No person or entity escapes the scrutiny of that penetrating question.

Have we reached the place as the body of Christ where we can relate to the statement in *Testimonies for the Church,* volume 9, that says, "The life of Christ established a religion in which there is no caste, a religion by which Jew and Gentile, free and bond, are linked in a common brotherhood, equal before God."

What an ideal that is! Equally, what a challenge that is. And the passage continues, "No question of policy influenced His [Christ] movements. He made no difference between neighbors and strangers, friends and enemies. That which appealed to His heart was a soul thirsting for the water of life" (9:191). This, then, is the theme of this book.

Conclusions

What precisely does this excellent book say about love? *First,* it teaches us that love is a divine principle and that genuine love for each other is the outworking of God's love for us. As all earth's energy comes from the sun, so all true love comes from God. Such love is more than respect or due regard. It is selfless humility in "working clothes"—God doing for others through us that which He ordains for our mutual benefit.

Second, we learn that love grows, that there are those used of God, who, like Peter of Acts 10, have not loved appropriately because they are deficient in understanding. Such individuals hindered by misinformation and a lack of profitable experience require only the kind of education that this book provides to correct their perspectives and enhance their loving and living.

Third, we learn that functioning in unity (or love) does not mean functioning in unison; that likeness is not sameness and that it is unity in diversity, not monolithic thinking or structures, that love requires. The varied backgrounds and experiences of the authors of this volume make it clear that each age, ethnic, and gender unit of humanity has its own particular outlook and needs.

True love does not find that offensive; it accepts such diversity as inevitable and wholseome and seeks to address the requirements of each in ways that best augment its prosperity. Genuine love does not chafe at genuine diversity. It blesses it with well-thought-out programs and helpful and creative initiatives; it honors all legitimate differences as good and refuses to force the diverse parts into any one mold.

Fourth, this books suggests to us practical ways of implementing the principles of love. Laced throughout its three sections are numerous ideas for love in action—hints and examples of how the authors fostered love's prerogatives and in consequence how we can individually pursue its lofty ideals. If love has worked for and through such a diverse educational and ethnic human variety as these, it can surely work for each one of us.

Fifth, the book reminds us that Jesus is both our inspiration and model for loving relations and that He who taught us to pray, "Our Father," and by whose sacrifices we are adopted into the family of God expects and in fact demands that we follow in His steps. In this sense, His life is not simply the "last" word. It is for His disciples the "only" word.

Calvin B. Rock, Ph.D., D.Min., is a vice-president for the General Conference. He chairs the boards for Loma Linda University, Loma Linda Medical Center, and the SDA work for China. He is an author, speaker, and former pastor and college president. He and his wife, Clara, have three daughters.

Glossary

The following are some key terms used in this book and in the area of diversity.

Acculturation. The process of becoming familiar and comfortable with, able to function with, and able to function within a different culture or environment, while retaining one's own cultural identity.

Affirmative action. Legally mandated programs whose aim is to (1) increase the employment opportunities of groups who have been disadvantaged in the past and (2) reverse historical trends of discrimination and create equality of opportunity.

Assimilation. The full adoption by an individual or group of the culture, values, and patterns of a different group, to the extent that attitudinal and behavioral affiliations with the original group are eradicated or no longer significant.

Attitude. A way of thinking that inclines one to feel and behave in certain ways.

Awareness. Bringing to one's conscious mind that which is only unconsciously perceived; for example, becoming conscious of the real differences among people and a sense that these may have to do with how people are or should be treated by others.

Bias. Preference or an inclination to make certain choices, which may be positive (bias toward excellence) or negative (bias against people), often with a resultant unfairness to someone.

Cross-cultural. Involving or mediating between two cultures, one's own and that of another.

Culture. A way of life. It is developed and communicated by a group, consciously or unconsciously, to subsequent generations. It consists of ideas, habits, attitudes, customs, and traditions that help create standards for a group of people to coexist. It makes a people unique. In its most basic sense, culture is a set of mental formulas for survival and success that a particular group of people has developed.

Differently abled. Refers to individuals with physical and/or mental endowments or impairments whose ability to participate in work requires aids or assistance. Used to replace the term *handicapped*, which has taken on a pejorative connotation.

Discrimination. The denial of equal treatment to groups because of their racial, ethnic, gender, religious, or other forms of cultural identity.

Diversity. The current term used to describe a vast range of cultural differences that have become factors needing attention in living and working together. It has to do with appreciating, respecting, valuing, and including people with differences. Often applied to the organizational and training interventions in an organization that seek to deal with the interface of people who are different from each other. Diversity is also referred to as "the biological, cultural, physical, and socioeconomic differences (such as race/ethnicity, age, gender, disabilities, class, education, values, sexual orientation, religion, etc.) that people bring to an organization, community, or society, which have the potential of giving rise to conflicts, but if managed well can result in a synergetic unity."

Dominant culture. Refers to the value system that characterizes a particular group of people that predominates over the value systems of other groups or cultures.

Equal employment or equal opportunity. Legally mandated guidelines whose objective is to guarantee that all people, whatever their background, are treated equally in such matters as pay, promotion, dismissal, etc.

Employment equity. The Canadian term for legally

mandated efforts, similar to affirmative action and equal employment in the United States.

Empowerment. The ability to feel capable and motivated in pursuing a goal. It is having the self-assurance needed to carry out and fulfill any endeavor. Empowerment can be self-initiated or the result of the proper kind of attention and support on the part of others.

Ethnicity. Refers to belonging to a group with unique language, ancestral, often religious, and physical characteristics. Broadly characterizes a religious, racial, national, or cultural group.

Ethnic group. Group of people who conceive of themselves, and who are regarded by others, as alike because of their common ancestry, language, and physical characteristics.

Ethnocentrism. Using the culture of one's own group as a standard for the judgment of others or thinking of it as superior to other cultures that are merely different.

Glass ceiling. An invisible and often perceived barrier that prevents some gender or ethnic groups (who are different from the dominant group) to become promoted or hired.

Gender. The cultural dimension and consequences of being male or female.

Macroculture, majority, or dominant group. The group within a society that is the largest and/or most powerful. This power usually leads to setting cultural norms for the society as a whole. The term *majority* (also *minority* below) is falling into disuse because its connotations of group size may be inaccurate.

Mediation. The use of an impartial third party to intervene as a facilitator in a difficult conflict or dispute. The mediator helps the parties listen, to come up with alternatives, and to arrive at a workable solution but does not have decision-making or coercive power.

Microculture or minority. Any group or person who differs from the predominant culture. Any group or individual, extending to second- and third-generations, who is born in a country different from their family origins and who has not adopted or embraced the predominant values and culture.

Multiculturalism. The existence within one society of diverse groups who maintain their unique cultural identities while accepting and participating in the larger society's legal and political system.

Native Americans. Popularly called American "Indians." People whose descendants became the indigenous or aboriginal people of North America.

Oppression. Oppression is the systematic and widespread institutionalized, day-to-day mistreatment of people based solely on the basis of group membership.

Paradigm shift. What occurs when an entire cultural group begins to experience a change that involves the acceptance of new conceptual models or ways of doing things and results in major societal transitions, e.g., the shift from an agricultural to an industrial society.

Perception. What exists in the mind as a representation (as of something comprehended) or as a formulation (as of a plan). Each person operates within a perceptual field or life space.

Person of color. Generally refers to the nondominant, non-White status segment of the population.

Prejudice. The inclination to cast a group of people in a favorable or unfavorable light usually without just grounds or sufficient information.

Psychological construct. The system that each of us creates to make sense out of our experiences and endow them with meaning. Originally inherited from our parents and our culture, it changes as we grow up and becomes more distinct through the events and turning points that individualize us. Essentially, one constructs a unique way of reading meaning into our private world or perceptual field, but life experience and learning should then cause us to alter and expand this psychological construct.

Quota. A numeric limit or objective used for the admission of immigrants or the hiring of a specific cultural group.

Race. A group of persons of, or regarded as of common ancestry. Physical characteristics are often used to identify people of different races. These definitions should not be used to identify ethnic groups.

Racist. One with a closed mind toward accepting one or more groups different from one's own origin in race or color.

Racism. Total rejection of others by reason of race, color, or, sometimes more broadly, culture.

Sexism. Sexism is the system of attitudes, assumptions, and behaviors that makes women subject to discrimination, poverty, unequal opportunity, and disrespect and that gives men power over women.

Stereotyping. Believing or feeling that people, groups, events, or issues typify or conform to a pattern or manner and lack any individuality. Thus a person may categorize behavior of a total group on the basis of limited experience with one or a few representatives of the group. Negative stereotyping classifies people in a group by slurs, innuendos, names, or slang expressions, which depreciate the group as a whole and the individuals in it.

Stigma. Stigma is any physical or social attribute—such as a physical deformity or disability, race, or criminal record, whether visible or hidden—which is used to devalue a person's social identity so as to disqualify the person from full or partial social acceptance.

Subculture. A group with distinct, discernable, and consistent cultural traits existing within and participating in a larger cultural grouping.

Synergy. The benefit acheived by the collaboration of two or more systems in excess of their individual contributions. Cultural synergy occurs when cultural differences are taken into account and used by a multicultural group.

Systemic. Refers to values, orientations, and habits that are institutionalized in an organization and that are (usually unconsciously) prejudicial to different cultural groups in the organization.

MAKE US ONE

Third Age. Refers to people who are fifty-five years of age and older. Popularly, but less appropriately, "senior citizens." This term has also been used to describe our present stage of development—the First Age having been the hunting and rural way of life, the Second Age the industrial stage, and the Third Age the post-industrial or information age.

Values. Sets of internal instructions, based in cultural and personal experience, that determine acceptable behavior for a group or individual. Such cultural priorities can be expressed in terms of moral, family, organizational, or even national values—namely, what a group considers important or desired behaviors for its members.

Visible minorities. Groups of people whose identity can be seen because of distinctive biological or physical characteristics. Replaces the less adequate term *people of color*.

*Note: Resources from which the above definitions are taken from are *Transcultural Leadership* by George Simons, Carmen Vazques, Philip Harris (Gulf Publishing Company, 1993); "Training in Diversity" by Caleb Rosado (1993), and "Diversity Definition," supplied by Delbert Baker (1994). It should be kept in mind that the above terms and definitions are culturally relative; that is, their use, meaning, and spelling are dynamic and subject to change in the context of a specific culture, time, and circumstance.

——BIBLIOGRAPHY——

This is a selected bibliogrphy of key books, supplements, and resources on diversity and race/ethnic relations.

Resources

A Tale of O. Good Measure, Inc, Cambridge, Mass.. A 27-minute videotape on diversity. "O" is an entertaining, captivating parable about what happens to any new or different kind of person in a group and how the situation can be managed.

Eyes on the Prize. This compelling public television series documenting the civil rights years is available on videotape at many local libraries.

Guide to Multicultural Resources (Charles A. Taylor, Editor), Highsmith Press, Fort Atkinson, Wisc., 1993. The guide is a concise directory, mediagraphy and almanac of current information on multicultural organizations, services and trends. Primary emphasis is upon key national organizations serving the U.S. and major state and local agencies and groups serving multicultural individuals and communities.

Face to Face: Seeking Racial Reconciliation, InterVarsity Christian Fellowship, Madison, Wisc. A thirty-minute videotape that is a good introduction to a group discussion on racism and Christians.

Harness the Rainbow: Diversity and the Bottom Line. Samuel Betances. United Training Media. Niles, Ill. A video that takes an honest look at diversity—what it is, its benefits, and offers ways to increase awareness and sensitivities.

We, the Americans *(Asians, Blacks, Hispanics, Pacific Islanders, etc.)* Series. U.S. Department of Commerce, Racial Statistis Branch, Population Division, Bureau of the Census. Washington, D.C., 1993.

Books
General

Allport, Gordon. *The Nature of Prejudice.* Reading, Mass.: Addison-Wesley Publishing Corp., 1979.

Bell, Derrick. *Race, Racism and American Law.* Third Edition. Boston: Little Brown and Company.

Blank, Renee, and Sandra Slipp. *Voices of Diversity.* New York: American Management Association, 1994.

Colson, Charles. *The Body: Being Light in Darkness.* Dallas, Tex.: Word Publishing, 1992.

Dittes, James E. *Bias and the Pious: The Relationship Between Prejudice and Religion.* Minneapolis, Minn.: Augsburg Publishing House, 1973.

Gilkey, Langdon. *Shantung Compound.* San Fancisco: Harper & Row, 1966.

Haseldon, Kyle. *The Racial Problem in Christian Perspective.* New York: Harper & Brothers, 1959.

King, Jr., Martin Luther. *Where Do We Go From Here: Chaos or Community?* Boston, Mass.: Beacon Press, 1967.

Knowles, Louis L., and Kenneth Prewitt, editors. *Institutional Racism in America.* Englewood Cliffs, N.J.: Prentice-Hall, 1969.

Peck, M. Scott. *People of the Lie: The Hope for Healing Human Evil.* New York: Simon & Schuster, 1983.

Perkins, John, and Thomas Tarrants, III. *He's My Brother.* Former Racial Foes Offer Strategy for Reconciliation. Grand Rapids, Mich.: Chosen Books, 1994.

Schermarhorn, R. A. *Comparative Ethnic Relations.* Chicago: University of Chicago Press, 1978.

Smedley, Audrey. *Race in North America: Origin and Evolution of a Worldview.* Boulder, Colo.: Westview Press, 1993.

Steinberg, Stephen. *The Ethnic Myth.* New York: Atheneum Press, 1981.

Takaki, Ronald. *A Different Mirror: A History of Multicultural America.* Boston: Little, Brown and Company, 1993.

White, Ellen G. *Christ's Object Lessons.* Hagerstown, Md.: Review and Herald Publishing Association, 1966.

Contemporary

America's Origional Sin: A Study Guide on White Racism. Sojourners (Special Supplement). Washington, D.C.: 1992.

Baker, Delbert W. *Talking and Listening.* Loma Linda, California: Loma Linda University Printing Service, 1994.

Barna, George. *The Barna Report: Absolute Confusion* (Vol. 3, 1993-94). Ventura, Calif.: Regal Books, 1993.

Barndt, Joseph. *Dismantling Racism: The Continuing Challenge to White America.* Minneapolis, Minn.: Augsburg Fortress, 1991.

Bell, Derrick. *Faces at the Bottom of the Well: the Permanence of Racism.* New York: Basic Books, 1992.

Buenker, John D., et al. *Multiculturalism in the United States: A Comparative Guide to Acculturation and Ethnicity.* New York: Greenwood Press, 1992.

Castuera, Ignacio, editor. *Dreams on Fire-Embers of Hope (From the Pulpits of Los Angeles After the Riots).* St. Louis, Mo.: Chalice Press, 1992.

Dialogues for Diversity: Community and Ethnicity on Campus. (Coordinated by the Accrediting Commission for Senior Colleges and Universities of the Western Association of Schools and Colleges.) Phoenix, Ariz.: The Oryx Press, 1994.

Gets, Lorine M., and Rudy O. Costa, editors. *Struggles for Solidarity.* Minneapolis, Minn.: Fortress Press, 1991.

Hacker, Andrew. *Two Nations: Black and White, Separate, Hostile, Unequal.* New York: Crown Publishers, Inc., 1991.

Kozol, Jonathan. *Savage Inequalities: Children in America's Schools*. New
    York: Crown Publishers, Inc., 1991.
Miller, Loren. *The Petitioners*. New York: Pantheon Books, 1966.
Morgan, Marlo. *Mutant Message, Down Under.* New York: HarperCollins
    Publishers, Inc., 1994.
Race and Attitudes Divide Us (Supplement of *The Plain Dealer*). Cleveland,
    Ohio: *The Plain Dealer*, 1992.
Rowan, Carl. *Dream Makers, Dream Breakers*. New York:Little Brown and
    Co., 1993.
Rutstein, Nathan. *Healing Racism in America: A Prescription for the Dis-
    ease*. Springfield, Mass.: Whitcomb Publishing, 1993.
Schaeffer, Richard T. *Race and Ethnicity in the United States*. San Fran-
    cisco: Harper & Row, 1995.
Spector, Rachel E. *Cultural Diversity in Health and Illness*. Third Edition.
    Norwalk, Conn.: Appleton and Lange, 1991.
Verkuyl, Johannes. *Break Down the Walls: A Christian Cry for Racial Jus-
    tice*. Grand Rapids, Mich.: William B. Eerdmans, 1973.
Wellman, David T. *Portraits of White Racism*. Cambridge, Mass.: Cambridge,
    1993.
West, Cornel. *Race Matters*. New York: Vintage Books, 1993.

Denominational

Baker, Delbert W. *The Unknown Prophet*. Hagerstown, Md.: Review and
    Herald Publishing Association, 1987.
Cleveland, E. E. *The Middle Wall*. Hagerstown, Md.: Review and Herald
    Publishing Association, 1969.
Graybill, Ronald D. *E. G. White and Church Race Relations*. Washington,
    D.C.: Review and Herald Publishing Association, 1970.
Kubo, Sakae. *The God of Relationships*. Edited by Rosa Banks. Hagerstown,
    Md.: Review and Herald Publishing Association, 1993.
Rosado, Caleb. *Broken Walls* (Race, sex, culture—in Christ, all barriers fall).
    Boise, Idaho: Pacific Press Publishing Association, 1990.
Tutu, Bishop Desmond . *Crying in the Wilderness*. Grand Rapids, Mich.: Wil-
    liam B. Eerdmans Publishers, 1982.
White, Ellen G. *The Southern Work*. Hagerstown, Md.: Review and Herald
    Publishing Association, 1966.

International

Axtell, Roger E., editor. *Do's and Taboos Around the World* (Compiled by the
    Parker Pen Company, 2nd Edition). New York: John Wiley & Sons, 1990.
Diversity: Brown and Yellow, Black and White. Takoma Park, Md.: *Spec-
    trum*, 23:5.
Elashmawi, Farid, and Phillip R. Harris. *Multicultural Management: New
    Skills for Global Success*. Houston, Tex.: Gulf Publishing Company, 1993.
Gioseffi, Daniela. *On Prejudice: A Global Perspective*. New York: Doubleday,
    1993.
Harris, Phillip R., and Robert T. Moran. *Managing Cultural Differences*. Third
    Edition. Houston, Tex: Gulf Publishing Company, 1991.

Horowitz, Donald L. *Ethnic Groups in Conflicts*. Berkeley, Calif.: University of California Press, 1985.
How to Bridge Ethnic Differences. A *Message* Magazine Supplement. Hagerstown, Md.: Review and Herald Publishing Association, 1987.
Marger, Martin. *Race and Ethnic Relations*. American and Global Perspectives. Third Edition. Belmont, Calif.: Wadsworth Publishing Company, 1993.
Prosser, Michael. *International Communication Among Natives and People*. San Francisco: Harper & Row, 1973.
Race Relations. Spectrum, 2:2, Spring 1970.
Smith, Anthony B. *The Ethnic Origins of Nations*. New York: Basil Blackwell, Inc., 1986.
Smith, Donald K. *Creating Understanding, A Handbook for Christian Communication Across Cultural Landscapes*. Grand Rapids, Mich.: Zondervan Publishing House, 1992.

Management/Leadership

Block, P. *The Empowered Manager*. San Francisco: Jossey-Bass, Inc., 1988.
_____. *Stewardship: Choosing Service Over Self-Interest*. San Francisco: Berrett-Koehler Publishing Association, 1993.
Cox, Jr., Taylor H. *Cultural Diversity in Organizations: Theory, Research & Practice*. San Francisco: Berrett-Koehler Publishers, 1994.
Deal, T., and A. Kennedy. *Corporate Cultures: The Rites and Rituals of Corporate Life*. Reading, Mass.: Addison Wesley, 1982.
Gentile, Mary C., editor. *Differences That Work: Organizational Excellence Through Diversity*. Boston, Mass.: Harvard Business School Publishing Corporation, 1994.
Greenleaf, Robert K. *Servant Leadership*. New York: Paulist Press, 1977.
Isaacs, Harold R. *Idols of the Tribe: Group Identity and Political Change*. Cambridge, Mass.: Harvard University Press, 1975.
Jamison, David, and Julie O'Mara. *Managing Workforce 2000: Gaining the Diversity Advantages*. San Francisco: Jossey-Bass Publishers, 1991.
Johnston, W., and A. Packer. *Workforce 2000. Work and Workers for the Twenty-First Century*. Indianapolis, Ind.: The Hudson Institute, 1987.
Kouzes, James M., and Barry Z. Posner. *Credibility: How Leaders Gain and Lose It, Why People Demand It*. San Francisco: Jossey-Bass Publishers, 1993.
Loden, Marilyn, and Judy B. Rosener. *Workforce America: Managing Employee Diversity as a Vital Resource*. Homewood, Ill.: Business One Irwin, 1991.
Morrison, A. M., et al. *The New Leaders. Guidelines on Leadership Diversity in America*. San Francisco: Jossey-Bass, Inc., 1992.
Naisbitt, J., and R. Aburdene. *Megatrends 2000: 10 New Directions for the 1990s*. New York: William Morrow, 1990.
Pritchett, Price. *Culture Shift*. Dallas, Tex.: Pritchett Publishing Company, 1993.
Pritchett, Price, and Ron Pound. *High-Velocity Culture Change*. Dallas, Tex.: Pritchett Publishing Company, 1993.

Rock, Calvin. *Church Leadership: A Call to Virtue*. Boise, Idaho: Pacific Press
    Publishing Association, 1990.
Ross, Marc Howard. *The Culture of Conflict*. New Haven, Conn.: Yale Uni-
    versity Press, 1993.
_____. *The Management of Conflict*. New Haven, Conn.: Yale University Press,
    1993.
Simon, George F., Carmen Vazquez, and Philip R. Harris. *Transcultural Lead-
    ership: Empowering Diverse Workforce*. Houston, Tex.: Gulf Publishing
    Company, 1993.
Thomas, Jr., R. *Beyond Race and Gender: Unleashing the Power of Your To-
    tal Work Force by Managing Diversity*. New York: Amacon, 1991.

Outreach

Campolo, Anthony. *Ideas for Social Action*. Grand Rapids, Mich.: Zondervan
    Publishing House, 1983.
Hesselgrave, David J.*Communicating Christ Cross-Culurally*. Grand
    Rapids, Mich.: Zondervan, 1991.
Kelsey, Geiorge D. *Racism and the Christian Understanding of Man*. New
    York: Charles Scribner's Sons, 1965.
Lingenfleter, Sherwood G., and Marvin K. Mayers. *Ministering Cross-
    Culturally*. Grand Rapids, Mich.: Baker Book House, 1986.
Mayers, Marvin K. *Christianity Confronts Culture*. Grand Rapids, Mich.:
    Zondervan Publishing House, 1987.
Williams, Cecil, with Rebecca Laird. *No Hiding Place: Empowerment and
    Recovery for Our Troubled Communities*. New York: Harper Collins Pub-
    lishers, 1992.

Reconciliation

Alderson, Wayne T., et al. *Theory R Management: How to Utilize the Value of
    the Person*. Nashville, Tenn.: Thomas Nelson, 1994.
Cohen, R. *Negotiating Across Cultures*. Washington, D.C.: United States In-
    stitute of Peace Press, 1991.
Ford, Clyde W. *We Can All Get Along: 50 steps you can take to help end rac-
    ism*. New York: Dell Publishing, 1994.
Jone, James M. *Prejudice and Racism*. Reading, Mass.: Addison-Wesley Pub-
    lishing Co., 1972.
Kehrein, Glen, and Raleigh Washington. *Breaking Down Walls*. Chicago:
    Moody Press, 1993.
Pannell, William. *The Coming Race Wars*. Grand Rapids, Mich.: Zondervan
    Publishing House, 1993.
Perkins, John. *With Justice for All*. Ventura, Calif.: Regal Books, 1982.
_____. *Let Justice Roll Down*. Glendale, Calif.: Regal Books, 1976.
Simons, G., et al. *Diversophy: Understanding the Human Race*. San Mateo,
    Calif.. Multus Inc. & George Simons International, 1992.
Simons, G. *Working Together: How to Become More Effective in a Multicultural
    Organization*. Los Altos, Calif.: Crisp Publication, Inc., 1989.
Skinner, Tom. *How Black Is the Gospel?* New York: Pillar Books, 1970.
Tannen, D. *You Just Don't Understand Me*. New York: William Morrow, 1990.

Washington, Raleigh, and Glen Kehrein. *Breaking Down the Walls: A Model for Reconciliation in an Age of Racial Strife.* Chicago: Moody Press, 1993.

Skills

Chester, Mark, and Hector Delgado. "Race Relations Training and Organizational Change." In *Strategies for Improving Race Relations*, edited by John W. Shaw, et al.

Gudykunst, William B. *Bridging Differences: Effective Intergroup Communication.* Newbury Park, Calif.: Sage, 1991.

Gudykunst, William B., Lea P. Stewart, and Stella Ting-Toomey, eds. *Communication, Culture, and Organizational Processes.* Newbury Park, Calif.: Sage, 1985.

Katz, Judith H. *White Awareness: Handbook for Anti-racism Training.* Norman, Okla.: University of Oklahoma, 1950.

Klopf, Donald W. *Intercultural Encounters: The Fundamentals of Intercultural Communications.* Englewood, Colo.: Morton Publishing Company, 1987.

Kochman, Thomas. *Black and White Styles in Conflict.* Chicago: The University of Chicago Press, 1981.

Ryan, William. *Blaming the Victim.* New York: Vintage Books, 1976.

White, Ellen G. *Mind, Character, and Personality,* Vols. 1, 2. Nashville, Tenn.: Southern Publishing Association, 1977.